T0162160

THE
ZAPATISTAS'
DIGNIFIED RAGE
FINAL PUBLIC SPEECHES OF
SUBCOMMANDER MARCOS

THE
ZAPATISTAS'
DIGNIFIED RAGE
FINAL PUBLIC SPEECHES OF
SUBCOMMANDER MARCOS

With additional contributions by
Lt. Col. Moisés and Commander Hortensia

EDITED BY NICK HENCK
★
TRANSLATED BY HENRY GALES

AK PRESS

DID YOU HEAR?

It is the sound of your world collapsing.

It is that of ours reemerging.

The day that was the day, it was night.

And night will be the day that will be the day.

—Subcommander Marcos
December 21, 2012

The Zapatistas' Dignified Rage: Final Public Speeches of Subcommander Marcos
© 2018 Insurgent Subcommander Marcos
Introduction © 2018 Nick Henck
Translation, foreword, and glossary © 2018 Henry Gales
Notes accompanying Marcos's writings et al. by Nick Henck and Henry Gales

This edition © 2018 AK Press (Chico, Oakland, Edinburgh, Baltimore)

ISBN: 978-1-84935-292-5
E-ISBN: 978-1-84935-293-2
Library of Congress Control Number: 2017936243

AK Press   AK Press
370 Ryan Ave. #100   33 Tower St.
Chico, CA 95973   Edinburgh EH6 7BN
USA   Scotland
www.akpress.org   www.akuk.com
akpress@akpress.org   ak@akedin.demon.co.uk

The above addresses would be delighted to provide you with the latest AK Press distribution catalog, which features books, pamphlets, zines, and stylish apparel published and/or distributed by AK Press. Alternatively, visit our websites for the complete catalog, latest news, and secure ordering.

Cover illustration by Mazatl, www.justseeds.org
Back cover photo courtesy of Marta Molina
Printed in the USA on acid-free, recycled paper

For Chómpiras — H.G.
For my wife, Yasuko, and our son, Louis — N.H.

Table of Contents

Acknowledgments

First and foremost, we would like to thank the tens of thousands of Zapatistas whose daily work keeps the movement alive and makes books like this possible. Another big thanks goes to the folks at AK Press for all their encouragement from the very moment we first approached them with this project. We would also like to express our gratitude to Jan Rus for granting us permission to reprint here his previously published translations entitled "Early January: Preparations and Visits" and "Late January: Toward a Free Market."

Glossary

See "Translator's Foreword" for further information about items marked **F**.

Above: Politicians, wealthy elites, and other power brokers. **F**

Autonomy: Since the 1994 ceasefire, the Zapatistas have devoted most of their energies toward creating governmental, educational, and health care institutions that are autonomous from official Mexican governmental institutions. This declared and practiced *autonomy* is similar to *independence*, since it involves a rejection of the official government's legitimacy and authority. A key difference is that there is no desire for separatism or for the formation of a new nation.

Balaclava: Also known as a *ski mask*; worn by all Zapatistas during official events and when being photographed. Marcos was never seen in public without a balaclava.

Below: Everyone not part of the political and economic elite. **F**

Calderón: Felipe Calderón Hinojosa, PAN politician and president of Mexico from 2006 to 2012. Calderón came to power in 2006 through electoral fraud and launched the "War on Drug Trafficking." By the end of his term, over sixty thousand people had died as a result, and no advances had been made toward curbing the influence of drug cartels in Mexico.

Calendar: Used by Marcos to talk about *time* or *conceptions of time*. **F**

Caracol: Literally a snail or a snail shell. The Zapatistas call their governmental/cultural centers "caracols" because, as with the shape and construction of a shell, they allow those outside to enter into the heart of the structure and allow those at its heart to go out into the world beyond. Each of the five Zapatista zones has one caracol and one Good Government Committee that meets there.

CCRI: Indigenous Revolutionary Clandestine Committee (Comité Clandestino Revolucionario Indígena), the semipermanent body of Zapatista leaders who oversee the organization's long-term vision and projects and coordinate public events. One of the Zapatistas' principles is "command by obeying" (*mandar obedeciendo*), meaning that leaders must respect the democratic decisions made by the Zapatistas at large.

Commander: In many left-wing guerrilla armies and in the CCRI, this is the highest rank. Marcos sometimes refers to the Zapatista commanders as his "bosses."

Compañero: Friend, acquaintance, classmate, coworker, or even someone the speaker has never met before, so long as there is some group association. In this book it is most frequently used to refer to Zapatistas and people who share the Zapatistas' political views. Sometimes shortened to *compas*. F

Don: Title of respect that can be added before someone's name. Marcos uses it to refer to older individuals who the Zapatistas have a great deal of respect for.

Don Durito of the Lacandon Jungle: A prominent character in many of Marcos's stories, Don Durito is a beetle who Marcos converses with from time to time.

EZLN: Spanish acronym for the Zapatistas' full name: Zapatista Army of National Liberation (Ejército Zapatista de Liberación Nacional).

Fox: Vicente Fox, PAN politician and president of Mexico from 2000 to 2006. Fox promised to dialogue with the Zapatistas and resolve the issue "in fifteen minutes," but he later signed a reform bill that contradicted many of the demands that the federal government had promised to meet.

Geography: Used by Marcos to talk about *places* or *conceptions of space*. F

Good Government Committee: Each caracol has a Good Government Committee (Junta de Buen Gobierno) that is responsible for overseeing projects in that zone and managing relationships with outside groups. Like the CCRI, these committees "command by obeying" and must consult their communities rather than making decisions themselves.

Insurgent: The Spanish word *insurgente* has been translated as *insurgent* because both words technically mean the same thing: someone who is part of a military group that fights against the sitting government. The cultural connotations of each word, however, are drastically different: in the United States, "insurgent" makes people think of Western-hating religious fundamentalists, but in Mexico it makes people think of the "insurgent army" that fought against Spain in the Mexican War of Independence.

Mestizo: In Mexico and other countries, this term is used for the race created by the cultural merger of Europeans and Mexican indigenous peoples. Currently, it is used for all Mexicans who do not actively identify with an indigenous culture, regardless of ethnic background. In certain regions of Chiapas, the term *ladino* is used instead.

Neoliberalism: Economic ideology that promotes privatization of government resources and operations, cuts to social programs, the elimination or reduction of regulations and subsidies, and free trade. The US government began to promote neoliberalism abroad in the mid-1970s and domestically in the late 1970s.

López Obrador: Andrés Manuel López Obrador, also known as AMLO, mayor of Mexico City from 2000 to 2005 for the PRD. In response to the electoral fraud used to deprive him of the presidency in 2006, López Obrador staged protests and held a faux inauguration ceremony in which he was sworn in as "legitimate president." He ran for president again in 2012 and shortly afterward left the PRD to form a new political party: Morena.

The Other Campaign: Campaign held by the Zapatistas alongside the 2006 presidential campaign, in which Marcos toured the country visiting other social movements that fight for similar goals across Mexico. For some time, those who support the Zapatistas were called "compañeros of the Other Campaign," but they are now called "compañeros of the Sixth

Declaration," since they have read and agree with the Sixth Declaration of the Lacandon Jungle.

PAN: National Action Party (Partido Acción Nacional); held the presidency from 2000 to 2012 (most of the speeches in this book were given from 2007 to 2009) and still controls many state governments.

Predawn: This is the best possible translation of the Spanish word *madrugada*, which refers to the time of night between midnight and sunrise. Marcos sets many of his stories in and makes many references to *la madrugada*.

PRD: Party of the Democratic Revolution (Partido de la Revolución Democrática); to the left of the PRI and PAN on many issues, including abortion, social spending, and LGBTQ rights. Since 1997, the PRD has controlled the Mexico City government but is currently in decline due to López Obrador's departure and the rise of his new party Morena.

PRI: Institutional Revolutionary Party (Partido Revolucionario Institucional); controlled the presidency and most of Mexico's government from 1929 to 2000 and retook the presidency in 2012. Its name refers to its claim of being the institutional embodiment of the Mexican Revolution.

P.S.: It is well-known that this is used to tack a sentence or two onto the end of a letter, but Marcos uses it to add entire pages of tangential material to his communiques and speeches.

Salinas de Gortari: Carlos Salinas de Gortari, PRI politician and president of Mexico from 1988 to 1994. Salinas de Gortari implemented neoliberal policies and signed the North American Free Trade Agreement (NAFTA) on Mexico's behalf.

Sixth Declaration of the Lacandon Jungle: Communique released by the CCRI in 2005 that outlines the Zapatistas' history and their perspective on fighting for political change. Today, it is still considered one of the most important documents published by the Zapatistas. An English translation is available at: sixthdeclaration.blogspot.com.

Support base: Term used to refer to the great majority of Zapatistas: civilians who do not participate in the Zapatistas' military arm and are not part of the CCRI.

Zapatismo: The Zapatistas' political principles and realization of these principles, in particular the idea that change must be made by working with the disempowered to fight against capitalism and inequality. Some analysts insist on calling this "Neozapatismo" to make clear the distinction between today's Zapatistas and the Zapatistas who fought under Emiliano Zapata in the Mexican Revolution.

Zedillo: Ernesto Zedillo Ponce de León, PRI politician and president of Mexico from 1994 to 2000. Zedillo attempted to deal with the Zapatistas by both using violent force and staging negotiations whose promises and accords were never honored by his administration.

—H.G.

Introduction

Background

For more than two decades now, Mexico's Insurgent Subcommander Marcos (Subcomandante Insurgente Marcos)—and the Zapatista indigenous movement of which he was military leader and spokesperson—have constituted a, if not *the*, primary beacon of hope among those deeply disillusioned with the havoc that capitalism is wreaking upon the earth. The Zapatistas rose up in arms on January 1, 1994, in Mexico's southeastern state of Chiapas, to decry and declare their resistance to the centuries of abuse, exploitation, racism, oppression, brutality, and neglect that had been heaped upon them by successive nonindigenous ruling elites.

Their resentment and despair had been brought to a head by President Salinas's recent neoliberal policies, which had been implemented to pave the way for Mexico's entry into the North American Free Trade Agreement (NAFTA). In particular, in February 1992, Article 27 of the Constitution was amended to permit the sale of communal village lands (*ejidos*) to stimulate both domestic and foreign investment in impoverished rural areas. While the amendment had the appearance of giving peasant communities the choice of either retaining their communal lands or selling them, the brutal reality, given the context of rural poverty and indebtedness, was that many communities were forced to sell these lands. Since for the Zapatistas, as Marcos has noted, "the land is not merchandise, but it has cultural, religious and historic connotations," the loss of these *ejidos* had a serious negative social as well as economic impact on indigenous communities in Chiapas.[1] Regarding NAFTA specifically, the Subcommander pointed out that now illiterate Mexican farmers with small, poor-quality, rocky, hillside plots of land would be forced to compete with US and Canadian farms: little wonder, then, that he concluded that "NAFTA is a death sentence for the indigenous people."[2] Moreover, preparations for entering NAFTA were, as Marcos would stress, creating enormous wealth disparities in Mexican society at large: while forty-one million Mexicans lived below the poverty line, the years 1991 through 1994 saw twenty-three new billionaires emerge in Mexico, half of whom were created by Salinas privatizing 252 state companies. Meanwhile, according to one observer, "an estimated sixty thousand small businesses [had] failed in 1990 alone . . . closed out of co-investment opportunities by the more lucrative partnership offers being pitched to foreign investors by Mexico's business elite, dominated by a group of thirty-seven Mexican moguls who controlled the country's top seventy corporations—an estimated 22 percent of Mexico's entire GDP."[3]

The Mexican government initially reacted to the uprising by attempting to crush it militarily. However, the Zapatistas' modest and (to most) just demands for work, land, housing, food, health care, education, independence, freedom, democracy, justice, and peace captured the public's sympathy, which in turn forced the government to issue a ceasefire and declare its intention to sit down and dialogue with the Zapatistas. Although the peace talks that followed two months later, in March 1994, ultimately failed to address the Zapatistas' demands to their satisfaction, in the months and years that followed the Zapatistas rapidly transformed themselves from a rebel army into an armed social movement whose political philosophy and practice, *Zapatismo*, soon attracted considerable interest worldwide. In the succeeding years, they (1) introduced and further developed autonomy within their own territory, living according to their own indigenous customs and practices, and significantly improving access to health care, education, justice, and agricultural support; (2) conducted lengthy, multistage negotiations with the government to recognize this autonomy, as well as indigenous rights in general; and (3) reached out to national and international civil society both through their spokesperson Marcos (who penned hundreds of communiqués and gave dozens of speeches and interviews) and by holding high-profile public mobilizations and events. These efforts included national and international gatherings (*encuentros*), the mass canvassing of public opinion (*consultas*), and marches, all of which were designed to keep the Zapatistas and their message alive, both on the ground in Chiapas (where they faced state repression and paramilitary violence) and in the public's imagination.

Ultimately, through these actions the Zapatistas inspired hope among many on the left who had been demoralized by both the failings of many socialist states and the electoral loss of the Sandinistas in Nicaragua. Their message gained particular traction, however, among those in the antiglobalization movement. Indeed, the Zapatistas' 1996 First Intercontinental Gathering for Humanity and against Neoliberalism tapped into and helped galvanize antiglobalization sentiment that had previously been experienced largely on an individual, small group, or national level but would subsequently coalesce around and be further consolidated through interventions by Peoples' Global Action and successive World Social Forums, both of which drew inspiration from the Zapatistas.

Turning to Subcommander Marcos specifically, throughout the last twenty or so years he has remained the most instantly recognizable, leading light of the antineoliberal globalization movement, and one who is, I would urge, imbued with considerable moral authority on account of having chosen to abandon a comparatively comfortable life as an urban university professor in favor of a markedly more arduous one as a rural guerrilla. Armed, in addition, with an extensive knowledge of literature (including poetry) that lends him a cultured demeanor and formidable rhetorical skills, a rigorous formative training in political philosophy, a sharp and analytical intellect, decades of lived reality with indigenous peoples, a highly charismatic personality, an acerbic wit, and an incredibly photogenic appearance, Marcos has proved a highly effective spokesperson for the Zapatista movement.

More than this, however, in the decade following the 1994 uprising the Subcommander acted as the liaison between rural indigenous communities in Chiapas and Mexico's urban mestizo society (and the wider world that lies beyond it), helped the Zapatistas navigate a series of negotiations with the Mexican government over the issue of indigenous rights, fronted several national and international gatherings (such as the 1994 National Democratic Convention and the 1996 Intercontinental Gathering for Humanity and against Neoliberalism), devised and formulated the mass canvassing of public opinion (including the 1995 International Consultation of Public Opinion and the 1999 Consultation of Public Opinion on Indigenous Rights), engaged with the national and global media, repeatedly confounded the government, forged direct links with prominent left-leaning individuals (including eminent literary figures), and headed the 2001 March for Indigenous Dignity, or Earth-Colored March, which traversed much of the country on its way to Mexico City. As a consequence of the crucial role played by Marcos, the literature about him has now reached considerable proportions and currently covers such diverse aspects as his literary output, his relationship with key Mexican intellectuals, his attitude toward intellectuals in general, his political philosophy, his discourse, his reading habits, and his iconic status. Indeed, Jorge Alonso notes that, "with over 10,000 citations, he [i.e., the Subcommander] has also made a dent in the academic world. Marcos' writings, as well as books based on him, have been referenced by a large number of researchers from different countries and in several languages."[4]

Here is not the place to retell more than twenty years of the Zapatista movement's public actions, and even less the decade of clandestine activity that preceded these. Instead, it will suffice to direct the reader to Gloria Muñoz Ramírez's *The Fire and the Word* (2008), a history of the movement largely in the Zapatistas' own words; the informative and highly readable account of the Zapatistas' actions covering the years 1994 to 2006 to be found in John Ross's trilogy: *Rebellion from the Roots: Indian Uprising in Chiapas* (1995), *The War against Oblivion: The Zapatista Chronicles 1994–2000* (2000), and *¡Zapatistas! Making Another World Possible: Chronicles of Resistance 2000–2006* (2006); and, covering the same period but specifically focusing on the Subcommander, my *Subcommander Marcos: The Man and the Mask* (2007). It is, however, necessary to note briefly two experiences that profoundly influenced the Zapatistas and their Subcommander so as to give context to their words contained in this collection: these are the legislative betrayal of 2001 and the "Other Campaign" of 2006.

Context

The election of Vincente Fox of the PAN (Partido Acción Nacional) to the presidency in 2000, the first time in over seven decades that a president who was not part of the PRI (Partido Revolucionario Institucional) had held that post, encouraged the Zapatistas to think that a potential political opening was emerging. More concretely, it offered a way out of the impasse that had been created by President Ernesto Zedillo's refusal to ratify the San Andrés Indigenous Accords. The agreement, which recognized a degree of autonomy for indigenous communities and allowed them to appoint their own officials and operate a limited justice system of their own, had been drawn up by the president's advisory team and had been signed by both his own negotiators and the Zapatistas; however, Zedillo had turned around at the last minute and refused to ratify the agreement, instead proposing a severely diluted counterproposal. This was followed by a period of increasing harassment by state security forces of indigenous villages (and of national and international foreign observers and supporters staying in them), as well as intensified paramilitary violence directed against pro-Zapatista communities.

With President Fox famously declaring that he would solve the problem of Chiapas in fifteen minutes—indicating that he believed a mutually satisfactory agreement could be rapidly concluded with the Zapatistas, thereby bringing peace to the state—and with the Zapatistas for their part proclaiming their willingness to resume dialogue with this new government, Marcos and twenty-three Zapatista commanders set off for a two-week tour of thirteen states that culminated in the nation's capital, Mexico City, on March 11, 2001. The March for Indigenous Dignity, or Earth-Colored March, was a tremendous success in garnering publicity and support. The Subcommander held rallies and gave speeches in different communities on an almost daily basis as the tour wound its way, three thousand supporters and the national and international press in tow, toward its final destination. Once in the capital's central square, a crowd of more than one hundred thousand would pack the plaza to witness Marcos and the Zapatistas enter triumphantly and then address their supporters. Over the next few days, Marcos gave numerous interviews and held dozens of public events, and in doing so was able to exploit the Zapatistas' high media profile to pressure the Mexican Congress into permitting Commander Esther to address its members. Taking the podium, she expressed the Zapatistas' grievances and petitioned for the signing into law of the San Andrés Indigenous Rights Bill that had been negotiated back in 1996 with the government of President Zedillo. This initiative having proven extremely effective in terms of public relations, Marcos and the Zapatista caravan returned to Chiapas to wait for the Congress to deliberate over, and pass a verdict on, the Indigenous Rights Bill; little did they know that what awaited them was betrayal by the legislative branch, which passed a version of the bill so substantially altered as to constitute a travesty of the original proposal and even a step backward for indigenous rights.

This legislative betrayal was to have a profound effect on the Zapatistas, who subsequently turned their backs completely on the institutional political path and chose to concentrate their efforts on making indigenous autonomy a lived reality instead of seeking to convince the government to bestow formal recognition on it. As the Zapatistas would explain in their Sixth Declaration of the Lacandon Jungle:

The politicians who are from the PRI, the PAN, and the PRD came to agreement among themselves and simply did not recognize indigenous rights and culture. That was in April of 2001 and there the politicians clearly demonstrated that they do not have any decency. . . . [W]e saw clearly that the dialogue and negotiation with the evil governments of Mexico was for nothing. In other words, there is no point in us talking with the politicians because neither their heart nor their word is straight, but instead they are twisted and tell lies. . . . We saw that they did not care about blood, death, suffering, the mobilizations, the consultations, the efforts, the national and international statements, the gatherings, the agreements, the signatures, the commitments.[5]

This stance taken by the Zapatistas would have significant ramifications when it came to the second formative experience mentioned above: the "Other Campaign" of 2006. With the presidential elections due to take place in the summer, Marcos emerged from relative seclusion to announce the launching of "The National Campaign with Another Politics for a National Program of Leftwing Struggle and for a New Constitution." The "Other Campaign," as the Subcommander would for the sake of brevity subsequently label it, represented an attempt to reach out to, and forge solidarity with, those who felt marginalized by the existing political system and excluded from the considerations of the current political parties. In short, it sought to appeal to the millions of Mexicans for whom the political class in its entirety had lost any semblance of credibility and for whom the political process as a whole lacked legitimacy. As the Zapatistas explained in the Sixth Declaration of the Lacandon Jungle:

We are going to listen to and talk directly, without intermediaries or mediations, with the simple and humble people of Mexico and, according to what we listen [to] and learn, we are going to build, together with those people who are like us, humble and simple, a national platform of struggle, but a platform that is clearly left-wing, i.e. anticapitalist, i.e. antineoliberal, i.e. in favor of justice, democracy, and freedom for the Mexican people.[6]

This emphasis on pursuing nonelectoral paths did not represent anything new in Marcos's thinking or the Zapatistas' position; indeed, the Subcommander had always said that there was much more to democracy than merely voting in periodic elections, arguing instead that free and fair elections (which the Mexican elections of 1988, 2006, and 2012 are widely perceived not to have been) are a necessary but far from sufficient precondition for constructing a truly democratic society.[7] Therefore, Marcos had not undergone any radical shift in his thinking during the run-up to the 2006 presidential campaign in viewing these elections as, at best, a distraction that diverted people's attention and energy away from creating authentic, grassroots democracy that aimed at bringing about a radical and fundamental transformation of society and, at worst, the tacit endorsement of an inherently illegitimate political system. The only discernible difference now perhaps was the Subcommander's explicit emphasis, based on recently having experienced the 2001 legislative betrayal, on the futility of expecting anything positive to come from the political class:

> In April of 2001, politicians from all the parties . . . formed an alliance in order to deny the Indian peoples of Mexico the constitutional recognition of their rights and culture. And they did so without caring about the great national and international movement which had arisen and joined together for that purpose. . . . It doesn't matter what they are saying now, when they are preparing for the elections (in other words, to secure positions that will make them profits): they are not going to do anything for the good of the majority.[8]

Nonetheless, despite Marcos having consistently retained this position, and the fact that he did not openly advocate voter abstention, the Subcommander's stance toward the upcoming elections generated considerable criticism, none more vehement than that emanating from sectors of the progressive Left, and in particular certain left-leaning intellectuals and journalists who until that point had proven generally supportive of the Zapatistas. Confronted now, however, with what appeared to be the very real prospect of victory for the center-left PRD candidate, Andrés Manuel López Obrador (AMLO), these former supporters of the Zapatista movement harshly condemned Marcos when he not only failed to endorse but instead actively criticized the presidential hopeful. It did not matter to them that, as Marcos would pointedly observe, AMLO's track record as mayor of Mexico City provided scant reason to hope that he would initiate and pursue substantial anticapitalist change; what they cared about was forging unity among the country's progressive forces so as to bring about, for the first time in Mexico's history, a PRD president. Marcos was therefore accused of being divisive at this vital juncture and thus of aiding and abetting the candidates of the right-wing PRI and PAN. In a November 2007 interview with journalist Laura Castellanos, Marcos pointed out what had happened:

> Until the failure of the indigenous law of the San Andrés Accords . . . we were in agreement with the progressive intellectuals who insisted on the political and institutional channel. . . . [A]fter . . . the San Andrés Accords . . . were not complied with . . . we judged that the possibility of interlocution was broken, there was no sense whatsoever in talking with the political class, in its entirety. That was what most bothered many people, that we wiped the slate clean and we didn't make the distinctions or nuances that they wanted.[9]

It is against this backdrop of the aftermath and repercussions of the legislative betrayal of 2001 and the "Other Campaign" of 2006 that Marcos's presentations, speeches, and communiqués collected here should be read, for these experiences left deep marks on the Zapatistas and their Subcommander. Specifically, they explain why throughout this collection we find repeated criticisms of Mexico's entire political class and a sustained defense, in the face of denunciations by progressive intellectuals and the institutional Left, of the Zapatistas' refusal to legitimate electoral politics in Mexico by endorsing candidates from any of the country's political parties.

The First International Colloquium in Memory of Andrés Aubry

"The First International Colloquium *In Memoriam* Andrés Aubry: Planet Earth, Antisystemic Movements" took place from December 13 to 17, 2007—that is, only a year after the first phase of the "Other Campaign" had ended and a mere three months after its second phase had been suspended, permanently as it would turn out.[10] It was named in honor of French-born ethnosociologist and historian Andrés Aubry, a veteran and tireless promoter of indigenous rights and culture for more than three decades who had been killed two months earlier, on September 20, in a traffic accident. Back in the mid-1990s, Aubry had been invited by Subcommander Marcos to become an adviser to the Zapatistas during the San Andrés discussions with the Mexican government, a role he had gladly accepted, and he had then headed a project to translate the accords into ten indigenous languages.

Fittingly, the Colloquium was hosted by the Indigenous Center for Integral Training–University of the Earth in San Cristóbal, which is an autonomous, nonformal learning center that promotes community empowerment, self-sufficiency, and ecological sustainability. It provides instruction in both practical disciplines as well as more academic ones, and it also houses the Immanuel Wallerstein Center for Research, Information, and Documentation, which was founded in 2004.[11] The center would also be the venue for the third stage of the Global Festival of Dignified Rage a year later and the Seminar on Critical Thought in the Face of the Capitalist Hydra, held May 2 to 9, 2015.

The Colloquium saw the Subcommander give a series of seven presentations under the general heading of "Neither the Center nor the Periphery." The opening session featured presentations by Marcos, eminent US world-systems analyst Immanuel Wallerstein, and Mexican social scientist Carlos Antonio Aguirre Rojas, who is also the founder and head of the journal *Contrahistorias*. Wallerstein and Aguirre had hailed the Zapatistas as representing an antisystemic movement of great significance.[12] Both men also clearly admired the Subcommander: Aguirre frequently published Marcos's words in his journal, and Wallerstein compared him to Gandhi and Nelson Mandela.[13] In addition to the presentations of Marcos, Aguirre, and Wallerstein, the Colloquium featured others by prominent speakers including British art critic, novelist, painter, and poet John Berger; Canadian award-winning writer, journalist, filmmaker, activist, and author of the anticorporate globalization classics *No Logo* and *The Shock Doctrine*, Naomi Klein; and other eminent participants whose names may be less familiar.[14] Not surprisingly, many of the almost two thousand attendees who came from thirty-four countries to hear these presentations were intellectuals and activists whose backgrounds and interests lay with social movements, feminism, indigenous rights and culture, autonomy, agrarian reform and practices, environmentalism, and antiglobalization.[15] In each of the seven sessions held there were two or three speakers, with the Subcommander giving the final presentation in each series.[16] In his contributions, Marcos made reference to, reflected on, and engaged with the works and ideas of the Colloquium's other speakers, at times responding to specific points and developing certain themes that had been articulated in other speakers' presentations.

When looking at these presentations as a whole, the first thing that needs to be stressed is their fundamentally anticapitalist character. Of course, almost from the very outset of the Zapatista rebellion Marcos's communiqués had repeatedly decried the evils of neoliberal capitalism, sometimes at considerable length—thus we have a series of conversations on this theme between the Subcommander and one of his literary creations, Don Durito of the Lacandon Jungle (1994–1996), and "The Seven

Loose Pieces of the Global Jigsaw Puzzle" (1997).[17] However, his primary and most immediate target had previously been the undemocratic, corrupt, authoritarian, neoliberal PRI government, which he continually lambasted and whose ideological underpinnings he set about systematically demolishing.[18] More recent years had witnessed the Zapatistas issuing communiqués such as the Sixth Declaration of the Lacandon Jungle (2005), "The (Impossible) Geometry of Power" (2005), and "The Pedestrians of History" (2006), in which Marcos trained his discursive big guns fully on capitalism as a whole. The Aubry Colloquium, by affording Marcos the opportunity to give a series of seven presentations, each of substantial length, alongside such anticapitalist icons as Naomi Klein and Immanuel Wallerstein, provided him with an ideal platform to convey in detail an elaborate analytical critique of capitalism. Marcos described its intrinsic nature (most notably, its interconnectedness with war, how it "impose[s] itself on and implant[s] itself in the periphery," its promotion of fear of the "other," its tendency to increasingly commodify resources, and how it contributes to environmental destruction and compounds natural disasters), its purported imminent demise, and, crucially, how it might be confronted and ultimately destroyed. The Subcommander quashes the idea, bandied around in leftist circles, that capitalism is in its death throes. He then makes clear that in order to successfully dismantle the capitalist system, what is required is the formation of "a broad movement . . . from the entire spectrum of anticapitalist opposition," in which there should be no privileging of one sphere of struggle over "other spaces of domination." Moreover, no single movement, and certainly not the Zapatistas, should claim for itself the role of vanguard in the antisystemic struggle.

Other predominant preoccupations and recurring themes clearly emerge from this set of presentations. The first is a concern with the "center and periphery" paradigm (that is, how a colonializing center dominates a dependent periphery). Marcos is especially interested in how the center tends to exert influence, and even exercise dominance, over the periphery specifically in the realm of theoretical production and dissemination, with the result that frequently sterile and abstract theories that are devised at the center (for example, in metropolises and first-world learning institutions) are then applied to and, even worse, forced upon the distant periphery (that is, where sites of struggle against social marginalization are located). The Subcommander's second concern—with theory, and more concretely its relation to both practice and reality—shines through strongly in his first, second, and final presentations.[19] Significantly, the Subcommander closes his series of presentations by rejecting an analytical framework that interprets the world according to the dichotomous center-periphery paradigm, insisting instead that another theory is needed, one that "must . . . break with the logic of centers and periphery, anchor itself in realities that erupt and emerge, and open new paths." Another major thread that the Subcommander stresses throughout the collection of presentations is collectivity. He calls attention to the collective nature of the Zapatistas, their essence being "the collective that we are," and insists that freedom has "to be made, built collectively." The last major theme to surface, one which is especially prominent in his sixth presentation, concerns "the gaze *toward* the Zapatistas and the gaze *of* the Zapatistas." Marcos notes how external gazes directed at the Zapatista movement emanate "from afar, from another reality," and, although they are myriad, each tends to focus on only one aspect of the Zapatistas, which is especially problematic since these external gazes are "a window for others to look at us." Worse still, Marcos points out, gazes directed *toward* the Zapatistas have been privileged over those *of* the Zapatistas, with the former enjoying "the privilege of being gazes that are disseminated and known," whereas "in contrast, our gaze . . . has the drawback . . . of only being known by the other from outside if you decide to or allow it."

Significantly, Marcos ends his series of presentations with the somber observation that the Zapatistas are experiencing renewed attacks by the military, the police, and paramilitaries, but, unlike in all previous instances, this time such acts of aggression have provoked no significant response from civil society either nationally or internationally.

In addition, throughout his presentations Marcos persistently lambasts AMLO, the PRD, progressive intellectuals, and the institutional Left for their denunciations of the Zapatistas in general, and himself in particular, for criticizing the supposedly center-left presidential candidate in the 2006 elections and for refusing to endorse (and thereby legitimate) electoral politics in Mexico. He also repeatedly mocks intellectual pretentiousness and snobbery.

Stylistically, the corpus exhibits Marcos's characteristic penchant for blending elements from diverse and often contrasting genres in order to create a postmodern patchwork. Thus, we encounter within these presentations fabulous tales involving the indigenous girl December, Shadow the Warrior, and Elías Contreras; revolutionary texts and anticapitalist tracts such as the "Revolutionary Agrarian Law" and "Some Theses on Antisystemic Struggle"; pithy maxims by the Subcommander's alter ego, the fictional beetle Don Durito of the Lacandon Jungle; "Some Not-So-Scientific Anecdotes" in which Che Guevara, Uruguay's national hero General Artigas, and the founder of that country's Tupamaros guerrillas, Raúl Sendic, all deceased, get together over music with Marcos and Daniel Viglietti; and a satirical aside, taking the form of a monologue, parodying certain attitudes expressed in some left-wing intellectual circles concerning the privatization of public space in Mexico City's historic center.

The National and International Caravan for Observation and Solidarity with Zapatista Communities

On August 2, 2008, the Subcommander, having been absent from public view since the Aubry Colloquium eight months earlier, gave a speech of welcome to over three hundred Mexican and foreign solidarity activists and promoters of human rights who had traveled to La Garrucha, Chiapas. The caravan took place in response to increased military intimidation and harassment on the one hand and actual paramilitary violence on the other, all directed toward Zapatista communities in Chiapas. The second stage of the "Other Campaign" had, it should be noted, been terminated abruptly and prematurely for precisely this reason, and the subsequent eleven months had witnessed evictions, incursions, paramilitary attacks, land invasions, persecution, and threats.[20] Significantly, many of these aggressive actions were carried out by the state police, presumably under orders from the PRD state governor, Juan José Sabines Guerrero, and by paramilitary groups such as the Organization for the Defense of Indigenous and Peasant Rights (OPDDIC), which has ties to the local PRD government.[21] Meanwhile, at the national level, pro-PRD intellectuals and journalists continued to voice very public criticisms of Marcos.[22] These circumstances form the local and national context for the Subcommander's speech, and it therefore comes as no surprise that here, as in both his preceding presentations at the Aubry Colloquium and his successive ones at the Festival of Dignified Rage, Marcos levels various accusations against AMLO and his supporters among the intelligentsia, the institutional Left, and the so-called progressive media.

The purpose behind convoking the caravan in La Garrucha, Marcos explains, was to help attendees "to understand directly what is happening with the Zapatista process, not only with the attacks we are receiving, but also with the processes that are being built here in rebel territory, in Zapatista territory." The Subcommander begins by sketching the history of the Zapatista Army of National Liberation (Ejército Zapatista de Liberación Nacional, EZLN) from its origins almost a quarter century earlier, as an orthodox leftist guerrilla *foco* that sought to spark an uprising to overthrow the government and install a socialist state, to its subsequent transformation through profound and prolonged contact and interaction with Chiapas's indigenous communities. Next, he emphasizes the vital role played by indigenous women who, seeing their children die each year of perfectly curable diseases, "began to push" for the EZLN to take decisive action. He then explains how, ultimately, the dilemma faced by the indigenous communities was whether to rise up, and in doing so draw attention to their plight with the hope that this might bring about an improvement in their conditions, or not to do so and face disappearing as indigenous peoples. Marcos also notes the fundamental lesson taught to the EZLN by the indigenous communities, one that is strongly related to the Zapatistas' rejection of electoral politics in general and of AMLO and his supporters in particular—namely, that of "the problem of power," and specifically how "solutions . . . are built from the bottom up."

The speech also contains several points that Marcos would go on to develop further in subsequent writings and speeches, including one that occurs in the presentations delivered at both the Aubry Colloquium and the Festival of Dignified Rage. Thus, we find the Subcommander noting how, having abandoned (or, rather, having been abandoned by) "Zapatologists" who had formerly acted as "solidarity intermediaries" between the Zapatistas and national and international civil society, and having since forged direct links with those "other belows" in rebellion the world over, the Zapatistas came to realize that "Zapatismo's connection was stronger with other countries than with Mexico.[23] And it was stronger in Mexico than with people from Chiapas." Marcos made another point in this speech that he would pursue and elaborate on later, about how surviving Zapatistas should repay their debt to those who have given their lives in the struggle. The Subcommander closes his address to the caravan stating: "We owe a debt to those who died fighting. And we want the day to come when we can say to them . . . just three things: we did not give up, we did not sell out, we did not surrender."[24] The final point is Marcos's repeated assertion, found in this speech but also in his Colloquium and Festival presentations, that the Zapatistas utterly reject a hegemonizing or homogenizing role for themselves within the broad spectrum of anti-capitalist movements or society at large.

Marcos's speech was followed by one delivered by Lieutenant Colonel Moisés, in which he outlines how autonomy is being constructed within Zapatista rebel territory. He begins by providing an account of how indigenous peoples in the area sought to organize and unite against exploitative local bosses and the government. He traces their first attempts at doing so by joining official peasant organizations, which resulted in their demands being ignored; their subsequent forming of legal, independent organizations, which were met with repression; and ultimately their joining the ranks of the EZLN. Moisés then gives a lengthy and detailed explanation of the structure, organization, institutions, and workings of Zapatista autonomy, with its emphasis on grassroots consultations, collective decision-making processes, and a governing principle of "command by obeying" whereby the autonomous authorities have "to obey and the people command." The speech is significant not only for its content but also because, with hindsight, it may be viewed as providing Moisés with experience in preparation for his presentation at the Festival of Dignified Rage less than six months later, and can even be interpreted as the initial step in his being groomed for promotion to subcommander four-and-a-half years later.

The Global Festival of Dignified Rage

During the "Other Campaign," the Subcommander had toured the country listening to the humble and downtrodden individually tell of their personal experience of dispossession and exploitation, but also of resistance to such treatment; in doing so, they exhibited a bitterness borne with dignity. Having heard such accounts firsthand, Marcos concluded: "Down here we are being left with nothing. Except rage. And dignity. . . . Rage and dignity are our bridges, our languages. Let us listen to each other then, let us know each other. Let our rage grow and become hope. . . . If this world doesn't have a place for us, then another world must be made. With no other tool than our rage, no other material than our dignity."[25] Taking this into account, and encouraged by the success of the Aubry Colloquium twelve months earlier, the Zapatistas convened the Global Festival of Dignified Rage, with its theme of "Another World, Another Path: Below and to the Left."[26] The Festival would take place from late December 2008 to early January 2009 and would commemorate several important milestones for the movement, including the twenty-fifth anniversary of the founding of the EZLN, the fifteenth anniversary of the Zapatista uprising, five years of the Zapatistas' Good Government Committees, and three years since the "Other Campaign" had begun. The Festival comprised three stages: the first was held in Mexico City from December 26 to 29; the second in Oventik, Chiapas, on December 31 and January 1; and the third in San Cristóbal de las Casas from January 2 to 5.[27]

The first stage was perhaps most akin to a festival in that, as Jorge Alonso notes, "around 2,500 people turned up every day, in addition to about a hundred artistic groups that shared their music, theater, dance, stories, poems, paintings, films, videos, and photography related to the struggles in Mexico and the world," so that ultimately "a total of 270 speakers from 57 collectives in 25 countries gave presentations at 39 locations, while another 1,155 people from 228 organizations from 27 states of the Mexican Republic presented their political and cultural proposals in 109 places."[28] In addition to these cultural exhibitions, open forums and, ultimately, a roundtable ran concurrently in which activists, intellectuals, members of collectives and grassroots organizations, as well as others met in the mornings to discuss the four wheels of capitalism (exploitation, dispossession, repression, contempt) and then again in the afternoons to deliberate on "other paths" (including "another city," "other social movements," "another history," and "another politics").

The second stage was held in the heart of autonomous Zapatista territory, at Oventik, deep in a predominantly indigenous Tzotzil and Tzeltal region of the highlands of Chiapas. There the Festival's participants were warmly greeted by the autonomous government and Zapatista support bases, after which they all celebrated the fifteenth anniversary of the event that brought the Zapatistas out of their clandestine darkness and into the public light: their January 1994 uprising.

Finally, the third stage shared points in common with the Aubry Colloquium in that it involved the Subcommander again delivering a succession of vehemently anticapitalist presentations, this time as part of a series titled "Seven Winds in the Calendars and Geographies of Below," once again at the Indigenous Center for Integral Training–University of the Earth in San Cristóbal, and alongside an array of other left-wing luminaries including both those who had previously participated in the Colloquium, such as Carlos Antonio Aguirre Rojas, Pablo González Casanova, Gustavo Esteva, Sylvia Marcos, Jean Robert, Sergio Rodríguez Lascano, and John Berger (who had to send a recording of his contribution as he could not attend in person), as well as those who had not, among them Michael Hardt, a US professor, political theorist, and coauthor (with Tony Negri) of several seminal works of political philosophy.[29] Some thirty-five hundred audience members were in attendance, once again comprising academics and activists from various national and international organizations and institutions. Unlike the Aubry Colloquium, however, this time Marcos was not the only Zapatista to give a presentation. He was joined by Lieutenant Colonel Moisés, who delivered the Zapatistas' fourth presentation on "An

Organized Dignified Rage," in which he discussed the Zapatista Autonomous Rebel Municipalities, their democratic structure, their collective nature, and their grassroots workings; and by Commander Hortensia, who gave their fifth presentation on "A Dignified and Feminine Rage," in which she talked at length, as she puts it, "about the work, participation, and organization of women in Zapatista territory." Moreover, in contrast to the Colloquium, this time the Zapatistas' speeches were followed by panel sessions in which the themes that had been covered and the points that had been raised were then discussed further.

The first point to note is that certain threads pertaining to both Marcos's Aubry Colloquium presentations and his August 2008 speech to the solidarity caravan can also be seen resurfacing in the Subcommander's words at the Festival. One such important instance involves the question of geography. In the Aubry Colloquium Marcos had talked of how theories emanating from metropolitan centers imposed themselves on rural peripheries, and in his Caravan speech he had noted "an inverse relationship in geography" whereby "those who lived farther away were closer to us, and those who lived closer were farther away from us." Here, in his opening speech at the Festival, the Subcommander develops this theme, discussing "the problem of . . . geographies," and more specifically how Power has done a good job of convincing people that geographical (that is, spatial) differences exist and of creating an apparent distance between countries when in fact there is no distance either between those places where Power tries to exert its dominion or between those places where resistance arises to counter this domination, with the result that Chiapas and Greece, on account of their resisting Power (that is, opposing capitalism's imposition), are not distant but instead close. The second theme that spans speeches at all three occasions has already been noted: namely, the Zapatistas' repeated rejection of a hegemonic or vanguard role for themselves among anticapitalist movements. Lastly, we also witness the resurfacing of such preoccupations as denouncing AMLO and those who support him, especially so-called progressive intellectuals, and the reassertion of the Zapatistas' refusal to pursue the electoral route or even participate in electoral politics.

Marcos also covered new ground in his presentations at the Festival. One theme that he makes much of in his first paper is violence. The Subcommander observes how "up above everyone takes out their dictionaries and finds the word 'violence' and counterposes it with 'institutionalism.' And without putting it in context—that is, social class—they accuse, judge, and condemn. . . . [U]p above they demand and insist: 'We must say no to violence, wherever it comes from' . . . making sure to emphasize it if the violence comes from below." He also makes clear that it was through the use of violence initially that the Zapatistas have been able to achieve what they have and that Power employs violence as one of its many means of exerting dominion, so that those who oppose Power must also retain violence as one possible weapon in their arsenal.

Another important theme is raised in Marcos's second presentation and concerns "calendars" that "Power . . . uses . . . to neutralize movements that attack or have attacked its essence, its existence, or its normality." The Subcommander notes that commemorative statues, ceremonies, monuments, and parades are all mobilized to ensure that those who died opposing Power stay dead and buried.

Next, Marcos trains his rhetorical guns on supposed "specialists," and in particular (though not exclusively) that "special species of specialists: professional politicians." He accuses specialists of arrogance, and of jealously guarding what they have learned. By contrast, insists the Subcommander, indigenous peoples are not specialists, but they are not ignorant either, even though they are frequently treated as such by others, and they are generous regarding the knowledge they have acquired. Finally, Marcos contrasts the advances in health, housing, education, and nutrition made by nonspecialist, indigenous Zapatista authorities, some of whom lack any formal education, with the comparative lack of progress being made in these areas in "the official municipalities that are governed by professional politicians, by political specialists."

The last two major themes taken up by the Subcommander are connected to one another. First, in his sixth presentation, Marcos acknowledges the support that the Zapatistas have received "from indigenous people, from women, from young people, and from gays, lesbians, transgender people, transsexuals—principally, although not always, sex workers." He points out that these groups are united by their common status as "others." More broadly, the Subcommander states his total opposition to the imposition of any norm that prescribes what constitutes "a normal person" and treats those outside this category with distrust, discrimination, mockery, and assault. Secondly, and very much linked to this defense of difference and diversity, is Marcos's insistence on the importance of heterogeneity within the anticapitalist struggle. The Subcommander urges that within the anticapitalist movement—even though each struggle has its own history and dreams, fights on its own fronts in its own ways, and recognizes its own strengths and limitations—there must nonetheless be respect toward others whose goal is similar though their methods may be different. He concludes by arguing that the anticapitalist movement's strength lies precisely in its diversity.

There remains a final point worth making concerning this set of presentations, which is that, just as at the Aubry Colloquium, so too on this occasion Marcos employs a variety of genres—anecdotes, stories, firsthand reportage, fables, children's stories, and myths—to convey, or in certain instances reinforce, the Zapatistas' messages. This leads Jérôme Baschet, in his introduction to a French translation of the Colloquium and Festival presentations, to extol the Subcommander's "narrative and linguistic abilities and his skill at weaving fable and story, humor and theory, social imaginary and tales of the everyday life of the native rebel communities into the heart of a discourse which is as political as it is poetical," and to note how "the first virtue of this use of language is that it breaks with conventions of customary political discourse, thanks to its humor, its irony and the continued recourse it has to a mixture of genres. . . . It is a matter also of breaking, by a concrete use of language, the abstractness of political theory, and it is here that the power of narratives works wonders."[30]

Marcos Bids Adiós

Little had been seen of Subcommander Marcos in the five years following the Festival of Dignified Rage. True, after a two-year lull, Marcos had picked up his pen again in early 2011 and began to issue a significant number of communiqués that included a four-part correspondence with eminent Spanish-Mexican philosopher Luis Villoro. However, the Subcommander had been largely absent from the public scene. While rumors swirled regarding his disappearance, looking back it seems highly probable that he was spending this period contemplating and preparing to take a backseat within the movement, stepping aside to make way for a younger, purely indigenous generation of Zapatista leaders and spokespersons. Indeed, on February 14, 2013, Marcos introduced a new subcommander to the world, former Lieutenant Colonel Moisés. This was a highly significant promotion because it represented the first appointment of a Zapatista subcommander in a quarter century, the first time since the death of Subcommander Pedro on the first day of their uprising that the Zapatistas had had more than one subcommander, and the advent of the first-ever indigenous subcommander of the EZLN.

Fifteen months later, in the very early hours of May 25, 2014, in the town of La Realidad, deep in the Zapatistas' heartland, Subcommander

Marcos delivered a speech before more than two thousand support-base members, six hundred solidarity supporters, and the alternative press in which he declared that he would henceforth cease to exist.[31] Those assembled had convened the previous day to pay homage to a Zapatista support-base member and teacher known as Galeano, who had been ambushed and brutally assassinated by paramilitaries a little over three weeks earlier, on May 2, only a few hundred yards from where Marcos was now speaking. Beyond bearing Marcos's message of farewell, the speech is important for a number of other reasons.

First, Marcos provides a succinct outline of the "multiple and complex" changes that had taken place in the composition and character of the EZLN over the last two decades; these changes were of generation, class, race, gender, and political theory and practice. Second, Marcos uses his speech not only to provide an explanation as to how "the character named 'Marcos' started to be constructed" but also to discuss how this persona subsequently took on a life of its own: he also addresses its function, assesses its efficacy, and relates its ramifications for the Zapatista movement.[32] He then goes on to disparage what he perceives to have been a frivolous obsession with the persona of Marcos, choosing to stress instead the importance of collective struggle over an emphasis on any one individual. Finally, the speech closes with a brief eulogy on Galeano in which the Subcommander explains that the Zapatistas hoped to cheat death by killing off the character of Marcos and offering him up in place of Galeano.

After having concluded his speech, Marcos lit his pipe and exited the podium, which was then plunged into almost total darkness. Subcommander Moisés, who had accompanied Marcos on the stage until this point, then announced that another comrade would address the audience, after which the voice that had once belonged to Subcommander Marcos could be heard introducing himself as "Insurgent Subcommander Galeano" and asking if anyone else present bore the name Galeano. A host of voices from the audience shouted out "We are all Galeano," echoing the refrain "We are all Marcos" that was chanted by protesters in the streets of Mexico City in February 1995 during demonstrations against the government's sudden attempt to capture (some would suggest, kill) the Subcommander. In response, the voice replied: "Ah, so that's why they told me that when I was reborn, it would be collectively."

Ultimately, this speech can be said to be momentous in that it marked the latest transformation of a man who was born Rafael Sebastián Guillén Vicente and subsequently underwent successive rebaptisms as Zacarías (on entering the clandestine Forces of National Liberation, the mother organization of the EZLN), Marcos (when he joined the ranks of the EZLN in Chiapas), "El Subcomandante" or "El Sup" (following his public appearance during the Zapatista uprising), and "Delegado Zero" (at the outset of the "Other Campaign").[33] It also marked a watershed moment for the EZLN: from this point on the Zapatistas would have two Subcommanders, two spokespersons, and the figure of Marcos, now reincarnated as Galeano, would share center stage with Moisés, as happened at the 2015 "Critical Thought in the Face of the Capitalist Hydra" seminar.

Appendix: The "Rewind" Trilogy and the "Pain and Rage" Communiqué

The "Rewind" series of communiqués was composed in the usual order (that is, number 1 was written first, number 2 second, and number 3 third), but they were released publicly at intervals in reverse order.[34] Thus, "Rewind 3" appears first and is dated November 17, 2003, which, as Marcos points out, marks the thirtieth anniversary of the founding of the EZLN in Chiapas. "Rewind 2" is dated December 22, 2013, which, although the Subcommander does not make mention of it, marked the sixteenth anniversary of the Acteal massacre in which forty-five indigenous men, women, and children were massacred by paramilitaries, as police looked on, while praying for peace in their chapel. "Rewind 1" was released on December 28, 2013, in the immediate run-up to the twentieth anniversary of the Zapatista uprising.

These communiqués contain numerous interesting observations (such as on the nature of fanatics and fanaticism, the relationship between biographers and their subjects, the issue of identity, the avoiding of imposed false dichotomies, and so forth) and are rich in incisive critiques (such as of the "paid" media, the institutional Left, and those who would impose modernity on the Zapatistas in the name of "progress"). Here, however, I draw attention to one theme and two interconnected emphases that are exhibited in the "Rewind" trilogy. Throughout the communiqués, Marcos talks about "life and death" and, more specifically, how the first is frequently (mis)represented (for example, in biographies and the "paid" media) while the latter is often hijacked, administered, and commodified (by "those who live at the cost of others' dying . . . justifying their own inaction . . . or sterile action"). The Subcommander also emphasizes two related points: the collective as opposed to the individual and, linked to this, the path as opposed to the person who walks it.

Looking back in hindsight, with the knowledge that less than six months after the Subcommander had released the last in the "Rewind" series he would give a speech announcing that he would henceforth cease to exist, we can perceive in these communiqués his preoccupations during this period in which, as he tells us in his farewell speech, he was planning the destruction of the Marcos character that the Zapatistas had created. In short, the "Rewind" communiqués foreshadow Marcos's farewell speech.

The final communiqué in the appendix, "Pain and Rage," represents the Zapatista Command's first official, public response to the murder of the Zapatista teacher Galeano and, in doing so, provides a report on the initial findings of its preliminary investigation. It is important not only because it supplies a context for the eulogy that Marcos delivers in his farewell speech but also because it provides a window on the day-to-day lived realities that the Zapatista communities face: namely, harassment, intimidation, violence, and even murder. The death of Galeano is described in vivid detail, its brutal, cowardly, and premeditated nature; the true motivation behind it (in contrast to the attempts to speciously portray it as having resulted from a bloody squabble between indigenous groups); and the widespread pattern of provocation into which it fits; laid bare for all to see.

Conclusion

The presentations, speeches, and communiqués translated here provide a vivid snapshot of both the politics taking place in Mexico in the twenty-first century and the impact that neoliberal capitalism is having on the most marginalized sectors of Mexican society. Crucially, it is a picture produced by those situated at the sharp end of capitalist exploitation—that is, by those who have direct knowledge and firsthand experience of its ravages. More than being the mere eyewitness testimony of those who face capitalism's inroads and impositions on a daily basis, however, these Zapatista texts communicate to us the inventive and illuminating strategies—theoretical, practical, and rhetorical—they have devised to confront its onslaught; they also afford effective future avenues for the antineoliberal globalization movement to pursue. Interestingly, they do so while employing an innovative, inspiring, creative, lively, and engaging political language that is very far removed from the impenetrable, esoteric, highly technical Marxist jargon of the old Left; the gray, bureaucratic platitudes of current government spokespersons; and the often sterile, stilted, dry, and detached academic prose of political scientists and theorists.

Finally, with regard to the Subcommander specifically, the speeches and communiqués included in our collection reveal Marcos's many facets—political philosopher, postmodern pamphleteer, promoter of indigenous and women's (and, indeed, human) rights, and champion of the downtrodden—and cement his status as an anticapitalist and antiglobalization rebel icon.[35] Indeed, what follow are some of the most penetrating analyses and devastating critiques of the capitalist system and its effects at both the local and global level that have been produced by the iconic and iconoclastic Insurgent Subcommander. Significantly, while there have been many poignant critics of capitalism, political parties, electoral democracy, academia, fear of difference, and many of the other things that Marcos here critiques, he was the only one providing such accounts who was also military leader and main spokesperson of an armed social movement made up of tens of thousands of people. Moreover, the Subcommander's tremendous ethical consistency, his living entirely in accordance with the ideals he has expressed in his writings and spoken word, ensures that for two decades he was arguably the foremost and most recognizable exponent of combining left-wing theory and practice. His words (and those of his fellow Zapatistas) therefore lie at the cutting edge of anticapitalist discourse.

With that having been said, it is now time to let Marcos's words speak for themselves.

Nick Henck
Yokohama, June 2017

ENDNOTES

1   Communiqué entitled "Chiapas: The Thirteenth Stele, Part Two: A Death," July 25, 2003, https://www.narconews.com/Issue31/article833.html.

2   Interview with Ann Louise Bardach, "Mexico's Poet Rebel," *Vanity Fair* 57 (July 1994): 68–74 and 130–35, at 132; and interview with Medea Benjamin, "Interview: Subcomandante Marcos," in *First World, Ha Ha Ha! The Zapatista Challenge*, ed. Elaine Katzenberger, 57–70 (San Francisco: City Lights, 1995), 67.

3   Michael Tangeman, *Mexico at the Crossroads* (New York: Orbis Books, 1995), 77.

4   Jorge Alonso, "A History of Challenging Messages," *envío*, no. 418 (May 2016), http://www.envio.org.ni/articulo/5188.

5   Available online both in English and Spanish: Zapatista Army of National Liberation, "Sexta Declaración de la Selva Lacandona," http://palabra.ezln.org.mx/comunicados/2005/2005_06_SEXTA.htm; and Zapatista Army of National Liberation, "Sixth Declaration of the Lacandon Jungle," http://sixthdeclaration.blogspot.com.

6   Zapatista Army of National Liberation, "Sixth Declaration of the Lacandon Jungle," http://sixthdeclaration.blogspot.com.

7   Several of the Subcommander's key statements on democracy are collected in Nick Henck, *Insurgent Marcos: The Political-Philosophical Formation of the Zapatista Subcommander* (Raleigh, NC: Editorial A Contracorriente, 2016), 136–38.

8   "A Letter from Marcos," Anarkismo.net, June 21, 2005, http://www.anarkismo .net/newswire.php?story_id=777.

9   In *Corte de Caja: Entrevista al Subcomandante Marcos* (México, DF: Grupo Editorial Endira, 2008), 54.

10   Immanuel Wallerstein, who coined the phrase "antisystemic movements," defines them as ones that are "struggling against the established power structures in an effort to bring into existence a more democratic, more egalitarian historical system than the existing one." Wallerstein, Keynote address delivered at the Thirty-Eighth Annual Political Economy of the World-System Conference, April 10, 2014, Pittsburgh, Pennsylvania; published as "Antisystemic Movements, Yesterday and Today," *Journal of World-Systems Research* 20, no. 2 (2014): 158–72, at 160, http://jwsr .pitt.edu/ojs/public/journals/1/Full_Issue_PDFs/jwsr-v20n2.pdf.

11   For more on this innovative and inspirational educational facility, see the interview with the center's general coordinator, Dr. Raymundo Sánchez Barraza: "Interview with Raymundo Sánchez Barraza: A University without Shoes," *In Motion Magazine*, December 18, 2005, http://www.inmotionmagazine.com/global/rsb_ int_eng.html. For a useful description of the center, known by its Spanish acronym CIDECI, complete with excellent photographs of its facilities, see "Visiting Another Unitierra – In San Cristobal, Chiapas," Enlivened Learning, January 16, 2003, http:// enlivenedlearning.com/2013/01/16/visiting-another-unitierra-in-san-cristobal-chiapas/.

12   See the chapter entitled "El carácter 'modélico' del neozapatismo mexicano dentro de los movimientos antisistémicos actuales," in Carlos Antonio Aguirre Rojas, *Antimanual del Buen Rebelde* (Barcelona: El Viejo Topo: 2015), in which Aguirre extols the Zapatistas' "model and exemplary character" within the antisystemic movement. For his part, Wallerstein labels the Zapatistas "the most important social movement in the world . . . the barometer and the igniter of antisystemic movements around the world" and "a major inspiration for antisystemic movements throughout the world." Immanuel Wallerstein, "The Zapatistas: The Second Stage," Commentary, no. 165 (July 15, 2005), http://www.binghamton.edu/fbc/archive/165en.htm; and Wallerstein, "What Have the Zapatistas Accomplished?," Commentary, no. 224 (January 1, 2008), http://www.binghamton.edu/fbc/archive/224en.htm.

13   Immanuel Wallerstein, "Marcos, Mandela, and Gandhi," Commentary, no. 59 (March 1, 2001), http://www.binghamton.edu/fbc/archive/59en.htm. Wallerstein likens the Zapatista movement to the Indian National Congress and African National Congress, given the ability of all three "to gain the widest support from world public opinion, thereby achieving what might be called moral hegemony," with the result that "Gandhi, Mandela, and now Marcos have taken on the flavor of world moral heroes."

14   For example, Jorge Alonso, Mexican anthropologist and correspondent for the Nicaraguan monthly magazine *envío*; Jérôme Baschet, a French medieval histori-

an, supporter of the Zapatistas, and author of several books on the movement; Pablo González Casanova, former rector of the National Autonomous University of Mexico, winner of Mexico's National Prize for Arts and Sciences (1984) and UNESCO's José Martí International Prize (2003), author of the celebrated *Democracy in Mexico* (as well as some forty other books), and longtime supporter of the Zapatista movement; Enrique Dussel, an Argentine philosopher and prolific writer; Gustavo Esteva, a Mexican grassroots activist, "deprofessionalized intellectual," former adviser to the Zapatistas, and founder of the Universidad de la Tierra (Oaxaca); Ricardo Gebrim, Brazilian lawyer and member of Landless Movement (MST); François Houtart, a Belgian priest and founding member of the World Social Forum's international council; Sylvia Marcos, a Mexican feminist scholar; Jean Robert, a Swiss-born architect, historian of technology, energy specialist, and adviser to the Zapatistas; Sergio Rodríguez Lascano, a former activist with Mexico's Revolutionary Workers' Party (PRT) and the Zapatista National Liberation Front (FZLN), and current editor of the Zapatista magazine *Rebeldía*; Peter Rosset, a U.S.-born internationally respected food security and agricultural issues expert, and researcher at the Center for the Study of the Americas; Jorge Santiago, the former director of Social and Economic Development for Indigenous Mexicans (DESMI) in San Cristóbal (Chiapas) and a leading proponent of the "solidarity economy" movement; and Gilberto Valdés, a Cuban professor of philosophy and specialist in social movements.

15   The original audio recordings of all the main presentations from the Colloquium can be found at http://www.coloquiointernacionalandresaubry.org/audios .html, and the Enlace Zapatista website, at http://enlacezapatista.ezln.org.mx/, has both the recordings and their typescripts. For useful firsthand accounts in English of some of the ideas presented by various speakers at the Colloquium—provided by a participant and an attendee, respectively—see Jorge Alonso, "Warning the World that Zapatismo Is in Danger," *envío*, no. 318 (January 2008), http://www .envio.org.ni/articulo/3718; and Quincy Saul, "Reflections on the Primer Colloquio [*sic*] Internacional In Memoriam Andres Aubry: Planeta Tierra: Movimientos Anti-sistemicos," Yo No Me Callo, September 15, 2010, http://smashthisscreen.blogspot. co.uk/2010/09/reflections-on-primer-colloquio.html.

16   The first session saw presentations by Immanuel Wallerstein, Carlos Antonio Aguirre Rojas, and Marcos; the second, by Sylvia Marcos, Gustavo Esteva, and Marcos; the third, by Gilberto Valdés, Jorge Alonso, and Marcos; the fourth, by Ricardo Gebrim, François Houtart, Peter Rosset, and Marcos; the fifth, by Sergio Rodríguez Lascano, Enrique Dussel, and Marcos; the sixth, by John Berger, Jean Robert, and Marcos; and the seventh, by Naomi Klein, Pablo González Casanova, and Marcos.

17   "The Story of Durito and Neoliberalism" (April 1994), "Durito II: Neoliberalism Seen from La Lacandona" (March 1995), "Durito III: The Story of Neoliberalism and the Labor Movement" (April 1995), "Durito IV: Neoliberalism and the Party-State System" (June 1995), "Durito VI: Neoliberalism, Chaotic Theory of Economic Chaos" (July 1995), and "Durito IX: Neoliberalism, History as a Tale . . . Badly Told" (April 1996). These are collected in *Conversations with Durito: Stories of the Zapatistas and Neoliberalism* (New York: Autonomedia, 2005).

18   For a detailed discussion of these ideological underpinnings, which include *mestizaje*, modernity, the rule of law, neoliberalism as the bringer of economic benefit to all, and the PRI government as sole legitimate heir to the Mexican Revolution, see my "Adiós Marcos: A Fond Farewell to the Subcommander Who Simply Ceased

to Exist," *A Contracorriente* 12, no. 2 (Winter 2015): 401–21, at 410–15; and my *Insurgent Marcos: The Political-Philosophical Formation of the Zapatista Subcommander* (Raleigh, NC: Editorial A Contracorriente, 2016), 99–104.

19   The relationship between theory, on the one hand, and both praxis and reality, on the other, is something that Marcos had deeply concerned himself with previously, for example in his "The World: Seven Thoughts in May of 2003." For a detailed treatment of the Subcommander's preoccupation with this theme, including discussion of how he explores this in his presentations at the Aubry Colloquium, see Henck, *Insurgent Marcos*, 105–13.

20   For a catalog of such acts of aggression, see Jessica Davies, "Threats to Autonomy: The Urgent Need for Solidarity with Zapatista Communities under Attack," *the narcosphere*, October 2, 2008, http://narcosphere.narconews .com/notebook/jessica-davies/2008/10/threats-autonomy-urgent-need-solidarity-zapatista-communities-under-.

21   See ibid. and Hermann Bellinghausen, "Desestabiliza Opddic zonas de Chiapas, denuncian juntas de buen gobierno," *La Jornada*, February 13, 2007, http://www.jornada.unam.mx/2007/02/13/index.php?section=politica&article=015n1pol.

22   To cite a specific instance, see Octavio Rodríguez Araujo, "El fin del liderazgo del Subcomandante Marcos," *Casa del Tiempo* 2, nos. 14–15 (December 2008–January 2009): 31–35, http://www.uam.mx/difusion/casadeltiempo/14_15_ iv_dic_ene_2009/casa_del_tiempo_eIV_num14_15_31_36.pdf. More generally, see Laura Castellanos, "Learning, Surviving: Marcos after the Rupture." *NACLA Report on the Americas* 41, no. 3 (May–June 2008): 34–39, https://nacla.org/article/ learning-surviving-marcos-after-rupture.

23   "Zapatologists" is the term that Marcos uses to denote supposed or self-styled experts on the Zapatista movement.

24   Marcos would reiterate this five years later, in his second "Rewind" communiqué. See the full text of the communiqué in the appendix on p. 241.

25   In his communiqué announcing the forthcoming Festival: "Comunicado del CCRI—CG del EZLN. Comisión sexta—comisión intergaláctica del EZLN. En inglés," Enlace Zapatista, September 18, 2008, http://enlacezapatista.ezln.org .mx/2008/09/18/comunicado-del-ccri-cg-del-ezln-comision-sexta-comision-inter-galactica-del-ezln-en-ingles/. In his October invitation to participate in the coming Festival, Marcos would talk of "a creative rage, that is, it points towards a transformation of the situation."

26   Part of the September 16, 2008, invitation to participate in the coming Festival is quoted and translated by El Kilombo: "Zapatistas Hold First Global Festival of Dignified Rage," El Kilombo, http://www.elkilombo.org/first-global -festival-of-dignified-rage/. See, too, the communiqué dated November 26, 2008, outlining the participants and agenda of the Festival: "Comunicado del CCRI—CG del EZLN. Comisión sexta—comisión intergaláctica del EZLN. En inglés," Enlace Zapatista, September 18, 2008, http://enlacezapatista.ezln.org.mx/2008/11/30/ comunicado-de-la-comision-sexta-y-la-comision-intergalactica-del-ezln-a-ls-participantes-del-festival-en-ingles/.

27   For a useful overview of all three stages of the Festival, including a brief discussion of the themes covered in the presentations delivered during the third stage,

see Jorge Alonso, "Zapatistas Organize the First Global Festival of Dignified Rage," *envío*, no. 330 (January 2009), http://www.envio.org.ni/articulo/3940. For a wealth of information on the Festival in Spanish, including full-color photographs, see the 250-page *Miradas, Ecos, y Reflejos de la Digna Rabia* (Spain: Europa Zapatista, 2009), produced by www.europazapatista.org and available at http://www.chiapas.at/beitraege/reflejos_de_la_digna_rabia.pdf.

28   Alonso, "Zapatistas Organize."

29   For example, Mónica Baltodano, a Nicaraguan former revolutionary and politician; Hugo Blanco, a Peruvian ex-guerrilla, author, and politician; Paulina Fernández Christlieb, a Mexican political scientist; Adolfo Gilly, an Argentine-Mexican professor of political science; Oscar Olivera, a Bolivian coleader of the antiprivatization protesters in the Cochabamba Water Wars; Luis Villoro, a Spanish-Mexican philosopher of considerable repute; Jaime Pastor, a Spanish Marxist intellectual and political figure; and Raúl Zibechi, a Uruguayan journalist, activist, and political theorist.

30   Jérôme Baschet, introduction to *Saisons de la Digne Rage* (Paris: Climats, 2009), 8, 36.

31   The transcript of the Subcommander's original speech in Spanish can be found at "Entre la luz y la sombra," Enlace Zapatista, May 25, 2014, http://enlacezapatista.ezln.org.mx/2014/05/25/entre-la-luz-y-la-sombra/. For audiovisual coverage, see "Entre la luz y la sombra: Últimas palabras del Subcomandante Marcos," Radio Zapatista, http://radiozapatista.org/?p=9766&lang=en; and, in four parts with English subtitles, "Between light and shadow. Sup Marcos' last public speech. English subtitles," posted by Maria Taurizano: https://www.youtube.com/watch?v=Tw38fm4nWRE (posted May 30, 2014), https://www.youtube.com/watch?v=R4BZnyEh6FI (posted May 31, 2014), https://www.youtube.com/watch?v=EfOz5X4xIks (posted June 11, 2014), and https://www.youtube.com/watch?v=r_cfG_cyBCE (posted June 11, 2014).

32   For a reasonably detailed discussion of Marcos's somewhat self-effacing assessment of how important it was for him to draw the gaze of the Mexican and foreign media, Mexican civil society, and an international audience and support base that has included Hollywood stars and directors, literati, intellectuals, artists, academics, journalists, and rock musicians, see Nick Henck, "Adiós Marcos: A Fond Farewell to the Subcommander Who Simply Ceased to Exist," *A Contracorriente* 12, no. 2 (Winter 2015): 401–21.

33   For these incarnations, see Nick Henck, *Subcommander Marcos: The Man and the Mask* (Durham, NC: Duke University Press, 2007); and for a detailed, firsthand account in English of Marcos's transformation into Subcomandante Galeano at the end of this May 25, 2014, speech, see Alejandro Reyes, "Adiós, Subcomandante," *Radio Zapatista*, May 26, 2014, http://radiozapatista.org/?p=9785&lang=en.

34   For a brief but useful discussion of the "Rewind" series, see Eugene Gogol, *Utopia and the Dialectic in Latin American Liberation* (Leiden: Brill, 2016), 406–13.

35   If the relevance of the term "pamphleteer" is less self-evident than the preceding and succeeding labels, consider that the function of a pamphleteer was, traditionally, to promote political and social issues, encourage public debate on these issues, disseminate a political program, satirize abuses of power, and lampoon the

powerful. On this basis, Marcos is a pamphleteer par excellence. In fact, Christopher Domínguez Michael and Enrique Krauze—both Mexican historians, essayists, and critics—have independently applied the label "pamphleteer" to the Subcommander. I qualify the term with the adjective "postmodern" both because Marcos's medium is the Internet (not the printing press) and because of his penchant for producing a discourse that is informed by, and itself takes the form of, myriad genres.

Translator's Foreword

Five years ago, I set out to produce translations of Zapatista communiques of higher quality than those in existence. It took me four months (on and off) to translate my first communique, and I learned a lot along the way. The translation wasn't all that bad, but it wasn't all that good either.

The fact of the matter is that it's real hard to produce translations that don't suck. No matter how good your Spanish is, the first time you translate you get stuck every few sentences or every few words on something you can't quite get to sound right in English. After a while I got the hang of it, and, at different points along the way, I genuinely believed I had succeeded at translating perfectly and with ease.

Thankfully, I had the good fortune of crossing paths with people who have dealt a blow to the temptation of complacency and led me to rethink and improve the way I translate. My personal reflections and the feedback of others have dramatically improved the quality of my work and also led me to opt for translations that are different from those that longtime readers of Marcos are used to.

Most notably, I have chosen to translate *Subcomandante Marcos* as *Subcommander Marcos* instead of leaving it in Spanish, as has been common practice since the Zapatistas' inception. I have done the same for other members of Zapatista leadership whose ranks have generally not been translated: Commander Ramona, Lt. Col. Moisés, Commander Hortensia, etc.

I see no reason to use the Spanish terms *subcomandante* and *comandante/comandanta* other than the sheer weight of tradition. *Subcomandante* and *subcommander* mean exactly the same thing; neither in English nor in Spanish is it a common military rank. The only real difference is that googling "subcomandante" yields results about the Zapatistas while googling "subcommander" yields results about Star Trek. I'm not sure what this unorthodox term means aboard the USS Enterprise, but as far as the Zapatistas are concerned, it refers to the fact that Marcos is subordinate to the Zapatistas' indigenous commanders, who he sometimes refers to as his "bosses."

In general, I have translated every word or term for which I could find a viable English translation, regardless of whether those words have traditionally been left in Spanish for one reason or another. While others familiar with Spanish may at times find these translations to be less than perfect, I find this approach to be far better than the alternative. Extensive use of unusual words creates a culture of exclusivity and barriers to understanding, or at the very least makes the text harder to read and unappealing for those who are not diehard Zapatista supporters.

English-speaking Zapatista supporters have a tendency to pepper their writing and speech with untranslated Spanish words. I myself used to do this because I believed that there was an "essence" to certain Spanish words that could never be captured in an English translation. This was a silly thing to do. It's true that there is often something about certain words that makes them special in a way that a translation cannot reflect. However, the practice of using copious amounts of Spanglish is no different than using unnecessary amounts of academic jargon, it is nothing more than another sleight of hand that intentionally or unintentionally keeps people out of the club.

Sure, you don't need to be fluent in Spanish to figure out that *comandante* means *commander*. The same cannot be said, however, of trying to pronounce this word and use it in conversation. As such, I believe that we must use as much English as possible when addressing an English-speaking audience. We must focus on using language that is accessible to the population at large and low on jargon.

Nonetheless, there are a few Spanish words that cannot be translated into English. The most common untranslatable word that you'll find in this book is *compañero* (the ñ is pronounced "n-y" like in *piñata*: "com-pahn-yair-oh"). *Compañero* can be used to refer to a friend, acquaintance, classmate, coworker, or even someone who the speaker has never met before, so long as there is some kind of shared ideological or group connection between the two people. There is simply no suitable equivalent in English; we don't have a word that can be used for both friends and complete strangers, in both cases implying some level of connectedness.

Since most Spanish nouns are gendered, *compañero(s)* is used for males or gender-neutral situations, while *compañera(s)* is used for females. There is also a fully gender-neutral contraction of the word: *compa* (*compañero, compañera*), and Marcos has coined the word *compañeroa* for those who do not identify with either gender.

Compañero/a is used quite heavily within the Mexican left-wing community. Marcos uses it constantly to refer to those who share the Zapatistas' strategy for political change: "from below and to the left." Change "from below" means working to organize the disempowered and change things from that level of society, rather than working to take political power or focusing only on changing laws and public policy. In the case of the Zapatistas, "to the left" means fighting against capitalism and the tremendous inequalities in wealth and power that it perpetuates, as well as fighting for a world where we accept and respect those who are different from us.

Specifically, those who align themselves with the Zapatistas are called "compañero/a(s) of the Other Campaign / Sixth Declaration." These are people who have read and adhere to the principles of the Zapatistas' Sixth Declaration of the Lacandon Jungle, which explains the Zapatistas' history and their perspective on fighting for political change.[1]

Marcos also makes numerous references to the "Right." However, it should be noted that Mexico has no equivalent of the American "right-wing" or "conservative" identity. There is no shortage of people with conservative views on gender, abortion, marijuana, or homosexuality; it's just that these people do not consider these views to be a crucial part of their identity. So when Marcos uses the term "right-wing," he is talking almost exclusively about those in positions of political power who are using violence and oppression to stop people from fighting for change.

This group of power brokers is also referred to as "those above," while the Zapatistas and people without political or economic power are "those below." Marcos constantly uses the words *below* and *above* to draw contrasts between the many and the few.

As indigenous peoples, a crucial part of the Zapatistas' politics is opposing the centuries-long racism against the indigenous exercised by Mexico's dominant race: mestizos. Marcos reflects this by making reference to the indigenous struggle and using symbolism to express indigenous pride. There are numerous references to earth-colored or brown, tying the skin color of Mexico's indigenous to the land and agricultural production. He also weaves in the political saying "five hundred years of struggle," which

---

1   An English translation is available at: sixthdeclaration.blogspot.com.

refers to the more than five hundred years of racial oppression that the indigenous in North and South America have fought against since Columbus's arrival in 1492.

Marcos ties the struggle of the Zapatistas and of indigenous peoples to similar struggles in other "geographies" and "calendars." *Geographies* is Marcos's unique way of saying "places" or "conceptions of space," while *calendars* is his way of saying "time" or "conceptions of time." Why he chooses to do this is certainly open to interpretation. One clear benefit is the continuity of having a single word to refer to all things place-related and a single word to refer to all things time-related. Another likely motive is to draw attention to the fact that our Western way of thinking about time is radically different from that of Mayan indigenous cultures like those that the Zapatistas come from; we view time as linear while they view it as cyclical and have a spiral-shaped calendar.

Mayan languages—several are spoken in Zapatista territory—are also drastically different from Spanish or English, and Spanish is a second language for many Zapatistas. This results in an ungrammatical Spanish and an unusual way of phrasing things, which Marcos relays when telling us stories about Elías Contreras and on other occasions. You will also notice this when reading the speeches given by Moisés and Hortensia, both of whom learned an indigenous language first and Spanish second.

I have spent much of the past year struggling to properly translate all the peculiarities that make what you're about to read so utterly unique. The above paragraphs touch upon a few of these and many more lie in the pages that follow.

I hope I have succeeded at recreating Marcos's witty eloquence and wacky irreverence. I hope you find it fascinating, hilarious, beautiful. I hope it helps us change in all the ways we desperately need to change.

I.

Neither the Center nor the Periphery

December 13–16, 2007

First International Colloquium *In Memoriam* Andrés Aubry

Indigenous Center for Integral Training–University of the Earth
(CIDECI–UniTierra)

San Cristóbal de las Casas, Chiapas, Mexico

Part I. Above, Thinking White: Theory's Geography and Calendar

> The problem with reality is that it doesn't
> know anything about theory.
> —Don Durito of the Lacandon Jungle

Elías Contreras, EZLN Investigation Commission, said that struggle—ours at least—could be explained as a struggle of geographies and calendars. I do not know whether this compañero, one more of the dead that we are, ever imagined that his theories ("his thoughts," he used to say) would be presented alongside as many intellectual luminaries as those who now converge in the southeastern Mexican state of Chiapas. I also do not know if he would have authorized me, an ordinary subcommander, to take some of those thoughts and present them publicly.

But, taking the evidence of our low media and theory ratings into account, I believe that I can afford to try to explain the rudimentary bases of this theory, so other that it is practice.

I'm not going to bore you by talking about the emotional mess of Elías Contreras, who, like all Zapatistas, chose to love with defiance. As if the emotional bridge that extends toward the other were not already in itself complex and complicated, Elías Contreras still added to it the distances and walls that separate calendars and geographies, in addition to knowledge of—that is, respect for—the other's existence. As if by doing so he (and with him, the collective that we are) decided to do everything possible for a deed as ancient, ordinary, and everyday as the existence of the human being to become something extraordinary, terrifying, wonderful.

However, instead of telling you about Elías Contreras's complicated and unbreakable love bridge for Magdalena (who was neither male nor female, which is already in itself a challenge to the gender struggle), I thought then about bringing you some of the music that gets played in Zapatista communities. For example, just last night I heard music that the master of ceremonies classified as a "corrido-cumbia-ranchera-norteña"[1] beat. What's it like? A corrido-cumbia-ranchera-norteña beat . . . if that is not theoretical defiance, then I don't know what is. And do not ask me how they play that or dance to it, because I can't even knock on a door right and, also, at my old age, on the dance floor I am as graceful as an elephant with an ingrown toenail.

A little over two years ago, in these mountains of the Mexican Southeast, during the preparatory meetings for what later would be called the "Other Campaign," a young woman said something to the tune of, "if your revolution does not know how to dance, don't invite me to your revolution." Sometime later, but then in the mountains of northeast Mexico, I again heard those same words from the mouth of an indigenous leader who strives to keep the dances and the entire culture of our ancestors alive.

After hearing the one and the other, at different times, I turned and looked at one of the commanders and told her: "They're talking to you, ma'am." The commander continued to look at the audience, but said quietly: "Err Marcos . . . Mother 'ucker, they'd have seen how when I get on a dance floor, I flatten the ground."

I will not be *liaring*[2] to you. The truth is that I thought I could bring you some stories about Shadow the Warrior, about Elías Contreras and Magdalena, about the Zapatista women, about the children who are growing up in a reality different (note: not better, not worse, just different) from their parents, marked by another resistance, and even tell you a story about a girl named "December" who, as her name suggests, was born in November. And I also wanted to play some music for you (no offense to the music out there), but the seriousness with which the Zapatistas approach theoretical issues is known to all, so I will only say that you'll have to find a way of connecting theory to love, music, and dance. Maybe theory will not be able to explain anything worth explaining, but it will be more human, because seriousness and rigidity do not guarantee scientific rigor.

Well, though, I am already getting off track again. I was telling you that Elías Conteras, EZLN Investigation Commission, said that our

---

1   *Corrido*, *cumbia*, *ranchera*, and *norteña* are popular genres of music in Mexico.
2   Here Marcos says *mentirando*, an intentional grammar error on his part that involves adding the equivalent of "–ing" somewhere it does not belong.

struggle could be understood and explained as a struggle of geographies and calendars.

In our participation as "opening acts" for the thoughts that in these days gather in this place and on these dates, geography and calendar—or rather, the long braid that is tied between them below—will be one of our word's points of reference.

Our eldest say that the very first gods, those who birthed the world, were seven; that seven are the colors: white, yellow, red, green, blue, brown, and black; that seven are the cardinal directions: above and below, in front and behind, one side and the other, and the center; and that seven too are the senses: smelling, tasting, touching, seeing, hearing, thinking, and feeling.

So seven will be the threads of this long braid—always inconclusive—of Zapatista thought.

Let's talk, then, about Theory's Geography and Calendar. To do so, let's think the color white up above.

We do not have the exact numbers, but in the complex calendar of theoretical thought from above, the calendar of its sciences, techniques, and tools, as well as of its analysis of realities, there was a moment in which lines were drawn from a geographic center and from there extended toward the periphery, like a stone cast into the center of a pond.

The conceptual stone touched the surface of theory and a series of waves was made that affected and modified the various adjacent scientific and technical tasks. The consistency of analytical and reflexive thought made, and makes, these waves remain definite . . . until a new conceptual stone falls and a new series of waves changes theoretical production. The sheer density of theoretical production may be able to explain why the waves—most of the time—do not reach the edge: reality.

Some have given the name "scientific paradigms" to these concepts capable of modifying, renewing, and revolutionizing theoretical thought.

In this conception of theoretical tasks, in this metatheory, people not only insist on the irrelevance of reality, they also brag that they have completely left it aside, in an attempt at isolation and hygiene that they say is worthy of applause.

The image of a sterile laboratory is not only limited to the so-called natural sciences or hard sciences, no. In the global capitalist system's latest leaps, this obsession with antireality hygiene reached the so-called social sciences. In the global scientific community, the "if reality does not behave as theory indicates, too bad for reality" thesis then began to gather momentum.

But let's go back to the peaceful pond of theoretical production and the stone that has altered its form and content.

The recognition of this apparent fragility in scientific conceptual scaffolding meant accepting that theoretical production was constantly being renewed, even within the attempted isolation from reality. The laboratory (a term now widely used by so-called social scientists to talk about struggles within societies), as disinfected and sterile as it may be, could never assemble the ideal conditions to guarantee the perpetuity that all scientific law demands. And it turns out that in this very endeavor, new concepts burst forth again and again.

In these conceptions, the idea (the concept, in this case) comes before the subject matter, and like so the responsibility for humanity's great transformations is assigned to science and technology. And the idea has, in each case, a producer or an announcer: the individual, the scientist in this case.

Ever since Descartes's idle reflection, theory from above has insisted on the superiority of mind over matter. "I think, therefore I am" also defined a center, the individual *I*, and the other as a periphery that is affected or unaffected by that *I*'s consciousness: affection, hatred, fear, sympathy, attraction, repulsion. What was out of reach for that *I*'s consciousness was, is, nonexistent.

So, the birth of this global crime called capitalism is a product of the steam engine and not of dispossession. And the capitalist phase of neoliberal globalization began with the appearance of computing, the Internet, cell phones, malls, instant soup, fast food—and not by starting a new war of planetwide conquest, World War IV.

In the field of technology, the same pattern repeats itself. And, it must be added, like scientific thought, technique is born "innocent," "free of all blame," "inspired in humanity's well-being." Einstein is not responsible for the atomic bomb, nor Mr. Graham Bell for the cellular fraud of the richest man in the world, Carlos Slim. Colonel Sanders is not responsible for the indigestion caused by Kentucky Fried Chicken, nor Mr. McDonald for the recycled-plastic hamburgers.

This, which some developed further and defined as "scientific objectivity," created the image of the scientist that still permeates the popular imagination: a man or woman, messy hair, glasses, a white coat, disheveled, surrounded by bubbling test tubes and flasks.

The self-proclaimed "social scientist" "bought" that very image, with some changes: instead of a laboratory, a cubicle; instead of flasks and test tubes, books and notebooks; instead of white coat, a dark one; the same disheveledness; but add tobacco, coffee, brandy or cognac (*in science too there are levels, my dear*), and background music, which were unthinkable in a laboratory.

Nonetheless, more than a few people, engrossed as they were in their objectivity and sterility, did not warn of the appearance and growth of "commissioners of science": philosophers. These "judges" of knowledge, as objective and neutral as those they observe, stripped away scientific criteria. Since reality was not the point of reference to determine if a theory was true or false, philosophy went on to fulfill that role. And so the "philosophy of science" appeared, the theory of theory, the *metatheory*.

But so-called social science, the bastard child of knowledge, found the philosophers overburdened or with demands difficult to fulfill (like "If A equals B and B equals C, then A equals C"), so it must increasingly put up with academy intellectuals as censors and commissioners.

. . .

Hmm . . . I think that above I have already demonstrated that I can be as opaque and incomprehensible as any respectable theoretician, but I am sure there is a simpler way of continuing with this.

So here I go, move to the side a bit, I don't want to splash you.

In short, as a result of this calendar and this geography, it turns out that up above theoretical production is nothing more than something fashionable that is thought, seen, smelled, tasted, touched, heard, and felt in academia's spaces, laboratories, and specialized institutes.

In other words, theory is something fashionable in theses (*Master's theses, my dear, in academia too there are levels*), conferences, specialized magazines, and books, the replacements for fashion magazines. Symposiums take the place of fashion exposés, and there the panelists do the same thing as models on the runway: they show off their anorexia, in this case, their intellectual frailty.

Take each moment from one of those paradigms' emergence and you will find an intellectual center where people vie for the scoop. European universities and American technological institutes repeat the fashionable list: Paris, Rome, London, New York (I'm sorry if I'm ruining any illusions, but Monterrey Tech, Ibero, and UDLA are not on the list).[3]

By this I mean that the scientific world built a glass tower (but with lead glass), with its own laws and decorated with the Churrigueresque[4] stained glass that intellectuals make ad hoc.

---

3   These are all prestigious private universities in Mexico.
4   A type of Spanish baroque architectural decoration characterized by its lavishness and elaborate attention to detail.

Reality cannot access that world, that tower and its penthouses, until it provides proof of graduate studies and a résumé—pay attention—as bulky as its wallet.

That is how the scientific community presents itself to the common people, and how it represents itself.

But an attentive and critical look, one of those that is in such short supply today, would allow one to see what is really happening.

If the new paradigm is the market and the idyllic image of modernity is the mall or shopping center, let us imagine then a series of shelves full of ideas or, better yet, a department store with theories for every occasion. It would not be difficult then to imagine a great capitalist or a ruler going through the aisles, comparing the prices and quality of various thoughts, and purchasing those best adapted to their needs.

Up above, all respectable theory must perform a double role: on the one hand, shift responsibility for an action with an argument, whose elaborateness doesn't make it less ridiculous; and, on the other, hide reality (that is, guarantee impunity).

In the explanation for tragedies, some examples come to light:

Mr. Calderón (some disoriented people still consider him president of Mexico), dressed up as a military man,[5] finds within lunatic theory the explanation for the catastrophes that devastated Tabasco and Chiapas (as happened before to Sonora and Sinaloa) and ordered his troops to secure for him the power to convince, something that he has not been able to build on that house of doctored cards that was the 2006 presidential election. His failure, reported so little in the media, was foreseeable: Teletón[6] gets more than the presidential administration. Shifting responsibility to the moon (who, it turns out, is resentful, as shall be told in the legend on the origin of Shadow the Warrior; but that will be, if it is so, another day), Calderón hides his responsibility and that of those who preceded him. Result: a commission is created to investigate . . . astronomy, and so give—along with poor weapons-bearers—some legitimate sustenance to that Huerta[7] emulator and, as he himself admits, lover of war video games. Surely if the moon refuses to admit its responsibility, the incumbent of the Fourth Reich will tell it, with a tough and determined look: "Come down or I shall make you come down!"[8]

---

5   Calderón would often wear a military-green jacket and cap since Mexico was fighting the so-called War on Drug Trafficking.

6   Teletón is an annual telethon that takes place early in December to raise money for children's rehabilitation centers.

7   During the Mexican Revolution, Victoriano Huerta launched a counterrevolutionary coup in 1913 against President Madero, whom he had executed. In the Mexican popular imagination, Huerta is widely regarded as a traitor who wrongfully seized the presidency by force.

8   Calderón infamously uttered this phrase during a photo op in devastated regions of

Mr. Héctor Aguilar Camín, the prototype of an intellectual not from above (what more could he want?) but instead a social climber, rewrote the "White Book" with which the Zedillo Justice Department[9] wished to explain—unsuccessfully—the Acteal massacre[10] (this December 22, ten years will have passed without truth or justice). Loyal to the day's boss, Aguilar Camín seeks, in vain, to divert the indignation that arises once again, hiding a state crime and shifting responsibility from the murderers . . . to the dead.[11]

Felipe Calderón and Héctor Aguilar Camín, one comically dressed as a military man and the other pathetically disguised as an intellectual. The former cursing the person who recommended that he buy the theory of the moon, and the latter going to governmental offices and military barracks offering to sell his useless detergent to wash off the bloodstains.

This, the white and untainted theory from above, is what is dominant in the decaying scientific world. Faced with each of its theoretical breakthroughs, also pompously called "scientific revolutions," progressive thought in general has found itself forced to row upstream. With a pair of criticism and honesty oars, left-wing thinkers (or theoreticians, although it is common to use this term in a disparaging way) must question the avalanche of evidence that, disguised as science, buries reality.

The point of reference for this critical task is social science. But if this is limited to the expression of wishes, judgments, condemnations, and prescriptions (as some theoreticians of the Mexican Left now let happen) instead of trying to understand in order to try to explain, one's theoretical production will not only turn out to be incompetent, but also—most of the time—pathetic.

That is when the distance between theory and reality not only becomes an abyss, we also witness the sad spectacle of self-proclaimed

---

flood-hit Tabasco in October 2007. As he was helping fill sandbags to be put in place to contain the overflowing Grijalva River, he became incensed that locals were merely watching instead of participating and shouted out this threat. Marcos again makes mention of this episode and the accompanying phrase in "Part III. Touching Green."

9   In Spanish, la Procuraduría General de la República (PGR).

10   On December 22, 1997, forty-five Tzotzil men, women, and children were brutally massacred by government-trained paramilitaries while attending church; the police were several hundred feet away but did not intervene. The "White Book" refers to the much-discredited "White Book of Acteal," compiled by then president Zedillo's attorney general and issued weeks after the massacre, which concluded that the bloodshed had been caused by ongoing disputes between indigenous communities. There is evidence to suggest that Zedillo himself may be partially responsible for the massacre; a lawsuit was filed against him in the United States, where he currently lives, but it was dismissed because of sovereign immunity.

11   Camín wrote a three-part piece entitled "Return to Acteal" published in *Nexos*, a monthly magazine that he coedits, which drew heavily on the "White Book" and other government and progovernment sources.

social scientists dragging themselves with remarkable joy into a conceptual void.

Maybe someone who is listening to or reading this knows about those commercials that advertise products to slim down without exercising and while also devouring garnachas and food rich in "hydrocarbons."[12] I know that it is unlikely that someone here would know about that, as I am sure you all are immersed in truly important theoretical matters, so allow me to give you an example: there is an ad for a cookie that, if eaten, can give women the figure of Angelina Jolie (sigh), and men can end up with the athletic body of Subcommander Marcos (hot tamales!) . . . Hang on! Did I write what I just said? Hmm . . . no, I don't think so, my modesty is legendary, so erase that part from your notes. What was I talking about? Ah, yes! About the cookie that will give you a spectacular figure all without doing any exercise other than lifting the product into your mouth and chewing it.

In the same vein, in the past few years an idea has gathered momentum in Mexico's progressive-intellectual circles: the idea that social relations can be transformed without a fight and without touching the privileges that the powerful enjoy. All you need to do is fill out a ballot and voilà! The country transforms, ice-skating rinks and artificial beaches, car races on Reforma Boulevard, double-decker beltways, and bicentennial construction projects galore[13] (have you noticed that no one talks about the centennial?[14]). Well, it isn't even necessary to oversee the election and prevent it from turning into a fraud and a movie documenting it.

The submissiveness with which this was obtained, digested, and disseminated by a large part of Mexico's progressive intellectuality mustn't seem strange, above all if one takes into account that the alternative— thinking, analyzing, debating, and criticizing—costs more.

The surprising thing is the viciousness and baseness with which they attacked and attack those who do not swallow that diet cookie, sorry, that millwheel.[15]

---

12 A garnacha is a corn tortilla fried in oil and usually topped with meat, cheese, and salsa, which is a typical type of street food in parts of Mexico, particularly its southern states.

13 A reference to the Mexico City government's glamorous events and public works projects.

14 The bicentennial of the Mexican War of Independence, which began in 1810, and the centennial of the Mexican Revolution, which began in 1910.

15 A reference to the expression "comulgar con ruedas de molino," which translates as "take communion with millwheels." Like communion bread, a millwheel is round, but it is much too large to swallow, implying that the person is highly gullible and will swallow anything. So, in this sentence, Marcos is saying that progressive intellectuals have attacked those who are not gullible enough to buy their theories.

I'll give you another example:

In Mexico City there has been an impeccable dispossession, and it has obtained the support and/or complicit silence of that intellectuality.

A "modern, left-wing" government has obtained what the Right had been unable to: stripping the city and the country of the Zocalo.[16]

Without the need for laws regulating marches or rallies, without the need for signatures that PAN members were to falsify, the government of Marcelo Ebrard[17] took the Zocalo, gave it to for-profit companies (we read somewhere that it was praised because it would have cost the Mexico City government nothing and everything would have been financed by private companies that, as a matter of fact, include one of the television stations "vetted" by the López Obrador crowd), an ice-skating rink gets built and voilà! For at least two months, no rallies or protests in the square that the 1968 student movement wrenched from official celebrations.

No more AMLO-CND,[18] no more mob invasions of the cathedral, no shouts except from people who fall down, no more rallies or marches, no more shouting, banners, indignation.

For the ten remaining months of the year, "leftish" Ebrard already has new projects thought out that make capital dwellers feel they are in another more "chic" metropolis.

Just a few days ago, the so-called National Front against Repression discovered that the march it had convened for the Zocalo could not be held because the ice rink was there.

They did not protest that dispossession, they simply changed the location. After all, there was no reason to interfere with the New York spirit in the air in Mexico City . . . nor with ice skate sales in the megamalls.

Not only was this dispossession not stopped, not only was it not criticized, it was applauded and celebrated with front-page color photos, features, and interviews, this "historic" event that saved Mexico City residents from the long lines to get a US visa, and from the cost of transportation and lodging in the New York of the movies that Marcelo Ebrard and his homegrown Cristina Kirchner wannabe watch.[19]

---

16 Mexico City's main square, on which the National Palace and the Metropolitan Cathedral are located.

17 Former mayor of Mexico City (2006–2012).

18 National Democratic Convention (Convención Nacional Democrática), convened by López Obrador to protest the fraudulent 2006 election result.

19 The inference here is that Marcelo Ebrard's wife, Mariagna Prats, wishes to follow a trajectory similar to that of Cristina Kirchner, who went from being the first lady of Argentina (2003–2007) to being president (2007–2015). At the time of this presentation, Ebrard was mayor of Mexico City, and Marcos is possibly insinuating here that his wife harbored delusions of grandeur.

If this is reminiscent of the "bread and circus" method, so expensive for PRI governments, then one forgets that there is still not enough food, because the only PAN[20] around is the party that is now tied to the fall of Calderón Hinojosa, which the entire political class is involved in privately and disassociated from publicly.

All this happens and is celebrated because Mr. Ebrard has not (yet) had his photo taken with Felipe Calderón and because he says he's left-wing . . . even if he governs like he's right-wing, with eviction and dispossession disguised as spectacle and order.

And these left-wing intellectuals?

Well, a round of applause for the eviction of neighborhoods (with drug-trafficking accusations that never were proven), another round of applause for the eviction of mobile street vendors in Centro Histórico (to finish giving it to private enterprise), another round of applause for the race queens at the auto race on Reforma Boulevard . . .

/ *What a change, my dear! From the all-included tents at the encampment against fraud, to the glamour of speed in a sport with so much mass appeal, so popular, and so unsponsored as are auto races; from the "cry of the free" against the spurious one, to aspiring to be the Winter Olympics subhost; no, my dear! It does not matter if that is not left-wing, but that it dazzles, dazzles! Look, I have those skates in several combinations: tricolor for the nostalgic, blue for the astonished, and yellow and black for the naive;[21] there are also some with childish colors, I mean, take whatever you can get, right? Now, yes, ice-skating is for slender people, so I'll include those cookies that make you thinner than being squashed on the Metro during rush hour. What? Are you a skater? Should I tell you? That's why this country does not progress, all over the place there are people who are dirty, ugly, bad, and, to finish the damage, ghetto scum. Hey, just give me the money from your unemployment benefits and I won't tell anyone . . .* /

Faced with the eviction of families in the rough neighborhood of Tepito, silence or frivolous and servile reasoning: "It's to fight crime," remarked an intellectual and failed UNAM[22] presidency hopeful, and a front-page photo showed a girl sitting on the few items of furniture that her family rescued from one of the evictions. The Rudolph Giuliani philosophy, imported (like the ice rink) from New York by López Obrador

---

20 In Spanish, this is a double entendre, since "pan" means "bread."

21 These colors represent those of Mexico's three main political parties at that time. The tricolor refers to the vertical green, white, and red bands of the PRI; blue is the color of the PAN; and yellow and black are the colors of the PRD.

22 National Autonomous University of Mexico (Universidad Nacional Autónoma de México).

with the "poor first" pretext, now made intellectual argument: that girl was a potential drug trafficker . . . now she is . . . no one.

There is no longer a desire to hide the fact that the so-called institutional Left is not left-wing, now it is presented as a virtue, in the same way that one announces a decaf coffee with the virtue of not keeping you awake and not tasting like coffee.

This is the Left that some progressive intellectuals present as the only acceptable, mature, responsible, desirable, and possible point of reference for social transformation.

Nonetheless, and fortunately, not all progressive thought is "well-behaved."

Some men and women have made uncomfortable and against-the-grain words from analytical and reflexive thought. In these days, we shall have the chance to listen to some of these thinkers. Not all are here, those here are not all there are, but knowing of their upstream navigation in the canal of knowledge is a relief for those of us who sometimes imagine that we are not alone.

And so, in this first round I welcome Immanuel Wallerstein and Carlos Aguirre Rojas.

Reflecting on something from their theoretical work, we present . . .

Some Theses on Antisystemic Struggle

ONE: The capitalist system cannot be understood and explained without the concept of war. Its survival and growth primarily depend on war and on everything associated with and implicit in it. Through it and in it, capitalism dispossesses, exploits, represses, and discriminates. In the neoliberal-globalization stage, capitalism wages war on all of humanity.

TWO: To increase their profits, capitalists do not only resort to reducing production costs or increasing commodity prices. This is true, but incomplete. There are at least three more ways: one is increasing productivity; another is producing new commodities; yet another is opening new markets.

THREE: Today, producing new commodities and opening new markets is achieved with the conquest and reconquest of social territories and spaces that before were of no interest to capital. Ancestral knowledge and genetic codes—in addition to natural resources like water, forests, and air—are now commodities with open markets or markets in the making. People found in spaces and territories with these and other commodities are, whether they like it or not, enemies of capital.

FOUR: Capitalism is not inevitably destined to self-destruct, unless it destroys the entire world. Apocalyptic accounts of how the system will collapse on its own are erroneous. We indigenous people have been hearing prophecies to that effect for several centuries.

FIVE: Destruction of the capitalist system shall only take place if one or many movements confront and defeat its core: private ownership of the means of production and exchange.

SIX: Real transformations of a society—that is, of social relations in a historic moment, as Wallerstein points out in some of his texts—are those directed against the system in its entirety. At present, patches or reforms are not possible. However, antisystemic movements are possible and necessary.

SEVEN: Great transformations do not begin from above nor with monumental and epic deeds, but with movements small in size and that appear irrelevant to politicians and analysts from above. History is not transformed by packed squares or enraged crowds, but, as Carlos Aguirre Rojas points out, by the organized conscience of groups and collectives that know and recognize one another, below and to the left, and build another politics.

It is necessary, we believe, to tear down theory and make it with practice. But Don Daniel Viglietti may explain that better tonight when he takes his part of the blame for me being behind this balaclava instead of being behind a guitar trying to play the corrido-cumbia-ranchera-norteña rhythm.

That's the way it is, I think it will always be that way. Daniel Viglietti will sing tonight, so there will be music and dance.

In these days, Elías Contreras, Magdalena, Shadow, December, and the Zapatista women may also arrive.

And maybe Andrés Aubry will smile seeing and listening to everything, happy to not be at this table where he never finished saying what he had to tell us, because he killed himself thanking people and, invariably, halfway through his presentation they gave him the "time's-up" slip.

So, before they give it to me, thank you, see you this afternoon.

Insurgent Subcommander Marcos.
San Cristóbal de las Casas, Chiapas, Mexico.

Part II. Hearing Yellow: Difference's Calendar and Geography

The dangerous thing about different people is that after a while, they start looking a lot like one another.
—Don Durito of the Lacandon Jungle

Women's Struggle, From the Center to the Periphery?

If before we talked about how in thought from above, there is an abyss between theory and reality, and about the accompanying theoretical bulimia that is becoming fashionable among a part of progressive intellectuality, now we would like to spend some time on that point regarding the supposedly scientific geography that is the center where the conceptual stone—that is, intellectual fashion—falls and where the waves that will affect the periphery begin.

It turns out that those theories and practices suggested in the center extend toward the periphery, not only affecting thoughts and practices in those corners, but also—and above all—imposing themselves as truth and a model to follow.

We have already talked about the emergence of new social actors or subjects, and mentioned women, young people, and other loves.[1]

---

1   LGBTQ, etc.

Well, new theoretical developments emerge regarding these "new" protagonists of daily history and—always in the broadcast center—are translated to political and organizational practices.

In the case of the gender struggle—or more specifically, in feminism—the same thing happens. In one of the metropolises an idea emerges on what it is, its character, its objective, its forms, its destination. From there, it is exported to points on the periphery, which in turn are centers of other peripheries.

This transfer does not take place without problems and "jam-ups" unique to different geographies.

Nor does it take place on equal terms, paradoxically. And I say "paradoxically" because one of the essential features of this struggle is its demand for equality, for gender equality.

I hope that the compañeras and compañeros who raise up this struggle, and who are listening to or reading my words, forgive the reductionism and oversimplification with which I am touching upon this point. And it isn't because I want to save my machismo, so natural and spontaneous, really, but because we are not talking about the efforts that you are carrying forward. We are not saying that your projects are unquestionable. They are and in more ways than one, but we are talking about another gender struggle, about another feminism: that which comes from above, from the center to the periphery.

In a few days, the Zapatista women will hold a gathering where their experience and word will have a unique space, so I will not elaborate more on this topic. Nonetheless, I would like to tell you the short story of a failed encounter.

In the first few months after beginning our uprising, a group of feminists (that's what they called themselves) came to some of the Zapatista communities.

No, no they did not come to ask, to listen, to understand, to respect. They came to say what the Zapatista women should do, they came to free them from the oppression of Zapatista machos (beginning, of course, by freeing them from Marcos), to tell them what their rights were—to give orders, that is.

They courted the women they thought were the bosses (incidentally, with very masculine methods, it turns out). Through them they tried to impose, from outside—in form and substance—a gender struggle without even pausing to find out whether or not it existed—and to what extent—in Zapatista indigenous communities.

They didn't even stop to see if they had been heard and understood. No, their "liberatory" mission had been accomplished. They returned to their metropolises, wrote articles for newspapers and magazines, published books, traveled abroad all-expenses-paid giving conferences, took government jobs, etc.

We are not going to question this, each person goes on vacation however they can. We only want to remind you that they did not leave the slightest mark on the communities, nor did they help the women in any way.

This initial failed encounter marked the subsequent relationship between Zapatista women and feminists, and brought about an unseen confrontation that, of course, the feminists attributed to the EZLN's vertical and militaristic machismo. This got to the point where a group of female commanders refused a women's rights project. It turns out that they wanted to offer some classes, designed by city dwellers, taught by city dwellers, and evaluated by city dwellers. The Zapatista compañeras were opposed, they wanted to be the ones who decided on the content, the ones who taught the class, and the ones who evaluated the results and what came next.

You can see the result yourself if you go to the La Garrucha Caracol and listen to, from the very lips of the Zapatista women, that and other stories. Maybe it would help you understand better if you brought the disposition and spirit of comprehension. Maybe, like Sylvia Marcos in the Bedouin women's Israel, you would understand that Zapatista women, like many women in many corners of the world, break the rules without throwing out their culture, rebel as women, but without ceasing to be indigenous and also, it mustn't be forgotten, without ceasing to be Zapatistas.

A few years ago, a journalist told me that he had run into a Zapatista woman on the side of the road and given her a ride into town. "Did she have a uniform or pants or boots?" I asked him worriedly. The journalist clarified: "No, she was wearing a nagua, an embroidered shirt, and was barefoot. Also, she was carrying her child in a shawl." "How did you know that she was a Zapatista then?" I insisted. The journalist responded in a natural way: "It's easy, Zapatista women stand differently, walk differently, watch differently." "How?" I reiterated. "Well, like Zapatistas," said the journalist, and he took out his recorder to ask me about the government's dialogue proposal, the upcoming elections, the books I had read, and other equally absurd things.

Nonetheless, it is necessary to point out that this distance has been shortened thanks to the work and understanding of our feminist compañeras from the Other Campaign; in particular and notably, our compañeras from The Other Campaign–Jovel.[2]

---

2   La Otra Jovel is a group of signatories to the Sixth Declaration based in San Cristóbal de las Casas, a city known as Jovel in the Tzotzil and Tzeltal languages.

According to my machista viewpoint, in both corners the difference between some and others has been understood and, therefore, a mutual recognition has begun that will become something very other, and that surely sends shivers not only through the entire patriarchal system, but also through those of us who are just beginning to understand the force and power of that difference, and brings us to repeat, albeit in another sense: "¡Vive le difference! ¡Viva la diferencia!"[3]

From that tension, gradually turning into a link and a bridge, a new calendar shall emerge in a new geography. A calendar and geography where women, in their equality and difference, have the place they conquer in their struggle, the most onerous, the most complex, and the most continuous of all antisystemic struggles.

Our oldest knowers tell that the very first gods, those who birthed the world, made the color yellow from the smiles of children. Remembering this, we have decided to tell you a story that is for children, but the adults are going to have to suck it up because . . . because . . . well, because it would look really bad if you left before this session of the colloquium ends.

Now, if you are going to leave, I ask you to not be meanies and to do it discreetly so that the organizers here don't feel so bad (I'm already used to it).

Well, for those who remain, here goes the story . . .

I've said this before, so I will only briefly repeat the story of December. She was a girl, like this, real little. She was born in the month of November and, since her parents only spoke an indigenous language, it was a shit show when they went to register her. The notary hastily asked where she was born, when she was born, what month it was (he was a bit hungover), and things like that. Her mother was just about to say what month it was when the civil registry employee again asked what her name was going to be. "December" is what the notary heard, and Rome was screwed because once they realized it, it was a mess to change the paperwork. So this girl who was born in November ended up being named "December." According to adults' customs and traditions, when they scold a girl or boy, they don't remember the child's name and begin to say different names until they get it. In December's case, the reprimands were less strict because the mother began with January, and when she got to December she had already forgotten why she was going to scold the girl.

3   "Long live difference!"

In another story, now distant, December met an owl and made friends with him. Then, she solved the crooked-flute challenge and made I-don't-remember-what-other mischief.

Well, here goes . . .

December and the Story of the Handless Book

One afternoon, almost evening, an evening like this one that announces a shower of lights, December was walking, just walking around. Perhaps she wasn't thinking anything, she just walked, picking up pebbles and twigs, and hung the pebbles from a tree, and piled the twigs next to the path, and gave them names: this was a "pebble tree" and that a "twig mountain." In other words, as the saying goes, December not only took to agitating her thought, she agitated the world too.

She also had some colored pencils, who knows who gave them to her. So, when she was not hanging up rocks and piling twigs, December took her colored pencils out of her bag[4] and started coloring whatever was around.

Well, it turns out that December was walking around, humming a corrido-cumbia-ranchera-norteña tune, when poof! There was a book sitting right there in the middle of the path.

December was happy. She took out her colored pencils and went very resolutely to grab the book and fill it with lines and dots and stick figures and even a doodle that was supposed to be a composite sketch of Panfililla, that was the name of her dog who was more like a mule (no offense to the mules out there).

December was already getting close to the book in the middle of the path, she was already imagining how the Good Government Committee would give her permission to paint a mural on the wall of the autonomous school, she already saw herself asking a woman from civil society to take a photo of her with Panfililla, standing by the mural, and she already thought that perhaps if Panfililla did not look like the mural painting then she would paint the corrections right then and there. Not on the school wall, but on Panfililla's body, of course.

December was thinking all this when, once she got closer to the book to grab it, whoosh! The book opened its cover and flew away.

"Wowzers!" said December, with a tone of voice that left no doubt about her plebeian origin, "So that book flyin.'" The book fluttered a few yards and perched further ahead, in the middle of the path. December ran to

---

4   *Morraleta*: a colorful, highly durable, woven poly-mesh bag commonly used in certain regions of Mexico.

grab the book, but, before she got there, it flew away again. Then December thought that the book wanted to play and so did she. So she chased the flying book all over the place, and, meanwhile, Panfililla had already wolfed down half a dozen pebbles and two dozen twigs and had laid down, digesting and just moving her ears around, while December chased after the book.

It took a while, but the time came when December got tired and worn out, and laid down next to Panfililla.

"And now what do we do, Panfililla?" asked December.

And Panfililla just moved her ear, because she was still trying to digest an amberstone and couldn't bark.

"I know, I have an idea," said December, "I'm gonna look for Mr. Owl and ask him."

Panfililla moved her ears as if to say, "OK, I'll wait for you here," while she saw that there was still half a pile of twigs left to wolf down.

So December went to visit her friend the Owl. She found him sitting in his tree, looking at a magazine with naked ladies.

Here the Owl interrupts the story and clarifies for the public:

"Don't believe Marcos, it was not a magazine with naked ladies, it was a lingerie catalog, for Victoria's Secret to be exact. It's not the same thing."

All right, so the Owl was looking at a magazine with *half-naked* ladies when December arrived and, without anesthesia or saying *heads up*, blurted right then and there:

"Hey Mr. Owl, why are there books that flyin'?"

"It's *fly*, not *flyin'*," Mr. Owl corrected, and added, "and no, books don't fly. Books are in bookstores, in libraries, on scientists' desks, and—when nobody buys them—on tables outside of colloquiums."

"There's one that does," answered December, and then told him what had happened before with the flying book.

Mr. Owl closed his catalog with ladies in undergarments—after having bookmarked the page he was on, of course—and said very resolutely:

"Very well, we'll look into it, just hang on a minute because I have to change into more suitable attire."

"All right," said December, and while waiting for Mr. Owl, she started hanging some pebbles that she managed to rescue from Panfililla's gluttony on the branches of trees.

Meanwhile, Mr. Owl opened a giant chest and began to look, murmuring, "Hmm, whip, no . . . garter belt, no . . . negligee, colder . . . hmm . . . here it is!" Mr. Owl suddenly exclaimed, and he took out a black balaclava.

He put it on and, grabbing a pipe, went to December and asked her:

"Well now, what do you think of my disguise?"

December looked at him puzzledly and, after a while, said, "What are you disguised as?"

"What do you mean what? As a Zapatista subcommander! If that book sees me as an owl, it's not going to let me get anywhere near, because us owls sure do want a lot of books; subcommanders, however, don't even use them to level out tables."

Here Marcos interrupts to clarify for the respectable public:

"Don't believe Mr. Owl, subcommanders do use books, sometimes, when the fire won't light . . ."

Ahem, ahem.

Well, so I was telling you that December and Mr. Owl, disguised as a subcommander, came down from the tree and headed toward where she had left Panfililla waiting.

When they got to where the dog was, they found her simultaneously trying to gnaw on half a slipper and digest the other half.

"My *Only at Macy's* slippers!"[5] a shocked Mr. Owl exclaimed, and he began to fight with Panfililla, trying to pry away the slipper half, which, it is worth noting, was the front half, so it could still pass as a minimalist version of a slipper.

December helped him, and whispered something into Panfililla's ear that made her immediately let go of the front half of Mr. Owl's slipper.

"Phew!" sighed a relieved Mr. Owl, and, while surveying the damage, he asked December:

"And what did you tell her to make her let go?"

December answered unperturbed, "That I would give her half of the other slipper."

"What!?" shouted Mr. Owl. "My slippers, my good name, my prestige, my intellectual status . . . !"

Just then, voilà! Close to where they were December discovered the flying book.

"Here it is!" December shouted to Mr. Owl.

Mr. Owl adjusted his balaclava as well as he could, lit his pipe, and said to December:

"Wait for me here, I'll have a look."

Mr. Owl got to where the flying book was, it didn't recognize him because of his subcommander disguise.

As we all know, books tell subcommanders what isn't written in them, so they were talking for a while.

---

5   Here Marcos uses "totalmente Palacio," the slogan for El Palacio de Hierro, a Mexican department store.

December was already falling asleep when Mr. Owl came back and told her:

"Done. The mystery has been solved."

"What happened?" December asked, yawning.

"Elementary, my dear December. It is, plain and simple, an extreme case of a *handless book*," said Mr. Owl.

"Handless book? And what's that?" asked December.

"Well, it's a book that doesn't want to be on a bookstore or library bookshelf, or on a desk, or cast aside in a corner, or leveling out a table. It is a book that wants to be in somebody's hands. Someone who reads it, writes it, draws it, who loves it, that is," explained Mr. Owl.

"Me!" said December joyfully.

"Are you sure? A book isn't just anything, it isn't like a slipper-eating dinosaur," said Mr. Owl while looking spitefully at Panfililla, who was already chewing on the pipe from Mr. Owl's subcommander disguise.

"Yes, I'm sure," responded December intently.

"Well, try to see if you can convince it," said Mr. Owl while he tried to pry the pipe from Panfililla.

"And how do I do that?" asked December.

"Very simple: get close, but not too close, and reach out with your hands. If it accepts, then it will go toward you," said Mr. Owl.

"All right," said Panfililla, sorry, December.

She cleaned her hands with her skirt because she remembered that she hadn't washed them, slowly went toward the flying book, and, when she thought she was close enough for the book to see her but not get scared, reached out with both hands.

So the book opened its cover, as if to fly off, but hesitated.

December reached out further and said:

"Come here, come here, come here."

So the book started to fly, but instead of going away, landed on December's hands.

She was very happy and hugged the book hard, so hard that the book farted a little: *prtt.*

A satisfied Mr. Owl applauded and Panfililla didn't bark, but burped out a badly-digested-slipper smell.

So Mr. Owl went off to keep looking at ladies . . . Sorry, to read and study a lot.

December started to color the book with her colored pencils and they did not live happily ever after because, in a moment of carelessness, Panfililla wolfed down the back cover, the index, the appendices, and seven endnotes.

The end.

Moral: Do not leave anything where dogs can get them, they may be dinosaurs in-disguise.

And now, I hope that soon Daniel Viglietti makes you forget this not-very-serious presentation, and that little girls remember it . . . forever and all eternity.

Thank you.

Insurgent Subcommander Marcos.
San Cristóbal de las Casas, Chiapas, Mexico.

Part III. Touching Green: Destruction's Calendar and Geography

> Burying capitalism is not enough, it must be put in the grave
> face down. So that if it tries to get out, it buries itself deeper.
> —Don Durito of the Lacandon Jungle

Several times here it has been said that American might is finished, the good news of capitalism's death as a global system has even been announced in advance. The collection of obituaries and places on the waiting list for history's funeral have included socialism, political economy, the political regime in Mexico, and the military capabilities of the global, national, and local oppressor.

We have been asked to stop worrying about what exploits us, dispossesses us, represses us, despises us. We have been urged to now discuss and agree upon what comes after this nightmare.

In a nutshell, "CLOSED DOWN" and "UNDER DEMOLITION" signs have been placed on buildings that—pardon our distrust cultivated carefully over the course of 515 years—seem to us Zapatistas to still be not only solid, but also fully functional and prosperous.

Arrogance tends to be a bad adviser for practical and theoretical questions. It was what fed the "Not one feather has been plucked from my rooster," "I'm up by ten points in the polls," "Smile, we're going to win," "Oaxaca shall not be Atenco."[1]

---

1   These were statements made in 2006 by PRD presidential candidate Andrés Manuel López Obrador. López Obrador narrowly won the 2006 presidential election but was deprived of the presidency through electoral fraud. Thus, these quotes are cited to mock the idea that we should be overly optimistic about the current state of affairs.

Let us not allow a similar arrogance to become encouragement for the idea that we should sit down to watch the enemy's corpse go by.

Later, in another one of these sessions, we will mention the issue of war. Now we would like to carefully focus on pointing out some destructions that are in progress and that, unlike those mentioned above, can be confirmed "in situ" (*Wowzers! Latin! I sure do seem academic now*).

More so than in a description or roll call, we would like to pause on an aspect that tends to be overlooked in those other destructions. And I'm talking about destructions of nature, be they through deforestation, pollution, ecological imbalance, etc., as well the misnomered "natural disasters." And I say "misnomered" because it is increasingly apparent that the bloody hand of capital accompanies these tragedies.

On other occasions we have already pointed out that capitalism, as a dominant trend in social relations, turns everything into commodities; that in capitalist production, circulation, and consumption, profit is the linchpin of its logic; and that the profit motive also seeks to make new commodities "appear" and to create or appropriate new markets.

It may strike you as too "orthodox" or "classic" (something that, as has been apparent in these fourteen years, Neozapatismo surely can be accused of) if we insist that capital is interested in profits, by any means and in any way, the entire calendar and across geography.

We understand.

But we ask those who look up, at least for a moment, to put aside your readings of *The Economist, The New Yorker, People*,[2] and Al Gore's keynote speeches; to put to rest for a few minutes your ghosts of the Gulag and the Berlin Wall; to put out for a moment the candles lit for the "lesser evil" former candidate; to put on standby your analysis that does not know the difference between a march and a social movement; and to concede that, maybe, it is probable, it is a suppository, it may be that, in effect, capital intends to turn everything into a commodity and commodities into profit.

Now take a look at, in detail, each of the various destructions that the planet endures and you will see how capital appears and usufructs. First in the causes of tragedy, and then in its consequences.

უ

---

2   Here Marcos lists the names of comparable Mexican magazines: *Vuelta, Letras Libres, Nexos*, and *TVNotas*.

Tabasco and Chiapas: Destruction's Geographies and Calendars

Several weeks after the Grijalva and Carrizal Rivers overflowed, putting 70 percent of the southeastern Mexican state of Tabasco's territory underwater, it would appear that a new era had begun: the era of reconstruction and unacceptable justifications. The numbers are chilling: one million impacted, and at least eighty thousand houses destroyed. In addition, the underlying danger of a new overflow.

In Felipe Calderón's PAN government, a serious discussion about what caused the flood has been avoided on the grounds of "not politicizing the situation": last November 8, the secretary of the interior said: "The emergency is the emergency and we have to resolve it, not find culprits."

Of course, it isn't possible to find culprits if a serious evaluation of what happened is not carried out. The reality is that, as the populace feels safer about its physical integrity, the discussion about what happened is the topic of—I would say dinner-table conversation but there are no tables—conversation in the shelters, in the streets, in the fields.

Similarly, in spheres of the country's various political currents, the topic begins to appear, not always selflessly. It is certainly absurd to ask not to politicize what happened there when behind everything is a series of public policies that have, in tandem with natural causes, allowed the situation that now exists in Tabasco to occur.

Felipe Calderón, with the cry of "I saw Al Gore's movie," took shelter behind an explanation that is very fashionable nowadays: climate change. "Let us not be mistaken, the disaster's cause lies in the enormous alteration in the climate," he said.

So there is no need to look for or locate any concrete responsibility. It would appear that for the self-proclaimed president, climate change is a quasi-divine tragedy that has nothing to do with the development model that has been applied and continues to be applied. It is very probable that this flood had something to do with climate change, what would be important to ascertain are the reasons for that.

Cecilia Vargas, a journalist from *La Verdad del Sureste*, tells us: "One of the flood's causes is the sale of land and construction of houses and commercial warehouses on marshlands, which must be filled in, covering the city's regulatory wetlands and impeding water circulation and absorption. In filled-in areas (or fills), strip malls were built with stores like Walmart, Sam's Club, Chedraui, Fábricas de Francia, and Cinépolis (built during the Roberto Madrazo and Manuel Andrade governorships)."

Or, as the indigenous inhabitants of the Chontal region pointed out: "Our grandparents say that it used to rain more or just as much, but there were no floods. Why now? They say that it's because of the buildings they're putting in, which cover the water's paths."

Then, Mr. Calderón, at the height of stupidity, blamed the moon for the tremendous tides it caused.

Nonetheless, María Esther, an inhabitant of the city of Villahermosa[3] and compañera of the Other Campaign, uses common sense—so foreign to "experts"—and points out a strange occurrence: "The Laguna de las Ilusiones, which is located right in Villahermosa, never flooded, and its level barely went up, unlike in other years. If the disaster's fundamental cause had been rain, the lake would have to have flooded, and that did not happen."

Cecilia Vargas agrees with María Esther: "The floods were a crime, because there was a discharge from the Peñitas Dam when it couldn't hold any more, and it was this water that filled Villahermosa." Then, she cites a document by the National Energy Committee from October 30, 2007, which points out that "the Peñitas Dam is on the brink of collapse because the water is only used to generate electricity at night, while electricity generation is gas-based and is carried out by private industries." Behind this is Repsol, the Spanish multinational that "wherever it sets foot, grass never grows again." The aforementioned document warns that "the penstocks need to be opened, because the dams' reservoirs are already full," and demands that the Department of Energy allow continuous hydroelectric generation.

The concrete fact is that if one walks around Villahermosa, they find that the hotel zone, the Tabasco 2000 neighborhood, and the city's other "rich" areas were not affected, thanks to the projects that—in recent years—were built there to prevent floods (the levee on the Carrizal River).

In the midst of disaster, politicians' moral statures are put to the test . . . and analysts' moral statures. This time has been no exception. In the midst of this tragedy, it has remained clear that the three main political parties in Mexico share responsibility for what happened.

The presidency, in the hands of the right-wing PAN, and the governorship, in the hands of a member of the corrupt Institutional Revolutionary Party, and the mayorships, mostly in the hands of the supposedly left-wing Party of the Democratic Revolution, have proven their profound detachment from society and from reality.

The clearest example of this situation occurred on October 31, when the self-proclaimed president of Mexico, Felipe Calderón, went to Tabasco

---

3   Villahermosa is the capital of the state of Tabasco, where the flood occurred.

to be given a tour in order to evaluate the situation. Seeing that there were people who were putting sacks on the riverbank to create a dike, he decided to help and worked for fifteen minutes, along with his wife and some members of his cabinet. This type of attitude, so close to how the PRI governed, used to have a strong social and media impact, but now it only causes indignation and rage.

But worse, after seeing that there were many people just watching and in light of the governor's "sobbing," Felipe Calderón was overcome with rage, and he threatened those who were only watching, telling them: "Come down and help or I shall make you come down!" And he immediately ordered the military to get men to help fill the sacks with gravel. People did not flinch, their faces took on a sense of contempt; soldiers also did not move, understanding that the order would only add fuel to the fire. All this caused the so-called president to leave the place and terminate his reconstruction chore, his fifteen minutes of work did not turn into his fifteen minutes of fame but instead fifteen minutes of shame. One of the people who was watching later commented, raising his voice, fearlessly: "It is easy to come here for fifteen minutes to take a photo, have the news channels record it, mingle with the common folk, and then go home and eat and sleep comfortably with your family."

Several weeks after the Tabasco tragedy began, what remains in the eyes of the inhabitants there is the great solidarity that their situation has awakened in the Mexican people. The majority of the food, beverages, and medicine that have reached them were collected by Mexican civil society.[4]

While the various provisions from various governments—whether federal or state or municipal—are consistently labeled with a logo identifying the political party that the government official is a member of, citizen aid has the characteristic of anonymity. It has nothing to do with the dispute between the federal government and the Mexico City government; neither Felipe Calderón nor Marcelo Ebrard cares at all about the victims' situation, the only thing they're interested in is getting their photos taken: one filling sacks of gravel, with the skill of a lawyer who graduated from a private university, and the other waving the starting flags, with a silly face, surrounded by cameramen and bought-and-paid-for journalists.

But, there is other aid that was present from the very first days in Tabasco's poorest communities, those near the border with the state of Chiapas: aid that was extended from poor community to poor community. An inhabitant of the area tells us:

---

4   People who are not affiliated with the government or political parties.

There was interest from the Zapatistas in knowing how we were doing, what each of our conditions were. They told us that if we needed to leave, we could count on the Zapatista autonomous municipalities to provide safe shelter.

They were difficult days, there was no communication; telephone lines, roads, and tap water were cut off. In many places there wasn't even electricity; food and drinking water were scarce. But in the midst of all this we had the certainty of knowing that we could count on having safe housing and food in the autonomous municipalities.

Communication between us was not easy. We knew more or less who had been flooded from each community's location; we knew that they were alive, albeit enduring this induced disaster.

So, the response was Zapatista-style: fast, effective, and safe. The support-base compas made a call for solidarity with us in Tila, Chiapas, and in the autonomous municipalities. We can say that the three dump trucks that came from Tila on November 3 were some of the earliest aid the state received, when we had no telephone communication and there was no roadway access except for heavy vehicles.[5]

We knew that, along with help from civil society and the Tila parish, aid was coming from the Zapatistas in the Northern Zone. We knew that the Zapatista compas were working day and night collecting. And the aid was not only timely, but wonderful. When there was no way to cook at home, only in some shelters, we got three dump trucks full of pozol [a traditional beverage of indigenous people in Chiapas and Tabasco], tostadas, and all of our traditional foods, not like different governments that gave us those horrible instant soups. In effect, they were the first ones to get here, and everyone admired and was thankful for this aid that was so timely and also so from below, so knowledgeable about our food, about what people already missed: pozol, tortillas. Then, two days later, another three dump trucks and several trips.

And then, full of emotion, she says:

But the Tacotalpa region was unreachable—not even dump trucks could get there. The Zapatista support-base compañeros told us not to worry, that special aid was coming for them, and that was how, in the middle of the Tacotalpa foothills, before the astonished looks of neighboring villages, a long line of more than fifty men, thirty women, and many children

---

5   Since the roadways are made of dirt, only dump trucks and other large, heavy-duty vehicles could travel along the damaged roads.

was seen coming down from the mountains, Zapatista support bases, who on two separate days brought down sacks—carrying them on their shoulders for several hours—with corn, beans, tostadas, pozol, pinole, sugar, oranges, mandarins, limes, squashes, yuccas, taro, bottles of water boiled from mountain streams, for the Tabasco compas. . . . This was through the El Campesino Autonomous Municipality, but we know that there was support from other municipalities that gave what they had good-heartedly and, as always, what they have is very great, very valuable, overcomes any difficulty however large it may appear.

For those of us who witnessed this, it was wonderful to see earth-colored men, children, women, elders, bring the nourishment that we needed here on this side of the low region. Later, two other trucks arrived with similar aid. But they came not only to provide aid, they also came to listen to our pain, for us to say what was happening, how we were doing, what really caused all this, how this tragedy is being experienced below. For us to release our pain, to begin to heal it.

There are no words for us to thank each and every Zapatista support-base compañero, who share—good-heartedly and with true humanism—their bread, their water, and their fight to build a world with room for many worlds.

Of course, none of this appeared in the Mexican mass media. In addition to being told about the ice-skating rinks, we were repeatedly told in the media that the entire political class accused each other of profiting from the tragedy. So, for example, the secretary of labor confronted the mayor of Mexico City, the former called the latter vile and the latter responded, calling the former a chump. The peculiar thing is that both of them were right.

Here you have a fundamental and irreconcilable difference between those of us who look to the movement still called the Other Campaign and those who coalesce around López Obrador.

They want a world with ice-skating rinks, artificial beaches, double-decker expressways, and first-world glamour.

We want a world like the one that came down from the Zapatista mountains to help the needy: a different world.

Something on Basic Geography and Calendar

There is in the Caribbean a long island, that green crocodile lying in the sun. "Cuba" is the territory's name and "Cuban" the people who live there.

Its history, like that of all the Americas' peoples, is a long braid of pain and dignity.

But there is something that makes that land shine.

It is said, not untruthfully, that it is the first free territory in the Americas.

For almost half a century, the Cuban people have borne a colossal challenge: building their own destiny as a nation.

These people have called their path and engine "socialism." It exists, it is real, it can be measured with statistics, percentage points, quality-of-life indices, access to health, to education, to housing, to nutrition, to scientific and technological development. In other words, it can be seen, heard, smelled, tasted, touched, thought, felt.

Its impertinent rebellion has come at the cost of it suffering economic blockade, military invasions, industrial and climate sabotage, assassination attempts against its leaders, slander, lies, and the most massive media smear campaign ever.

All these attacks have come from a center: American power.

The Cuban people's resistance does not only require knowledge and analysis, but also respect and support.

Now that deaths are talked about so much, it must be remembered that forty years of trying to bury Che Guevara have gone by; that Fidel Castro has been declared dead several times now; dozens of calendars of the Cuban Revolution's extinction have gone by, so far uselessly; that in the geographies plotted in savage capitalism's current strategies, Cuba does not appear, no matter how hard they strive.

Not so much as effective aid, but as a sign of recognition, respect, and admiration, the Zapatista indigenous communities have sent a little bit of non-GMO corn and another littler bit of gasoline. For us, it has been our way of making those people know that we know that the most onerous difficulties they bear have a point of origin: the government of the United States of America.

As Zapatistas we think that we must extend our gaze, our ears, and our heart toward these people.

May it not, as with us, be said that the movement is very important and essential and *blah, blah, blah*; and when, like now, we are attacked, there is not even a single sentence, nor a statement, nor a sign of protest.

Cuba is something more than the Caribbean's outstretched and green crocodile.

It is a point of reference whose experience will be vital for peoples who fight, above all in these times of obscurantism that are experienced today and will drag on for some time still.

Against destruction's calendars and geographies, in Cuba there is a calendar and a geography of hope.

And so we now say, without shrieking, not as a slogan, but with feeling: Long live Cuba!

Thank you very much.

Insurgent Subcommander Marcos
San Cristóbal de las Casas, Chiapas, Mexico
December 2007

P.S. Which confirms that the Moon is resentful and tells the legend of the origin of Shadow the Warrior:

Shadow, the Lifter of Moons

I'll tell it how they told it. It was a long time ago, a very long time. There is no calendar to situate it. The place where it happened has no geography to mark it. Shadow the Warrior was not yet a warrior nor was he even Shadow. He was riding along the mountainside when they gave him the news.

"Where?" he asked.

"There, where the cleft in the mountain," was the vague reference that they gave him.

Shadow, who was not yet Shadow, rode off. The news traveled the glens from end to end:

"The Moon. It fell. Just like that. As if it fainted and then fell. It came very slowly, like it didn't want to. Like don't watch me. Like don't notice. But we watched it. As if it stopped on the hill and then rolled to the bottom of the gully. There it went. We saw it clearly. Well it was light. It was the Moon."

Shadow reached the gully's edge, he got off his horse. Slowly he went down to the bottom. He found the Moon. He wrapped a tumpline round it. He carried it on his back. Moon and Shadow went up the mountain. Shadow on the path, Moon on Shadow. They got to the highest point on the hill. To launch it from there back into the sky, said Shadow. So that Moon would again walk the paths of the night. I don't wanna, said Moon.

71

I wanna stay here, with you. My light will be warm for you in the cold night. Cool in the scorching day. You will bring me mirrors that multiply my brightness. I will stay with you, here. Shadow said no, the world, its men and women, its plants and animals, its rivers and mountains, need the Moon to see their steps well in the darkness, to not get lost, to not forget who they are, where they come from, where they're going. They argued. They were there for a while. Their murmurs were brown lights, bright shadows. Who knows what else they said. They took a while. In the pre-dawn hours Shadow stood up and launched the Moon back into the sky with his tumpline. The Moon left angry, irritated. In the heights, in the place that the first gods gave it, the Moon remained. From then on Moon cursed Shadow. It said:

"From now on you shall be Shadow. Lights you shall see but shall not be. Shadow you shall walk. Warrior you shall be. For you there shall not be face, nor home, nor rest. You shall have only path and struggle. You shall overcome. You shall find, you shall, someone to love. Your heart shall speak in your mouth when you say, 'I love you.' But Shadow you shall remain and will never find someone to love you. You shall look, you shall, but will not find the lips that know how to say, 'you.' So you shall be, Shadow the Warrior, until you are no more."

Since then, Shadow has been who he is now: Shadow the Warrior.

Who knows when and where he was and shall be.

That calendar still needs to be made, that geography still needs to be invented.

Saying "You" still needs to be learned.

What needs to be done still needs to be done.

See you tomorrow.

Marcos.

Part IV. Tasting Brown: Land's Calendar and Geography

> The indigenous view the land as a mother. Capitalists view it
> as someone with a lack thereof.
> —Don Durito of the Lacandon Jungle

Some Not-So-Scientific Anecdotes

Yesterday at midday, Daniel Viglietti and his band arrived. Viglietti, as everyone knows, is a citizen of the Latin America from below who travels with a Uruguayan passport and a subversive guitar. There was music and words. We sent with him a greeting to Mario Benedetti, another person responsible for thwarting my career as a musician of perplexing rhythms. Viglietti told us that the rain gatherer for the memory of below—Eduardo Galeano—had been sick but was now better. We sent our best wishes to Don Eduardo and, if he gets sick again, an offer to treat him at the Oventik Clinic, where medicine is not abundant but brown Zapatista joy is, which does not cure but does soothe.

I don't mean to brag, but Viglietti and I composed, together, some verses for one of his songs, and also did a duet: he sang and I held the notebook with the music. The Insurgent Lieutenant accompanied us in the chorus, and she knew all the songs without need for a notebook. When it came time for unspeakable confessions, he knew that in reality I was, because of those antics of the geography of below, a Uruguayan born in

Chiapas. Raúl Sendic and the great General Artigas were also there, but I'm not authorized to disclose it.[1] And Che Guevara dropped in for a while, quizzical and leaning his elbows on some verses of dreams and predawn.

When we got to the "A Desalambrar"[2] part, Daniel explained to us that when he sang it for the first time to his father, his father warned him of the consequences of singing it in the countryside. "If they take out the fences there is going to be mayhem, Daniel, because the cattle are going to get out and go who knows where or get mixed up," he said in more or less those words.

That was when I told him a small part of what I'll tell you now in greater detail:

Near the La Garrucha Caracol, in the Tzeltal Jungle Zone (which, by the way, is where the Zapatista Women's Gathering with Women of the World is going to be held at the end of this month), before the uprising, there were multiple ranches.

Located on the best land in the Lacandon Jungle canyons—with abundant water, flat and fertile ground, nearby roads, private airstrips—each of these estates had thousands of acres dedicated almost exclusively to extensive cattle ranching.

The large trees—ceibas, huápacs, cedars, mahoganies, ocotes, hormiguillos, bayaltés, walnuts—fell to make way for the bovines that were a bonanza for livestock associations, slaughterhouses, distributors, and all levels of government.

The indigenous (Zapatistas, non-Zapatistas, and anti-Zapatistas) had been cast off to the mountainsides and peaks, on rocky terrain, always on steep slopes. There they were supposed to make their coffee plantations in small clearings that the mountain, generous with its guardians, made from time to time on its uneven slopes. Crops grew between rocks and thorns, clinging as well as they could to the sharp inclines that fell down the gorge, as if the mountain had become tired of standing up and suddenly let itself fall, just like that, to sit down on the lands where the boss commanded and "the lord of the gallows and axe" was not a metaphorical figure.

The entire family worked on small coffee plantations. Elders, men, women, and children cut, cleaned, dried, processed, and packed coffee in large sacks. To sell it, these same elders, men, women, and children had to

---

1   Sendic was a Marxist lawyer who founded Uruguay's Tupamaros guerrillas, who were active in the 1960s and 1970s. Artigas is Uruguay's national hero, a revolutionary, patriot, and democrat who fought for the country's independence during the first half of the 1800s.

2   "A Desalambrar" is a song by Chilean folk singer Victor Jara that Daniel Viglietti has recorded and frequently plays. "A Desalambrar" means "[let's] take down the fences," and it's lyrics talk about removing the fences that keep the land in the hands of a privileged elite.

load it, if they had a little luck, onto their beasts of burden. But since there was also a scarcity of animals, elders, men, women, and children were the beasts of burden that carried—on their shoulders—sixty, eighty pounds of coffee. Two or three workdays each with eight to ten hours of walking. They got to the roadside and waited for a car (that's what they call three-ton trucks), which charged them the equivalent of twenty or thirty pounds of coffee that they had carried on their backs.

When they arrived at the municipal seat, coyotes (that's what the Zapatista compas call middlemen) ambushed the vehicles and practically robbed the indigenous people, they lied to them about the coffee's weight and price, taking advantage of the fact that these indigenous people's Spanish was little or nonexistent. The reply that they were being cheated smashed against the coyote's argument: "If you don't want to sell, go back." The small payment they obtained ended up in cantinas and brothels, which had their best "season" during the coffee harvest.

Between one coffee harvest and the next, the indigenous, men, women, and children had to work their mountain fields and find employment as peons on the large estates that ruled over the large valleys opened by the Jataté and Perlas Rivers between these mountains in the Mexican Southeast.

Ranchers followed a single pattern to build on their landholdings. The Big House, the house where the rancher lived during the days that he was on his land, was made of construction material, was spacious, and had large verandas going around it. Next to it was the kitchen. Then, an ample space fenced in by barbed wire. Outside the fence that marked the limits of the "lord's" space lived the peons with their families, and houses made of adobe, wood, and grass roofs. Only the overseer or foreman, and the women who were in charge of the kitchen or housecleaning and the lord's things, could enter the "Big House's" space inside the barbed-wire fence. At night and when the "lord's" wife was not there, marriageable girls would also enter, over whom the rancher exercised the so-called *droit du seigneur* (which consisted of the estate owner having the right to deflower a woman before she was wed).

/ *I know it seems like I am telling you a Bruno Traven novel or am taking a text from the late nineteenth century, but when what I am telling you occurred, the calendar read December 1993, just fourteen years ago.* /

Not only had indigenous peons put in the barbed wire that separated them from the "lord," they also fenced off the large pastures where cattle grazed that later would be succulent steaks and complex stews on the tables of the rich in San Cristóbal de las Casas, in Tuxtla Gutiérrez, in Comitán, in Mexico City.

The barbed-wire fence was not only to control the rancher's cattle. It was also, and above all, a status symbol, a geographic line that separated two worlds: the caxlán's or rich white's world, and the indigenous world.

With methods that would make the Border Patrol or Minutemen cringe, estate owners created and applied their own customs law: if an animal, one of the few that there were in the communities, crossed onto the rancher's land, it became his property and the "lord" could do whatever he wanted with it: sacrifice it and leave it for the vultures, sacrifice it and bring it to his table, put his brand on it, or give it to the foreman for him to then do whatever he wanted. If, on the contrary, one of the "lord's" animals crossed onto the village's side, they had to return it to the rancher's land; if anything happened to it, the village had to pay for it and, additionally, return the wounded or dead animal to the ranch.

I know that I am going on a long while to point out something very simple: before the uprising, the land was owned by estate owners or ranchers who, incidentally, are the powerful's most retrograde sector. If someone truly wants to know how the reactionary radical Right thinks and acts, talk to a Chiapanecan rancher. And I'll give you one of their names, a man who—at least until not long ago—was one of Andrés Manuel López Obrador's allies in Chiapas and, along with Kibbles Albores[3] and the PRD, brought Juan Sabines to power (the one who threw Zapatista families who were evicted from the Montes Azules a few months ago, first into a disbanded brothel and then into a coffee warehouse—incidentally, without progressive intellectuals uttering even a word of protest). The rancher's name is Constantino Kanter, and he was the author of that now-famous phrase, said when the calendar read May 1993: "In Chiapas, a chicken is worth more than an indigenous person's life."

But let's not dwell on this, since it is known that the memory of above is selective and remembers or forgets according to what suits it calendar- and geography-wise.

The point is that something happened. I'm not sure if you know, but I'll tell you because it appears that some don't know or have forgotten, or at least act like they have. Well, the point is that on January 1, 1994, several thousand indigenous people rose up in arms against the supreme government.

You are not going to believe me, but it was here, in this geography and this calendar. And they say, it will have to be confirmed, that they called themselves "Zapatista Army of National Liberation" and that they used balaclavas to cover their faces, as if to show that they were nobody.

---

3 Roberto Albores Guillén was governor of Chiapas from 1998 to 2000. Marcos gave him the nickname "Croquetas," which in this context means "Kibbles."

According to some references from that calendar's newspapers, the insurgents simultaneously took seven municipal seats. It appears, I am not very sure, that one of those municipal seats that fell into the rebels' hands was this arrogant city of San Cristóbal de las Casas.

They fought against the federal army, and the central government of the time—which was led by Carlos Salinas de Gortari and made up of several figures that today may be found in the PRD and the López Obrador CND's ranks—classified them as "lawbreakers" (surely for having broken the laws of gravity, because what is down must not go up).

/ *I ask you to note that we are not talking about people with whom we have strategic or tactical differences, nor conceptual differences regarding reform or revolution. We are talking about our persecutors, about our executioners, about our murderers. If we had betrayed our dead and had supported that so-called option against the Right, we would now be in a "downturn" and a frustration similar to that described by compañero Ricardo Gebrim of the Landless Workers' Movement in Brazil.*

This morning I read that the legal aberration that—in violation of the Constitution—legally sanctions fascism (as was duly pointed out here yesterday by Don Jorge Alonso) was voted for by representatives of all the PRD's factions and groups, including those tied to or dependent on Andrés Manuel López Obrador. I hate to say I told you so, but I told you so. Those who overlooked everything, for the sake of stopping the Right, are now frustrated and in a "downturn." Those of us who were able to sense what is now happening have . . . something else. /

Anyway, it is something that will have to be researched in libraries and newspaper archives, which is where serious theoretical work must originate.

What I want to tell you is what also happened in those calendars, but in another geography that is not the cities'—in the ranches' geography.

It turns out—it is not very certain but there is evidence for it—that the insurgents prepared long in advance, and even made some rules or memorandums that they called "Revolutionary Laws."

One of them, called the "Revolutionary Women's Law," was already mentioned here by Sylvia Marcos a few days ago. She is a serious researcher, so it is very probable that, in effect, these aforementioned laws did exist (maybe they still do).

Well, another one of these laws was called, or is called, the "Revolutionary Agrarian Law."

Although not every respectable theoretician does this, I have taken the trouble of researching and have found something out there that progressive intellectuals call a "pamphlet" and that looks like a little newspaper that those small radical and fringe groups make. It is called "The Mexican Awakener: Informative Arm of the EZLN."[4] It is the first issue (I am not sure if there are subsequent issues), and it is dated December 1993, exactly fourteen calendars ago.

There I found what I'll read to you word for word (I respect the original wording only to demonstrate that these insurgents had no respectable and well-known theoretical counsel, and so it may be plainly seen that they were pretty much just ghetto scum, or that they asked their people—people with no preparation, apparently—what they were going to write):

Revolutionary Agrarian Law

Poor peasants in Mexico continue to demand that the land be for those who work it. The EZLN reclaims the Mexican countryside's just struggle for land and freedom, following in the footsteps of Emiliano Zapata and opposing the reforms to Article 27 of the Mexican Constitution. The following REVOLUTIONARY AGRARIAN LAW is issued to standardize the new agrarian redistribution that the revolution brings to Mexican lands.

1. This law is valid throughout Mexico and benefits all poor Mexican peasants and agricultural workers regardless of their political affiliation, religious beliefs, sex, race, or color.
2. This law affects all agricultural properties and national or foreign agricultural businesses within Mexico.
3. All tracts of poor-quality land in excess of 100 hectares[5] and of good-quality land in excess of 50 hectares shall be subject to revolutionary-agrarian reallocation. Owners whose land exceeds the aforementioned limits shall have the exceeding quantities taken from them and be left with the minimum allowed by this law, being able to continue as small landholders or join the peasant movement of cooperatives, peasant associations, or communal land.
4. Communal and ejido[6] land, or land held by people's cooperatives, shall not be subject to agrarian reallocation, even if it exceeds the limits mentioned in Article 3 herein.
5. Land reallocated by this agrarian law shall be divided among landless peasants and agricultural workers who request it, as COLLECTIVE PROPERTY, to form cooperatives, peasant associations, or

---

4   The Mexican Awakener: *El Despertador Mexicano*.
5   Approximately 247 acres.
6   Collectively owned plots of village land that were introduced as a result of the Mexican Revolution.

agricultural and cattle-production collectives. Reallocated land must be worked collectively.

6. Collectives of poor, landless peasants, as well as agricultural workers, men, women, and children who adequately prove that they own no land or own poor-quality land have a PRIMARY RIGHT to request land.

7. To make use of land for the benefit of poor peasants and agricultural workers, reallocations of large estates and agricultural monopolies shall include the means of production, such as machines, fertilizers, warehouses, financial resources, chemical products, and technical consulting. All of these means must be turned over to poor peasants and agricultural workers with special attention for groups organized into cooperatives, collectives, and associations.

8. Groups that benefit from this Agrarian Law must preferably engage in collective production of food necessary for the Mexican people: corn, beans, rice, vegetables, and fruits, as well as raising cattle, poultry, hogs, and horses, and their derivative products (meat, milk, eggs, etc.).

9. In times of war, part of the production from land reallocated by this law shall be allocated toward supporting orphans and widows of revolutionary combatants and supporting the revolutionary forces.

10. The objective of collective production is primarily to satisfy the people's needs, to instill collective consciousness of work and benefit in the law's beneficiaries, and to create units of production, defense, and mutual aid in the Mexican countryside. When a region does not produce a certain good, it shall exchange with another region that does produce said good, under conditions of justice and equality. Surplus production may be exported to other countries if there is no national demand for the product.

11. Large agricultural companies shall be expropriated and be turned over to the Mexican people, and shall be collectively administered by their workers. Farming equipment, implements, seeds, etc., found idle in factories and businesses or other places shall be distributed among the rural collectives in order to make the land produce extensively and begin to eradicate the people's hunger.

12. Individual hoarding of land and means of production shall not be allowed.

13. Virgin jungle areas and forests shall be preserved, and reforestation campaigns shall be carried out in the principal areas.

14. Springs, rivers, lakes, and oceans are collective property of the Mexican people and shall be cared for, preventing contamination and punishing misuse.

15. To benefit poor, landless peasants and agricultural workers—in addition to the agrarian redistribution set forth herein—trade centers shall be established that purchase the peasantry's products at a fair price and sell goods that the peasantry needs for a dignified life at fair prices. Community health centers shall be established with all the advances of modern medicine, with trained and mindful doctors and nurses, and with free medicine for the people. Recreational centers shall be established for the peasants and their families to have dignified relaxation without canteens or brothels. Free educational centers and schools shall be established where peasants and their families are educated regardless of age, sex, race, or political affiliation and may learn the necessary technical skills for their development. Housing and roadway construction centers shall be established with engineers, architects, and necessary materials for peasants to have dignified housing and good roads for transportation. Utility-provision centers shall be established to guarantee that peasants and their families have electricity, running water, sewage, radio, and television, in addition to everything necessary to facilitate household work: a stove, refrigerator, washing machine, mill, etc.

16. There shall be no taxes for peasants who work collectively, nor for ejido members, cooperatives, or communal lands. ALL DEBTS OWED BY POOR PEASANTS AND AGRICULTURAL WORKERS TO THE OPPRESSOR GOVERNMENT, TO FOREIGNERS, OR TO CAPITALISTS FOR CREDITS, TAXES, OR LOANS, ARE HEREBY CANCELLED.

This law ends with Article 16. There are more laws, but that's beside the point. I would like to point out these offenders-of-grammar-and-good-taste's lack of perspective on modernity, as there is no reference to free trade or agricultural commodities that, God save Lord Monsanto, capitalism has happily brought to the world.

Anyway, it appears that in territories where the rebels gained control, this law was implemented and the ranchers were expelled from their large properties and this land was divided among the indigenous and, so they say, the first thing they did was tear down the fences that protected the estate owners' houses.

They also say that they made this attack on private property singing "A Desalambrar," authored by a certain Daniel Viglietti (who was still seen a few hours ago in this geography, accompanied by people of very dubious reputation; several people present covered their faces, which leaves no doubt that they were hiding something).

Rumor has it that some years later the insurgents created their own forms of self-government and formed what they call "agrarian commissions" to supervise land redistribution and this law's implementation.

What we do know is that they have come across and continue to come across more than a few difficulties, and they resolve them according to their own abilities and means instead of going to advisers, specialists, and intellectuals who tell them what they should do, how they should do it, and evaluate for them what has been done and undone.

There is another piece of information, as scandalous as can be. According to trustworthy sources—that cannot be revealed because they use balaclavas—on a predawn day like any other, these men, women, children, and elderly uncovered their faces and sang and danced, always with rhythms that have no known categorization. They say that they knew they were not less poor than before and that problems of all sorts were upon them—death being one of these problems—so we do not know the motive, cause, or reason for their joy.

According to the latest information, they have kept dancing, singing, and laughing for fourteen calendars, and they say that it's because there is now another geography in their land. This only shows that they are ignorant, because INEGI's topographic maps do not document any territorial change in this southeastern Mexican state of Chiapas.[7]

Simple Answers to Complex Questions

> Predawn is the most Che Guevara-esque region of dreams.
> —Daniel Viglietti

Question 1: Have there been fundamental changes in the lives of Zapatista indigenous communities?

Answer 1: Yes.

Question 2: Did these changes take place beginning with the January 1, 1994, uprising?

Answer 2: No.

Question 3: When did these changes take place, then?

---

7   INEGI is the National Institute of Statistics and Geography (Instituto Nacional de Estadística y Geografía).

Answer 3: When the land became property of the peasants.

Question 4: Do you mean that when the land passed into the hands of those who work it, the processes that can now be seen in Zapatista territory began to unfold?

Answer 4: Yes. The starting point for advances in government, health, education, housing, nutrition, women's participation, trade, culture, communication, and information was recovering the means of production, in this case, the land, animals, and machines that were in the hands of large property owners.

Question 5: Was the Revolutionary Agrarian Law implemented in all territory that the Zapatistas claimed control over?

Answer 5: No. Because of their inherent characteristics, in the Chiapas Highlands and Northern Zones this process was minimal or nonexistent. It only took place in the Tzeltal, Tzotz, Choj, and Border Jungle Zones. But the changes spread to all zones through the underground bridges that unite our communities.

Question 6: Why do you always look happy, even if there are errors, problems, and threats?

Answer 6: Because, with struggle, we have recovered the ability to determine our fate. And that includes, among other things, the right to make mistakes ourselves.

Question 7: Where do you get those strange rhythms that you sing and dance to?

Answer 7: The heart.

Thank you and see you tonight.

Insurgent Subcommander Marcos
San Cristóbal de las Casas, Chiapas, Mexico
December 2007

Part V. Smelling Black:
Fear's Calendar and Geography

When it seems like nothing remains, principles remain.
—Don Durito of the Lacandon Jungle

Old Antonio used to say that freedom also had to do with the ear, the word, and the gaze. That freedom was our not being afraid of the gaze and word of the other, of those who are different. But also our not being afraid of being looked at and heard by others. And then he added that you can smell fear, and that fear gave off different smells below and above. He also said that freedom was not in a place, but that it had to be made, built collectively. That, above all, it could not be built on fear of the other, who, although different, is like us.

I mention this because we think that more than the number of people in a movement, more than its media impact or the forcefulness of its actions, more than how clear and radical its platform is, the most important thing is a movement's ethics. That is what gives it internal coherence, defines it, gives it identity . . . and future.

We have previously talked, and will talk, about what the fundamentals of our Zapatista ethics are.

Now we would like to, briefly, touch upon the nonethics of above, the ethics of fear.

Upon fear—and, more specifically, upon fear of transformation—the system has been constructing, quite patiently, an entire building of reasons not to fight.

There is a "no" for every person, fairly simple or complex according to its intended bearer.

We are going to put aside, for a moment, the material conditions that allow and distinguish what we may call "the empire of fear"—one of the capitalist system's defining characteristics—and concentrate on its existence, cast of characters, and hierarchy.

Let's suppose that one of the most well-developed fears is fear of the other, of what is different, of the unfamiliar.

I will only do a quick breakdown, hoping that these points may be developed later:

—Fear of Gender. But not only women's fear of men and vice versa, also women's fear of women and men's fear of men.
—Fear of Generations. Between elders, adults, young people, children.
—Fear of the Other. Against homosexuals, lesbians, transgender people, and other realities that do not cease to exist simply because they are unfamiliar to us.
—Fear of Identity or Race. Between indigenous people, mestizos, nationals, foreigners.

The freedom that we want must also conquer these fears.

ॐ

It has been said here before, correctly, that antisystemic struggles must not limit themselves only to what the orthodox call the substructure or base of capitalist social relations.

Claiming that the core of capitalist domination lies in the ownership of the means of production does not mean that we ignore or are unaware of other spaces of domination.

It is clear to us that transformations must not focus only on material conditions. That's why for us there is no hierarchy of spheres; we do not claim that the fight for land has priority over the gender struggle, nor that the gender struggle is more important than the fight to recognize and respect difference.

Instead, we think that all types of emphasis are necessary and that we must be humble and recognize that currently there is no organization or movement that can boast about covering all aspects of the antisystemic—that is, anticapitalist—struggle.

This recognition is the basis for our Sixth Declaration of the Lacandon

Jungle. It sets out by recognizing and accepting the breadth of our dream and the narrowness of our strength.

For example, we have pointed out some aspects of the gender struggle within Zapatismo, and in the next gathering you will hear about it first-hand.[1] But we recognize that there are more substantial advances in other collectives, groups, organizations, and individuals that have this objective.

We think that the inherent reality of our existence as the EZLN presents more than a few obstacles and hurdles that cannot be resolved with our internal logic. That's why we seek and ask for an egalitarian relationship with compañeras and compañeros who have advanced further in the gender struggle.

But we don't want you to confuse teaching with ordering, or learning with obeying. We believe that it is possible to build a respectful relationship where our reality advances with profound transformations in this regard; and we know two things: that we cannot do it by ourselves and that we need this relationship.

We offer nothing in return, nothing material I mean. Nor do we offer organic unity or chain of command in one direction or the other.

What we offer is a willingness to understand, respect, and learn.

What you can—and, I believe, should—give us will have its own assimilation process, and something new will emerge.

This new thing will not be a copy of your proposals or a justifiable repetition of our imperfect reality (above all with regard to the gender struggle), but a new way, our way, to take on that struggle and carry it forward.

What I'm saying about the gender struggle—which is where, as the EZLN, we recognize that we have the greatest lag—is true for all struggles and ways that we do not know of, do not encompass, or will never be able to cover.

The EZLN is an organization that has flatly refused to hegemonize and homogenize its relationships with other groups, collectives, organizations, peoples, and individuals, not even with other realities, organized or not.

Not even in the indigenous movement, which is where our strength and primary identity are, have we accepted the vanguard role to represent the entire indigenous movement in Mexico.

To our obvious shortcomings in the women's struggle, one can add insurmountable gaps: workers in the cities, urban popular movements,

---

1   Here Marcos is referring to the Zapatista Women's Gathering with Women of the World (Encuentro de las Mujeres Zapatistas con las Mujeres del Mundo), which featured presentations by Zapatista women and other invited guests.

young people, other loves,[2] and a true constellation of struggles that the Other Campaign has revealed in its tours and activities.

The antisystemic movement that we intend to build in Mexico sets off from this fundamental premise: it must be with the other—with those who are different and share pains and hopes—that one recognizes the capitalist system as being responsible for their situation of injustice.

And this, we think, is only possible with mutual understanding that turns into respect.

That's why the Sixth Declaration and the Other Campaign in Mexico have followed the steps that they have taken thus far: a roll call, a presentation where each person said who they were, where they were, how they saw the world and our country, what they wanted, and how they intended to do it.

In this process of understanding, some knew that this was not their place or their time. That this was not their calendar or their geography. They may say one thing or another, but this is the fundamental cause of their current distance.

It is not nor has it been the EZLN's objective to create a movement under its hegemony, homogenized with its times, ways, and no ways.

We wanted—and want—a broad movement that includes the entirety of our country's below, but with clear, transparent, definitive, and defining objectives: radical and profound transformation of our country, destruction of the capitalist system.

We have not lied, not before, not now.

We are not interested in Band-Aid solutions or reforms, plainly and simply because they do not aid anyone and do not reform even the most superficial elements.

We have told those willing to listen quite bluntly: What we are interested in is having our rights recognized, being allowed to be what we are and how we are—in sum, being left in peace.

We are not interested in government jobs and appointments, or statues and monuments, or museums, or going down in history, or prizes, or honors, or ceremonies.

What we want is to be able to get up each morning without fear being part of the day's agenda.

Fear of being indigenous, women, workers, homosexuals, lesbians, young, elderly, children, others.

But we think that this is not possible within the current system, within capitalism.

---

2   LGBTQ, etc.

We have looked for and have found thoughts and experiences that are different but similar.

We have been part of, above all students in, the most beautiful pedagogic exercise that Mexican skies and soils have ever beheld in their entire history.

It has been, and is, an honor to call compañeras and compañeros those peoples, organizations, groups, collectives, and individuals from the entire spectrum of anticapitalist opposition in our country.

We are not many, it is true. But we are. And in these times of opportunistic vagueness, of illusions and evasions, this—being—is and shall be the piece that the dream we dream needs in order to get going on its long path to reality.

෭෨

Elías Contreras Explains His Very Peculiar Version of Love and Such Things to Magdalena

I think we can imagine everything. Imagine the conversation, calendar, and geography in which it took place. Imagine that Magdalena and Elías Contreras, EZLN Investigation Commission, are talking about nothing in particular. But imagine that, when our ears and gazes arrive, what we see and hear is the following . . .

There is a night that has rushed in on the afternoon, casting it out of the day too early, extending its shades of black and shadows to all corners, leaving only a few lights and twinkles.

This dark invasion has been so quick that it surprised Elías Contreras and Magdalena on their walk back from the fields.

They are already close to the village, but the night is so heavy and so unforeseen that the fleeting lights that inhabit it are not yet ready.

As if fire beetles, stars, moon, and glimmers had remained in another calendar or had gone to the wrong geography and had not arrived in time for night, which was now lord and master in the mountains of the Mexican Southeast.

Elías Contreras knows. He knows, from having walked them, the paths that the night creates on the paths of day. That is why Elías takes Magdalena by the hand; Magdalena has been paralyzed with a gasp of fear after seeing only blackness.

Magdalena is in these lands because they[3] have come to help Elías Contreras with the fight against evil and evildoers, but this is not their battlefield. They are a city dweller. And in the city, or at least in the city where Magdalena lived, night is never absolute. With so many lights fighting for space, night there is a just a pretext for each one of them, each light, to define itself.

Elías's hand has calmed Magdalena. For a few moments, that hand is their only grip on reality. Almost immediately, Elías places Magdalena's hand on his lower back, so that Magdalena is holding Elías's belt.

"Don't let go," says Elías.

Fear makes Magdalena not mutter a word and just think:

"No freakin' way."

Elías leaves the real path and its large puddles and mud, and goes into the trees. Elías walks slowly, taking care that Magdalena does not trip.

In Magdalena's blinded gaze, horrors and ghosts appear that are not of this land: police officers surrounding Magdalena, putting a smelly bag on their head. Punches and mockery in the car. Not seeing, not knowing. Noises fading away. The discussion between them about the money to steal. Taking turns raping. The noise of the car pulling away. Fainting. The dog sniffing the blood from the wounds . . .

"We're here," says Elías's voice, and Magdalena is still trembling when he makes them sit on a log.

After a little while Magdalena recognizes where they are. Elías knows what he's doing. The place where they are has a brown light that does not quite illuminate but does define objects and distances.

It seems like Elías thinks that Magdalena is trembling because they're cold, and he wraps a raincoat around them; anticipating rain, he had it in his bag.[4]

"Where?" asks Magdalena.

Elías seems to know that what Magdalena wants to know is the source of that faint and blurry light.

"They're mushrooms," says Elías, igniting a match whose light erases everything and leaves only his gaze. "During the day they take in light, and at night they release it little by little, so that it lasts, so that it goes on, so that the darkness does not win later."

---

3   Since Magdalena does not fully identify with either the male or female gender, the gender-neutral singular pronouns "they," "them," and "theirs" are used. While traditionally used only for plural subjects, these pronouns are now accepted for singular subjects when there is the need for gender neutrality.

4   Morraleta: a colorful, highly durable, woven poly-mesh bag commonly used in certain regions of Mexico.

Answering a question that does not arrive, Elías says:

"These ones are not edible, they're only for seeing."

It isn't Elías's voice but his aroma that calms Magdalena. A mixture of corn, branches, earth, tobacco, sweat.

"Here we are going to wait a bit for the night to get its rhythm and stop racing along," says Elías.

Magdalena, sitting next to him, grabs Elías's arm and rests their head on his shoulder.

They are thinking about something, because suddenly they let go of Elías:

"Hey Elías, have you ever been with a woman?"

Elías gags on the cigarette smoke, and his body's nervous tensing-up is noticeable. His voice is barely a whisper when he responds:

"Err . . . well, yes, in meetings . . . and projects . . . and parties . . . the compañeras come . . . and we talk about the struggle . . . and about the projects . . . and we talk . . . yes . . . in meetings . . ."

"Don't play stupid, Elías, you know what I'm talking about," Magdalena interrupts.

If there were a little more light, we would see that Elías's face is a traffic light: first it turned red, then yellow, and now is turning bright green.

"Err . . . Mmh . . . Err . . . In other words, as they say, you're asking if I've ever made a love?"

Magdalena laughs readily after hearing Elías's way of referring to having sexual relations.

"Yes," they say still laughing, "I'm asking if you've ever made a love."

Elías's colors now go the other way: from green to yellow and then to red.

"Well, yes, but not exactly, a little, in other words, sort of, barely . . ."

It is a cold night, like the one we are in now, but Elías Contreras, EZLN Investigation Commission, already has his shirt soaked with sweat.

Magdalena is enjoying Elías's embarrassment and does nothing to lessen it.

On the contrary, they lengthen their silence so that Elías has to use words . . .

"Well, Magdalena, I'm not going to be *liaring* to you. I don't remember well, suddenly I do or suddenly I don't . . . But I remember that I read a book I found that was called 'Are you already thinking about love?' and there I got a good look at what it's like."

Magdalena, while neither male nor female, is a real mule (no offense to anyone listening to or reading this), and Elías's nervousness made them forget about the ghosts that were besieging them a few minutes ago, so they ask . . .

"Is that so? And what's it like?" and scoot closer to Elías.

Elías is now the same color as the phosphorescent mushrooms that cover the surrounding trunks and branches.

But Elías Contreras is the EZLN Investigation Commission, he has dealt with a multitude of dangers and unforeseen circumstances, so he breathes deeply while he thinks to himself: "A cigarette, I'll light a cigarette. Where did I leave my cigarettes? I'll light a cigarette and it'll give me time to get my thoughts together. I'll light a cigarette. And if the match doesn't light? Well, as Marcos says, Rome was screwed. Well now, and if the cigarette doesn't light?"

Then Elías begins his explanation:

"Well, Magdalena, it turns out that there is, as they say, that thing, whatever it's called, and the other thing, and it's like that, as if you're not thinking anything, but all of a sudden as if you start thinking something and so then, it turns out . . ."

Elías doubts himself, then says:

"Well, I think I'd better explain it to you another way because what if you don't understand . . ."

Magdalena is smiling a mischievous smile hidden by the darkness when they say:

"OK."

Elías begins:

"Well, so it turns out that there is something called means of production, because babies aren't just babies right away, but first they're products. So products are made with means of production. Ah, and also with raw materials.

"So then it turns out that there's the man's means of production, which is like, as they say, a something for producing products, but not exactly or alone, but another means of production is needed, and so then he talks to the girl and they make an agreement for the production and provide, as they say, the raw materials and they produce the product and one always gets tired, but like good tiredness, happy.

"But it's not like he goes up and says to the girl, 'Hey, let's do production of a product,' but, as they say, he goes around her, and the two go around, around, and then later they make their agreement, and then later it takes a few months and the product comes out and then they name it because they're not going to go around telling it, 'OK, product, go get water or wood,' but it has to have a name.

"So the name is important, but not very important because if someone is a Zapatista, later they can choose their name in the struggle,[5] but they have to think about it, well, because later they don't know if it'll stay that way.

"For example, there's Marcos, who chose the name Marcos, and Rome was screwed because his name is always going to be Marcos. In contrast, I chose Elías, but not everyone knows, so I can choose another name.

"And that's all I have to say and I hope you understood, Magdalena, and if you didn't, then later on, another day, I'll explain it to you because it's late and we have to get to the village."

Magdalena's belly hurts from holding back their laughter while listening to Elías's explanation, but they sit up and say:

"All right, you'll explain it to me another day."

The night is already clearer when Elías Contreras walks uphill arm in arm with Magdalena. It's Elías who breaks the silence:

"Hey Magdalena. Don't be afraid if you're with me."

Magdalena stops briefly to ask:

"How did you know that I was afraid?"

"Fear smells," says Elías, starting to walk again.

"It smells like nightmares, like bad dreams, like shame and sorrow."

It's already early morning when they get to the edge of the village. Magdalena asks:

"And what does joy smell like?"

Elías Contreras, EZLN Investigation Commission, extends his arm as if he were reaching toward the future and says:

"Like this."

An aroma of dignified and rebellious plants and land blows in and is so strong that it can almost be seen and touched and tasted and heard and thought and felt.

As if the future had leaned out into today, for a single instant, and had shown its most fantastic, terrifying, and wonderful treasures—that is, its potential.

Thank you, good night. See you tomorrow.

Insurgent Subcommander Marcos
San Cristóbal de las Casas, Chiapas, Mexico
December 2007

---

5   *Nombre de lucha*, a chosen name similar to a pen name or a nom de guerre.

Part VI. Seeing Blue: Memory's Calendar and Geography

If we below are just insects for those above, then let's bite them!
—Don Durito of the Lacandon Jungle

More than a few times we have said that our Zapatista uprising is against oblivion. Allow me then to try to remember something.

Several moons ago, passing through one of the zones in irregular Zapatista territory, a group of officials—insurgents and commanders—met to look at a few problems.

One of these issues was that many years ago, at the request of one of the zone leaders, some communities had contributed something to set up a cooperative that, they were told, sometime later would return what they had given.

Of course, as with any time there's an error, no one remembered who had made the request, how much had been contributed and by whom, what had happened with the cooperative, etc. When it came time to establish responsibility, we came across a black hole.

"The problem," said one of the insurgent officials, "is that we don't remember very well exactly what happened. But in the communities, they do remember everything, and they're pissed off because they're not being given reports.

"That's the problem. In the communities, they don't forget anything."

Another official said what I was going to say:

"What do you mean that's the problem? On the contrary, that is our strong point. If they forgot things in the communities, they'd barely be part of the fight."

"Exactly," the first official responded.

I looked at the commanders. There was no need to ask anything, they told me right then and there:

"We want the General Command to investigate in order to solve the problem."

"Okeydokey," I told them.

I gave the order to look for Elías Contreras and give him all the information there was.

Several days later, Elías's report arrived.

In effect, in one of those rare periods of low military pressure, the zone leader, anticipating that it would not last long, proposed forming a cooperative to have something when the siege again tightened.[1] That zone's CCRI agreed, and the proposal was made to some communities, which accepted. Sure enough, the time came when military pressure returned and everything that the cooperative had accumulated was sent to communities that were receiving refugees. Up to that point, neat and tidy and problem free. But . . . I'll cite part of Elías Contreras's report:

"The problem, Marcos, is that neither the leader nor the committee members informed the communities. So several years went by, not many, but more than a few, and in the communities they remembered it and they're asking the General Command to see what happened so that things aren't the same as with the PRI, where they do dumb things and just don't inform anyone.

"And I'll tell you what I think. Well, Marcos, of course I'll tell you that—as the saying goes—they fucked up, because it may be that sometimes there's no good food, or there's no clothes, or there's no medicine, or it just seems like the day never ends with all the problems there are, but memory is never absent."

Penalties were divided up among those who had erred, a report was made for the communities, and instructions were issued for a census to be taken of who had contributed and how much, and arrangements were made for them to be reimbursed from the war fund for what they had given.

The commissions went to the communities in question. A little while later they came back and reported. Everything had been set straight, except in the community of San Tito. And what happened is that a compañero, who is of age, refused to receive the reimbursement for what he had

---

1   Ever since the ceasefire in 1994, the Zapatistas have been subject to attacks by the Mexican military and government-backed paramilitaries. The frequency of these attacks varies by year and by community; in some communities it is rare, and in others it is frequent.

contributed. They explained again and again, and he lashed back about how he wouldn't accept it, period. The commissions spent three days and three nights there and couldn't convince him at all. Since they then had to go back to do other work, they left his money with the community head, with the recommendation to convince him later.

I asked the official who accompanied the commission what had happened. This was what he told me:

"It's Chómpiras. I don't know if you remember him, Marcos. He's the one who helped take out the wounded from the Ocosingo market, that time in '94. And then two of his children were killed during the betrayal of '95.[2] He is one of the first ones who joined the fight in these parts. He really reminds me of Mr. Ik. He hardly says anything. He's always quiet. But, err, Marcos, when we told him, he hardly stopped talking. He even scolded us. Well, he told us that he has a better memory than any of us. Damn kids, he told us [the official is almost thirty years old]. Don't we know that Mr. Ik explained that the fight ain't over 'til it's over and then everything's set straight. That he is not going to accept anything because he gave it for the fight and the fight ain't finished."

"And what did you do?" I asked him while I lit my pipe.

"Nothing. What could we do? We ran away because he chased us off with a machete. And he said that he's going to go to you and accuse us of having no memory. That's what he said."

👹

In one of this colloquium's presentations, in Don Jorge Alonso's, we were told that there is more than one angle for analyzing reality—there are different ways of approaching it. We want to take advantage of the double proximity of Jean Robert and John Berger, who know something about this, to take that correct assertion and talk about the gaze.

Rather, about two great gazes and about the privileges of one over the other.

I mean the gaze *toward* the Zapatistas and the gaze *of* the Zapatistas.

It may be attributable to their education, to their history, to their clearheadedness, or to that strange sensitivity that, from time to time, you find in some people, but there is an enormous difference between the way

---

2   This refers to the sudden attempt in February 1995 by President Zedillo to have the federal army capture the Zapatista leadership, in violation of the ceasefire and amnesty previously declared by the government. While Zedillo later abandoned the goal of capturing Marcos and other leaders since the effort had failed to gain popular support, many Zapatistas suffered as a result of widespread military persecution.

that people who work directly with indigenous communities see us and the way that other people see us from afar, from another reality.

I don't mean their indulgent-or-nonindulgent, questioning-or-nonquestioning, defining-or-nondefining way of looking at us. I mean the part of us that they choose to look at and the attitude they do it with.

Andrés Aubry, whose story brings us here, had his way of looking at us; in other words, he chose a part of what we are to see us. The last two times that I saw him exemplify this:

In one, in a private meeting between us and Jérôme Baschet, we talked about books and other nonsense.

Aubry was lively, eloquent, as if with friends.

In the other, at that roundtable where he launched one of the harshest and most accurate critiques against academia that I have ever heard, again and again Andrés turned around and looked behind him, where several hundred compañeras and compañeros, autonomous authorities, committee heads, and organizational leaders from the five caracols listened in silence.

Andrés was nervous, uneasy, as if before harsh judges or a synod.

From the other end of the table, I looked at him and understood him.

There are some who worry about academia's evaluation of their proposals. Aubry couldn't have cared less about that. It was the Zapatistas' evaluation that worried him.

This was the same Andrés Aubry who, during that Color of the Earth March in 2001's calendar, did not look toward the stages that there were in the geography that we went through, nor at the crowds that went to the events. Instead, he looked at the small groups that, scattered along the roads and highways, came out just to see us go by or to say hello.

Still, when we were in the tug-of-war over the Congress of the Union giving the floor to a faceless indigenous woman, Aubry hit the mark of a previous calendar when he said, in more or less these words: "The march, not this, the march there, in the mountains, in the small villages, in those who do not speak, things are going to happen."

Andrés Aubry did not look at us like other people who work in communities or with indigenous people do, like we are the perpetually evangelized, eternally children regardless of the calendars that go by, daughters and sons who make their parents ashamed or proud, or mirrors hung from oneself to cover the lives of those who we come into contact with, mirrors shown or not shown depending on the audience or situation, with a type of new-style opportunism. Those who listen to an accurate presentation or clear analysis by a compañera and compañero and complacently nudging their neighbor—or openly—say: "He, she, learned with us, not the Zapatistas."

No, Aubry looked at us as if the Indian peoples were a strict teacher or tutor. As if he was conscious of the fact that history could be turned upside down at any time. Or as if this had already occurred in the Zapatista communities and the indigenous were the evangelizers—the teachers—and when in their presence, PhDs, a tall stack of books written, the sloppily European or purposefully missionary fashion sense and attitude were all worthless.

Yesterday something was said here that must have caused Andrés Aubry to roll over in his grave. Someone said that our communities are ignorant. I don't know what those of us who consider ourselves students of these "ignorant" communities must be. I will come back to this later.

I think—when I see him, I'll ask him—that Andrés Aubry saw the part of Zapatista communities that is turned inward. As if this community had decided not only to turn the world around but also turn its perception around, and had made its essence—what defines it—look inward, not outward. As if the balaclava was multipurpose armor: strength, protection, external mirror, and—at the same time—a cover for something in the making.

I have recognized this way of looking at us in others: Ronco, Don Pablo, Jorge, Estela, Felipe, Raymundo, Carlos, Eduardo, someone else, nobody, to mention just a few. Forgive me if only one female name appears, but it appears that there is no gender quota on this type of gaze.

Not all gazes that look at us are so recognizable and appreciated as Aubry's.

There are also gazes for which we are—who would say it in full-fledged neoliberalism!—an opportunity for profit in the short, medium, or long term. The gazes of the political, ideological, scientific, moral, journalistic usurer. I will talk about them later.

All these types of gazes—so different from one another, so different when choosing the part of us to look at—nonetheless have something in common: they are gazes from outside.

Additionally, it must be said, they have the privilege of being gazes that are disseminated and known in other geographies and calendars.

In contrast, our gaze, our looking at you, has the drawback (and, at the same time, advantage, but I'll talk about that later) of only being known by the other from outside if you decide to or allow it.

If our gaze is one of gratitude, of recognition, of admiration, of respect, or one that coincides with what you see, then it is disseminated, known, and people remark about its wisdom, clarity, relevance.

If, however, it is one of critique and questioning, the arguments and reasons given do not matter: that gaze must be silenced, covered, hidden.

So people point out our disorientation, our intolerance, our radicalism, our errors.

Well, not "ours," but "Marcos's errors," "Marcos's mountain sickness," "Marcos's intolerance," "Marcos's radicalism."

In one of the presentations for the book *Fiery and Sleepless Nights*,[3] a journalist explained to me the fierce closed-mindedness and repeated slander against our word in places once open and tolerant, saying, "It's that you don't understand how to be consistent."

In a nutshell, what I want to point out is that in the last three years, your gaze toward us is what has been known most.

Photos, movies, recordings, reports, interviews, chronicles, articles, essays, theses, books, conferences, and roundtables have been done with your gaze looking at us.

I'm not going to take time to point out details like how some people have written entire books on Zapatismo without having gone further than San Cristóbal de las Casas, that some present themselves as if they were living in the communities when in reality they lived in this cold and arrogant Jovel,[4] or the extreme case of Carlos Tello Díaz, who wrote a so-called history of the EZLN with material provided by government intelligence services that, allow me to say, are not at all intelligent.

Instead, I want to point out that your gaze is not only from the outside, and not only chooses a way to look at us (an angle, said Don Jorge), it also chooses to look at only a part of what we are.

Yesterday I pointed out that we recognize that we are not capable (nor do we want to be) of covering all aspects of the antisystemic movement in Mexico.

It seems to me that your gaze looking at us must recognize that it is not capable of covering everything that our movement was, is, means, and represents.

We ask you not for humility (although I believe that for more than a few of you, taking a workshop on the topic wouldn't hurt), but honesty.

Your gaze—social scientists, intellectuals, theoreticians, analysts, artists—is a window for others to look at us.

Generally, one is not conscious of the fact that that window is showing only a small part of Zapatismo's big house, so it wouldn't hurt to warn those who look at us through you.

---

3   Sometimes translated as "Nights of Fire and Sleeplessness."
4   The Tzotzil and Tzeltal name for the city of San Cristóbal de las Casas; it means "place in the clouds."

A few years ago, a city-dweller compañera gave her own account of Zapatismo's history since January 1, 1994, and said, "I've been there for everything!"

It wasn't true. In her account, she forgot to specify that she only included Zapatismo's public, external events and activities.

It didn't include things and events that no words can describe: daily and heroic resistance in the communities, the insurgent troops' stubborn patience, the organizational leaders' silent coming and going through our territories. The Zapatismo that sustains and gives meaning to what is seen, heard, touched, tasted, spoken, thought, and felt.

I know that my position as subcommander gives me a privileged place to look by looking at us. But I'll be honest with you: I am not able to cover all the details, and, as Ronco confessed to us this morning, I never stop being amazed by, and again and again marveling at, how little a battered heart—full of patches and scars that fortunately do not heal—can cover.

I tell you this with that heart in my hand: in Zapatismo, the gaze is not an individual but a collective privilege.

And I add that in our gaze looking at you, the endeavor has always been trying to understand you, not judge you.

"Why?" is the question lying in our gaze when it looks at you.

"Why do they say that? Why do they think that way? Why do they do that?"

The truth is that our questions almost always go unanswered, but all right, OK, you win some, you lose some. When all is said and done, there is the certainty that with us, there are more questions and doubts than certainties and answers.

I am telling you this, but not to ask for something in return. Believe me that in the majority of your cases, in addition to respect, we feel gratitude.

It's only so you look at everything that later includes, and excludes, a gaze.

Correct me if I'm wrong, but I believe that it was Paul Eluard who said that "Le monde est bleue comme une orange," which my *sans papier* French translates as: "The world is blue like an orange."

I have also seen some of those photos of the world that are taken from space. The earth looks, in effect, blue and, yes, could very well be an orange.

Sometimes, in the predawn hours when they find me wandering around without possibility for rest, I am able to climb up on a wisp of smoke and, from very high up, I look at us.

Believe me that what can be seen is so beautiful that it's painful to look at.

I'm not saying that it's perfect, nor that it's finished, nor that it has no gaps, irregularities, wounds to close, injustices to remedy, spaces to liberate.

Eppur si muove. And yet it moves.[5]

As if everything bad that we are and carry were mixed with the good that we can be, and the entire world redrew its geography and its time were remade with another calendar.

Well, as if another world were possible.

Then I come here and hear someone say that our communities are ignorant.

I fill my pipe with tobacco, light it, and then say:

"Damn! What an honor to be able to be a student of so much and such scrumptious ignorance!"

Thanks a million.

Insurgent Subcommander Marcos
San Cristóbal de las Casas, Chiapas, Mexico
December 2007

---

5   Here Marcos quotes what Galileo is said to have muttered under his breath when forced to recant his theory that the earth orbits around the sun, accepting instead the church's theory that the earth is still and the sun orbits around it.

Part VII. Feeling Red: War's Calendar and Geography

> The difference between the hopeless and the necessary is that there is no need to prepare for the former. And only preparation makes it possible to determine the latter.
> —Don Durito of the Lacandon Jungle

Before, outside of this colloquium and in it, we have mentioned capitalism's warmongering nature.

Now we would like to add that war is not only a way—essential, it should be mentioned—for Capitalism to impose itself on and implant itself in the periphery.

It is also a business in and of itself. A way to make a profit.

Paradoxically, it is more difficult to do business in times of peace. And I say "paradoxically" because capital is supposed to need peace and tranquility to develop. Maybe that was so before, I don't know; what we see is that now it needs war.

That is why peace is anticapitalist.

It isn't talked about much—in Mexico, at least, it does happen—but the military industry's economic weight and gargantuan profits (which it obtains each time the supposedly dying American superpower decides to "save" the democratic world from a fundamentalist threat . . . other than its own, of course) are not at all negligible.

With theoretical matters—just as Jean Robert pointed out a few hours ago, correctly in our opinion—it is necessary to continually question "the ground" that a scientific approach steps on. We think that the concept of "war" in antisystemic theoretical analyses can help solidify ground that is still marshy.

But it is not only a theoretical question. Robert Fisk and Naomi Klein both have made enormous contributions toward lifting the veil that hid the Iraq War's set design. Not from their desks or sitting in front of a screen that manages the great media monopolies' information, but by personally going to the crime scene, both come to the same conclusions.

In more or less these words, they tell us: "Well! It turns out that Iraq is not being freed from Hussein's tyranny, but, quite simply, business is being done. And even the invasion's apparent failure is a business too."

I'm going to recommend a book to you. This is it. *The Shock Doctrine: The Rise of Disaster Capitalism*, by Naomi Klein. It is one of those books that is worth having in your hands. It is also a very dangerous book. Its danger lies in the fact that what it says is understandable.

As I write this I imagine that Naomi Klein has already laid down the cornerstones of what is presented in her thinking, so I will not repeat it. I'll just point out that it deals with aspects of capitalist operation that are overlooked or ignored by more than a few left-wing theoreticians and analysts in the world.

Don Pablo González Casanova is another one of those people who have made advances in dismantling capitalism's old and new realities in Mexico and the world, and is a gaze generous in time and respectful in its analysis of our comings and goings as Zapatistas.

We have here two representatives from two generations of analysts of the capitalist system, sober, brilliant, and also with something that tends to be forgotten in the theoretical and intellectual medium: they are pedagogues—that is, they make themselves understood.

Don Pablo González Casanova is a scholar. He is the only intellectual I have seen the indigenous Zapatista compañeros and compañeras talk to trustingly. Having spent over twenty-some years living in our communities, I know how difficult it is to earn their trust. When everyone turned their backs on us, he stayed by our side.

Our collective admiration and respect for Don Pablo are also personal. I often say that when I grow up, I want to be like Don Pablo González Casanova. In addition, I must add that he is one of those people that causes chauvinist relapses and makes us say that it is an honor to be Mexican.

We the Zapatistas, along with Don Pablo, would like to give Naomi Klein this doll with a snail shell. In our communities, the snail shell is how the collective is summoned. When the men are in the fields and the women are doing their work, the snail shell calls them to the assembly and then they become a collective. That is why we say that it is "our summoner." We give you this so that you may remember us and so that your gaze reaches us.

Don Pablo, I'd like to give you this book by Naomi Klein. It is a truly brilliant analysis of the current phases of capitalism and contains new elements for understanding the new paths that capitalism is following. I'm giving it to you because I already have another copy.

※

I'd like to take this opportunity to inform you of something.

This is the last time, at least for a while, that we'll come out for events like this; I mean colloquiums, gatherings, roundtables, conferences, as well as, of course, interviews.

Some of the people who have moderated these collective conferences have presented me as the EZLN's spokesperson, and this morning I read that someone refers to me—in addition to spokesperson—as Zapatismo's "ideologist." Wowzers! "Ideologist." Hey, and does that hurt a lot?

Look, the EZLN is an army. A very different one, true, but it is an army.

And in addition to the part of Marcos that you want to see (I mean, aside from my gorgeous legs), as spokesperson, "ideologist," whatever, I think that you are now old enough to know that Marcos is also the EZLN's military leader.

Unlike a few years ago, our communities—our compañeras and compañeros—are being attacked.

It had already happened before, true.

But it is the first time since that predawn morning in January 1994 that the societal response, national and international, has been insignificant or nonexistent.

It is the first time that these attacks have unabashedly come from supposedly left-wing governments, or that they have been perpetrated with the institutional Left's open support.

In today's newspaper, one can read that the Chiapanecan ranchers' emblematic figure I told you about yesterday, Mr. Constantino Kanter, was just appointed as a government official in Juan Sabines's PRD government, to a position where financial resources can flow to paramilitary groups problem-free.

It is also the first time that Flor y Canto[1] has been closed, the spaces where the common folk found out about what was happening with our movement, and about our reflections and calls to action.

---

1   The Flor y Canto Center for Indigenous Rights in Oaxaca, Mexico.

And not just that.

A few months ago, in Mexico City during one of the roundtables that we participated in, one of those rank-and-file López Obrador supporters, modern-day "brownshirts" (whose middle managers are cretins and grunts the likes of Jaime Avilés, from the newspaper *La Jornada*), questioned the Zapatistas (Commander Miriam, Commander Zebedeo, and me) by asking—with a smug and questioning tone, in more or less these words—why we didn't allow the "progressive people of this country to move forward with Mexico's democratization." That's what she said. We had just finished laying out a number of reasons for our distance from the PRD and López Obrador, which the well-dressed woman did not hear, of course.

The five or six people who had been sent responded to our arguments first with lies (that AMLO had distanced himself from Governor Sabines and other people who had aligned themselves with Felipe Calderón, that the CND was anticapitalist, and things like that) and then with their chant: "Es un horror, estar con Obrador" [It is terrible to be with Obrador].[2] Commander Zebedeo asked me later what we were doing there and who those people were that didn't even listen to what we were saying.

Several days later, the puss (my apologies to cats) who presides over the Party of the Democratic Revolution, Leonel Cota Montaño, accused us of having caused—with our criticisms—López Obrador's electoral defeat (that's what he said) in the 2006 presidential elections.

Before, practically since the Sixth Declaration of the Lacandon Jungle's launch, enlightened López Obrador supporters found that the spaces to attack us were wide open, while at the same time they shut us out.

We were told about everything over the course of this calendar. To paraphrase Edmundo Valadez, "the shit had permission," and the so-called progressive and left-wing intelligentsia said, drew, and wrote things that would have brought shame to our country's most reactionary press, but took place in the institutional Left and its satellites without them so much as blinking.

In the words of a "left-wing" intellectual, after the electoral fraud of 2006, "We are not going to forgive Marcos for this."

I am pointing out a simple and verifiable fact. A fact that, in addition, we foresaw even before that June 19, 2005, when we publicly released our Sixth Declaration of the Lacandon Jungle, and that we prepared for.

Incidents have also occurred that warn us and alert us, above all during

---

2   Marcos is mocking the original rhyming chant, "Es un honor estar con Obrador," which translates as "It is an honor to be with Obrador."

the last tour that we did for the Indian Peoples of the Americas Gathering, in Vícam, Sonora.

We know and understand that you think that things only happen if the media or a specific media outlet reports it. I'll inform you that that's not the way it is, for a while now many things have occurred that are silenced or ignored.

We understand that our positions are not received with the same openness and tolerance as some years ago.

We understand that a political position and vision are supported and publicized and then made into a "retreat" to leave out any dissident questioning or position.

We also understand that for some media outlets we are only newsworthy when we are killing or dying, but—at least for now—we prefer for them not to have anything to write about, and we'll try to continue moving forward with consolidating the civil and peaceful force that is still called the Other Campaign and—at the same time—be prepared to resist, on our own, the reactivation of attacks against us from the army, police, or paramilitaries.

Those of us who have waged war know how to recognize the paths on which it prepares and nears.

The signs of war on the horizon are clear.

War, like fear, also has a smell.

And its foul odor can now be inhaled in our lands.

In the words of Naomi Klein, we must prepare for the shock.

As a matter of fact, in these two years that we have been out and about, our theoretical, reflexive, and analytical production has been more abundant than in the twelve previous years. The fact that it has not been made known in the everyday media does not mean that it does not exist. Our approaches are there, in case someone is interested in discussing them, questioning them, or comparing them with what is happening now in the world and in our country. Maybe, if you stick your head out the window a bit, you will see—as a warning—what reality is today.

Anyway, that's the way it is. Maybe now you'll understand the "we're counting on you" tone of our presentations.

༄

When we Zapatistas speak, we put first our red heart that beats collectively.

Understanding what we say, do, and will do is impossible if our word is not felt.

105

I know that feelings do not fit into theory, at least into the kind of theory that is now stumbling around.

That it is very difficult to feel with your head and think with your heart.

That the theoretical masturbations created by raising this possibility are not minor, and that bookstore and library bookshelves are full of failed or ridiculous attempts at what I am telling you.

We know and understand.

But we insist that the assertion is correct; the mistaken thing is where attempts to resolve it are being made.

Because for us Zapatistas, the theoretical problem is a practical problem.

It isn't about promoting pragmatism or about returning to the origins of empiricism, but about clearly indicating that theories not only must not be isolated from reality but also must look within it for the sledgehammers that are sometimes necessary when one comes across a conceptual dead-end.

Rounded, complete, finished, coherent theories are good for taking a licensing exam or for winning prizes, but they tend to shatter at the first gust of reality.

At this table, we have heard lights and sparks that give us Zapatistas encouragement and room to breathe.

That explosive mixture of knowledge-made-feeling that John Berger dazzled and moved us with;

Jean Robert's clear and uncompromising inquiry;

Sergio Rodríguez's relentless, solid analysis;

the serene clarity of François Houtart's reflections;

the honest story of what happened and will happen with a movement that we not only respect but also admire—the Landless Workers' Movement—told by compañero Ricardo Gebrim;

Jorge Alonso's rich and *encompassing* thought;

Peter Rosset's enthusiastic description;

the brilliant reference that Gilberto Valdés made from theoretical discussions that are taking place now in revolutionary Cuba;

Gustavo Esteva's beneficial theoretical provocations;

Sylvia Marcos's noble lucidity;

Carlos Aguirre Rojas's theoretical-analytical advances;

Immanuel Wallerstein's far-reaching illuminations;

and, a short while ago, Don Pablo's amiable wisdom and the disturbing light that Naomi Klein shines on capitalist cynicism.

We also salute the compañeras and compañeros who moderated this colloquium's sessions.

My respects to those who worked on translating the presentations,[3] and my sincere apologies for the problems caused for you by Mr. Owl, December, Magdalena, and Elías Contreras's Zapatista "ways" of talking.

Nonetheless, there is something more that cannot be seen, because what it does is seen.

I'm talking about the compañeras and compañeros who we call *sound and lights*, and above all, all the young indigenous people who study and work here at CIDECI with Dr. Raymundo Sánchez Barraza.

Since we have already talked about the gaze, I think the least we can do is not only to see their work (they are basically the people who have made this colloquium possible), but also to see them.

Thanks also, a very special and loving thanks, to the EZLN Sixth Declaration Commission's support team. Thank you, Julio. Thank you, Roger.

I know you find it strange that I am saying this, since there is still the ceremony for Andrés Aubry tomorrow and the declaration-enigma of his doctoral degree.

For this event, taking place midday tomorrow, my bosses from the Indigenous Revolutionary Clandestine Committee–Highlands Zone shall arrive, along with autonomous authorities and work commissions from the Oventik Good Government Committee.

They shall then have our word, and through their voice, as now through mine, we shall speak the all that we are.

❧

As the last part of our extensive participation in this colloquium, I would like to explain what we want to point out with the overall title, "Neither the Center nor the Periphery."

We think that it isn't only about avoiding traps and concepts—in this case, of a theoretical and analytical nature—that the center puts and imposes on the periphery.

Nor is it about inverting and changing the gravitational center to the periphery, to then "irradiate" the center.

Instead, we believe that this other theory, some of whose general traits have been presented here, must also break with the logic of centers

---

3   Those who provided verbal, simultaneous translations during the event itself for attendees who did not speak Spanish.

and periphery, anchor itself in realities that erupt and emerge, and open new paths.

If these types of gatherings are repeated, I believe you will agree with me that the presence of antisystemic movements—as now with the Brazilian Landless Workers' Movement—are particularly enriching.

Well, I think that's everything.

Oh! Before it slips my mind: we're counting on you.

Thank you to everyone.

Insurgent Subcommander Marcos
San Cristóbal de las Casas, Chiapas, Mexico
December 2007

2.

National and International Caravan for Observation and Solidarity with Zapatista Communities

August 2, 2008

Caracol III: La Garrucha

Francisco Gómez Autonomous Municipality (Ocosingo Municipality), Chiapas, Mexico

Subcommander Marcos's Words for the National and International Caravan for Observation and Solidarity with Zapatista Communities

La Garrucha Caracol, August 2, 2008

Good afternoon, good evening. My name is Marcos, Insurgent Subcommander Marcos, and I am here to introduce you to Insurgent Lieutenant Colonel Moisés. Within the EZLN General Command, he is in charge of international work, what we call the Intergalactic Commission and the International Sixth Declaration, because of all of us, he is the only one who has the patience for you all.

Vamos a hablar despacio, para la traducción. We will speak slowly, for the translation. Nous allons parler doucement, pour la traduction.

We want to thank you for having come all the way here to understand directly what is happening with the Zapatista process, not only with the attacks we are receiving, but also with the processes that are being built here in rebel territory, in Zapatista territory.

We hope that what you see, what you hear, is worthwhile so you can take that word very far away, to Greece, to Italy, to France, to Spain, to the Basque Country, to the United States, and to the rest of our country, with our compañeros from the Other Campaign.

We hope you are not going to be like the so-called International Civil Commission for Human Rights Observation, which only came here several months ago to wash the PRD Chiapas government's hands by saying that the attacks our people suffered did not come from the state government, but from the federal government.

I would like to give a talk to introduce what Lieutenant Colonel Moisés is going to tell you about. We are pleased that his being in this zone coincides with your visit here. He is the compañero who has most closely followed the process of building autonomy within the Zapatista communities.

I wanted to explain, in broad strokes, the history of the EZLN and the Zapatista indigenous communities in this territory, in Chiapas, that is. I'm talking about the Chiapas Highlands, the Oventik Caracol Zone; the Tzeltal-Tojolabal-Tzotz-Choj Zone, belonging to the Morelia Caracol; the Chol Zone, which belongs to Roberto Barrios, in the north of Chiapas; the Tojolabal or Border Jungle Zone, which is the La Realidad Caracol; and this zone, the Tzeltal Zone, which is the La Garrucha Caracol.

Tomorrow, you are invited to visit a village where people have been EZLN support bases for many years. You will have the honor of being guided by Commander Ismael, who is here. This compañero, along with Mr. Ik—the late Commander Hugo, or Francisco Gómez, which was his civilian name—was going through these canyons, talking about the Zapatista word, when no one else was with us.

He is going to take you. You are going to see where the soldiers were looking for marijuana. We want you to see if there's marijuana. If you find any, don't smoke it, make a denunciation so it gets destroyed. No, there's no marijuana. But they don't believe us—maybe they'll believe you . . . Nope, even less likely! When you see them, they aren't going to believe anything you say.

Commander Tacho is also with us today, here to my right. He is also one of the commander compañeros who was with Mr. Ik, Commander Hugo, when the EZLN was just starting in this canyon. And he is part of the EZLN Sixth Declaration Commission. He was with us in the northeast of Mexico, going through Indian communities with compañeros and compañeras of the Other Campaign in Mexico, in that part of the country.

How did it all begin? Twenty-four years ago, almost twenty-five, a small group of urbanites—or city dwellers, as we call them—arrived not to this part of the jungle, but much deeper in, to what is now known as the Montes Azules Reserve. In that zone there was nothing, nothing but four-legged wild animals and two-legged wild animals, us. And this small group's conception—I am talking about 1983–1984, twenty-four or twenty-five years ago—was the traditional conception of liberation movements in Latin America: a small group of enlightened people who rise up in arms against the government. And that causes many people to follow them, rise up, and overthrow the government, and a socialist government is established. I am being very schematic, but basically it is what is known as "guerrilla foco" theory.[1]

That small group—of those of us who remained—had that traditional, classic, or orthodox conception, if you want to call it that, but it also had an ethical and moral burden that had no precedent in guerrilla or armed movements in Latin America. That ethical and moral inheritance came from other compañeros who had died confronting the federal army and the Mexican government's secret police.

All those years, we were alone. There were no Zapatista compañeros in the communities here. No one from Greece came to see us. Nor from Italy nor France nor Spain nor the Basque Country. Gosh . . . Not even from Mexico! Because this was the most forgotten corner of this country. Something that was a downside would, further along, turn into an advantage: the fact that we were isolated and forgotten allowed us to go through a devolutionary process. The orthodox will know of a book that talks about "the transformation of monkey into man."[2] In that time, it was the opposite: man transformed into monkey, which is what we were. Even physically—well, that's why I wear a balaclava. It is for questions of aesthetics and good taste that I must cover my face.

This small group survived the fall of the Berlin Wall, the crumbling of the socialist bloc, and the capitulation of the guerrilla war in Central America, first with the FMLN (Farabundo Martí National Liberation Front) in El Salvador, then with what was once called the Sandinista National Liberation Front in Nicaragua, and, later on, with the Guatemalan National Revolutionary Unity, the URNG.

What made it survive were two elements, according to us: One was the obstinance or stubbornness that those people probably had in their DNA. And the other was the moral and ethical burden that they had inherited from compañeros and compañeras who had been murdered by the army right in those mountains.

Things were left at that, with two options: A small group that spends decades holed up in the mountains, waiting for a time when something happens and they can act within social reality. Or end up, like some

---

1   The theory that a small, committed group of revolutionaries can start violent action against a sitting regime that will eventually lead to revolution.
2   Friedrich Engels's 1876 essay entitled "The Part Played by Labor in the Transition from Ape to Man."

portion of the radical Left in Mexico then, as congresspeople, senators, or legitimate presidents of the institutional Left in Mexico.

Something happened that saved us. It saved us and defeated us in those first years. And what happened is sitting here on my left, Lieutenant Colonel Moisés, Commander Tacho, Commander Ismael, and many other compañeros who turned the EZLN—a focalist and orthodox guerrilla movement—into an indigenous army.

Not only was it an army made up of an indigenous majority. Majority . . . that's an understatement because, in reality, out of every hundred combatants, ninety-nine were indigenous and one was mestizo. Not only that, this army and its design suffered a defeat in its guide-based approach to leadership, which had been a classic revolutionary, authoritarian structure where a man, or group of men, become the savior of humanity, or of the country.

What happened, then, is that this approach was defeated when we came face to face with the communities and realized that not only did they not understand us, but their proposal was better.

Something had happened in all those years, all those decades, all those centuries. We were dealing with a movement for life that had been able to survive conquest attempts from Spain, France, England, the United States, and all the European powers, including Nazi Germany from 1940 to 1945. What had made these people resist—our compañeros and compañeras initially, and today our bosses—had been an attachment to life that had a lot to do with a cultural burden. Language, dialect, the way of relating to nature presented an alternative not only for life, but for struggle. We were not teaching anybody how to resist. We were turning into students of that someone's school of resistance, someone who had been doing it for five centuries.

Those who came to save the indigenous communities were saved by them. And we found direction, destination, path, company, and speed for our step. Which, then and now, we call "the speed of our dream."

The EZLN owes a great debt to you, to people like you in Mexico and throughout the world, but our fundamental debt is in our heart: in the indigenous heart. In this community and in thousands of communities like it, inhabited by Zapatista support-base compañeros.

At the time when our small guerrilla group made contact with the communities, there was a problem and a struggle. I, the guerrilla group, have a truth, and you are ignorant; I am going to teach you, I am going to indoctrinate you, I am going to educate you, I am going to train you. Error and defeat.

When the language bridge was first being built and we began to modify our way of talking, we began to modify our way of thinking about ourselves and of thinking about the place we had in a process: Serving.

Once a movement that proposed putting the masses at its service, making use of proletarians, of workers, of peasants, of students to take power and lead them to supreme happiness, we were gradually turning into an army that had to serve the communities. In this case, the Tzeltal indigenous communities, which were the first ones we set up camp in, which was in this zone.

Contact with the communities meant a reeducation process that was stronger and more terrifying than the electric shocks that are customary in psychiatric clinics. Not everyone could put up with it, some of us could, but we still keep complaining this late in the game.

What happened next? What happened is that the EZLN turned into an army of indigenous people, to serve indigenous people, and went from the six of us who started the EZLN to over six thousand combatants.

What set off the January 1, 1994, uprising? Why did we decide to rise up in arms? The answer lies in the children. It was not an analysis of the international context. Any of you would agree that the international context was not favorable for an armed uprising. The socialist bloc had been defeated, the entire left-wing movement in Latin America was in a period of retreat. In Mexico, the Left was sobbing about defeat after Salinas de Gortari not only had committed fraud, but also had bought a good part of the Mexican Left's critical conscience.

Any marginally reasonable person would have told us: the conditions aren't right, don't rise up in arms, hand over your weapons, join our party, etc., etc. But there was something inside that made us defy those forecasts and those international contexts.

The EZLN then proposed, for the first time, defying the calendar and geography of above. The children, I said. It just so happened that in those years, since the beginning of the nineties, since 1990, there had been a reform that prevented peasants from being able to access land. As you're going to see tomorrow, when you go up the hill that goes toward the community of Galeana, that was the land peasants had: steep slopes, full of rocks. The good land was in the hands of the ranchers. In the next few days, you are also going to see those ranches and are going to be able to see the difference in land quality.

There was no longer the possibility of getting access to a plot of land. And at the same time, diseases began to kill off the children. From 1990 to 1992, there was no child in the Lacandon Jungle who reached five years of age. Before turning five, they died of curable diseases. It was not cancer, it was not AIDS, it was not heart disease—they were curable diseases: typhoid, tuberculosis, and sometimes a simple fever would kill children under five.

I know that in the city this might well be an advantage: fewer donkeys, more cobs, as the saying goes. But in the case of an indigenous people, the death of their children means their disappearance as a people. In other words, in the natural process, adults grow, age, and die. If there are no children, that culture disappears.

The mortality of indigenous people, of indigenous children, intensified the problem. But what made things here different from other Indian communities is that here there was a rebel army. The women were the ones who began to push for this. Not the men. I know that the tradition in Mexico—mariachis, Pedro Infante, and all that—is that we men are very macho. But it was not like that. The ones who began to push—something must be done, no more, and enough is enough—were the women, who were watching their sons and daughters die.

A type of murmur began in all the communities: something must be done, enough is enough, enough is enough, in all languages. Back then we were already in the Highlands Zone too. And there we had two compañeras that had been, and still are, the backbone of that work: the late Commander Ramona and Commander Susana.

This concern, this discomfort, began to emerge in different places . . . Let's call it by its name: this rebellion in the Zapatista women, the idea that something needed to be done. We did what we had to do then, which was to ask everyone what we were going to do. Then, in 1992, there was a consultation—no television, no Mexico City government, no nothing that there is now—and community by community it happened and assemblies were held, like this one right now. The problem was put forth. The dilemma was very simple: if we rise up in arms, they are going to defeat us, but it is going to draw attention and improve conditions for the indigenous. If we do not rise up in arms, we are going to survive, but we are going to disappear as Indian peoples.

The logic of death is when we say: they have left us with no other option. Now, after fourteen, almost fifteen years, those of us with the most time here say: it's a good thing we didn't have any other option.

The communities said: that's what you're here for, fight, fight with us. It was not just a formal relationship of command. Because formally it was the opposite: formally, the EZLN was in command and the communities were the subordinates. But de facto, in reality, it was the other way around:

the communities sustained, cared for, and made the Zapatista Army of National Liberation grow.

Back then, the participation of a mestizo compañero was also important, a compañero from the city, Insurgent Subcommander Pedro, who fell in combat on January 1, 1994.

When we brought this dilemma and the communities said "let's rise up in arms," the military calculus that we made—Lieutenant Colonel Moisés may remember this well because there was a meeting with all the Zapatista leaders in these mountains here behind the community, up high, in an encampment that we have—the proposal I made was this: we have to think about what we are going to do, because when we get something going, there's no turning back.

If we start to ask people if we should rise up in arms or not, then we are not going to be able to stop it. We knew and we felt that the answer was going to be yes. And we knew and we felt that those who would fall would be those of us who had met in these mountains, here above La Garrucha.

What happened happened. I'm not going to tell you about January 1, 1994, because you began to know about us—well, some of us, because there were some who were little kids—and an era of resistance opened, we say, where the transition was made from armed struggle to civil and peaceful organization of resistance.

Something happened in this whole process that I want to draw attention to: the change in the EZLN's position regarding the problem of power. And this definition surrounding the problem of power is what is going to leave the deepest mark on the footprint in the Zapatista path. We had realized—and this we includes the communities, not just the first group—that solutions, like everything in this world, are built from the bottom up. And our entire previous proposal, and the orthodox Left's entire proposal up to then, was the opposite, it was: from above things are solved for below.

For us, this below-for-above change meant not organizing ourselves, not organizing other people to go vote, nor to go to a march, nor to shout, but to survive and turn resistance into a school. This was what the Zapatista compañeros did, not the original EZLN, that small group, but the EZLN that now had this indigenous component. What is now known, broadly speaking, as building Zapatista autonomy is a process that Lieutenant Colonel Moisés is going to elaborate on in a little bit.

Before that, I want to point out a few things. It is said, not unjustly, that in the last two years—2006, 2007—Subcommander Marcos diligently and successfully worked on destroying the media image that had been built around him. And it captures people's attention that some who were close before have now distanced themselves and become definitively anti-Zapatista. Some of them went to their countries to give talks and were received as if they were the ones who had risen up in arms. They were the Zapatologists, willing to travel all-expenses-paid, to receive applause, caravans, and one favor or another when they traveled abroad.

What happened? I'm going to tell you how we see it. You will have your vision. At the time when the EZLN rose up . . . I'm going to explain myself: here in the indigenous zones, people talk a lot about "the coyotes." The coyotes, I want to make a distinction because for the Yaquis and the Mayos, the coyote is a real badass, it is emblematic. In Chiapas it isn't. The coyote is the intermediary. It is someone who buys low from indigenous people and then resells high on the market.

When the Zapatista uprising took place, something that we call "solidarity intermediaries" emerged. Solidarity coyotes, in other words. They are people who said, and still say, that they have a dialogue with Zapatismo, that they have the red telephone, that they are the ones who know what things are like here, and all that means political capital. They come and bring a little something, they pay a little, and go and present themselves as emissaries of the EZLN: they get paid a lot.

The appearance of this group of intermediaries—where there were politicians, intellectuals, artists, and social-movement actors—hid from us the existence of other things, of other belows. We sensed that the Spain of below was out there, that the Basque Country in rebellion was out there, that rebel Greece was out there, that insurrectionary France was out there, that the Italy of struggle was out there, but we did not see them. And so we feared that you would also not see us.

These intermediaries organized and did things when we were fashionable, and charged their political capital. Just like someone who organizes concerts, says that they are to benefit us, and keeps a portion: they charge something like a salary, or the organization's cut of the proceeds.

There was another below. We always had that idea: Zapatismo has always stated that it is not the only rebel, nor the best. And our conception was not to create a movement that hegemonized all rebellion in Mexico or all rebellion at the global level. We never aspired to have an international, the fifth international or I don't know which one you're on . . . Alejandro? Now it's the Sixth Declaration, but this is different, this is the Other International. Alejandro knows about internationals.

What happened? I'm going to tell you some things that will not be new to you. The tale of an institutional Left is perfectly clear to the Spanish, with Rodríguez Zapatero or Felipe González; for the Basque Country—Gora Euskal Herria—more still; for rebellious Italy it is also nothing new; and Greece, well, it can tell us a lot about that; in France since Mitterrand, the man, the same goes.[3]

In Mexico, no. There continues to be that expectation: that it is possible for the Left we suffer from now, if it takes power, to do so scot-free. Which means: it is going to be able to attain governmental power without ceasing to be left-wing. Spain, Italy, France, Greece, practically every country in the world can give an account of the opposite, of left-wing, principled people—not necessarily radicals—who when they come to power are no longer so. The speed varies, the depth varies, but unfailingly, they change. It is what we call power's "stomach effect": it digests you or turns you into shit.

In Mexico, this approach toward power by the Left or what calls itself the Left . . . right now I am remembering it came out in a newspaper that I was not here, that I was in Mexico City at leftist parties—I didn't know there was a left-wing in Mexico City and that they throw parties . . . there still is, but it is an Other left-wing. When the possibility of power presents itself, this process of power's digestion and defecation of that Left began to emerge. To us Zapatistas, and everyone who was in the center . . . Pardon me if I break any hearts, but that center is not in the center, it's stuck to the right. It's the other side, to the right . . . well, to your right . . .

So we had to, we were asked by this group of intellectuals, artists, social leaders, to turn back history to 1984, when we thought that a group, or a person, if it came to power, transforms everything downward. And we were asked to place our trust, the future, our life, and our process in an enlightened one, in one person, along with a band of forty thieves that is the Mexican Left.

We said no. It's not that the legitimate president seems unpleasant to us, it's just that we plainly and simply do not believe in that process. We do not believe that someone, not even someone as good-looking as Subcommander Marcos, is capable of making that transformation—well, my legs. We could not, and so the split took place.

I want to bring something to your attention: back then, we said what was going to happen. What is happening now. When we said it, they said that we were playing into the Right's hands. Now that they are repeating, with our very words, what we said two years ago, they say that it is to serve the Left.

---

3   Marcos is making the distinction here between the former French president François Mitterrand and his wife, Danielle, who had visited Marcos in Chiapas in 1996 and who was to the left of her husband on the political spectrum.

Zapatismo is uncomfortable.[4] As if in power's puzzle there came a piece that did not fit and must be disposed of. Of all the movements there are in Mexico, one of them—not the only one—Zapatismo, is uncomfortable for these people. It is a movement that does not allow itself to conform, does not allow itself to give up, does not allow itself to surrender, does not allow itself to sell out. And in movements from above, that is the logic, that is what's rational. It is "realpolitik," as they say.

So, this distancing took place, which little by little began to fundamentally permeate toward international sectors in Latin America and in Europe. In that trajectory, nonetheless, more solid relationships were built. To mention some: the compañeros of the CGT[5] in Spain, the rebellious cultural movement in the Basque Country, the social Italy, and, more recently, the rebellious and unsubmissive Greece that we have encountered.

This rush to the right is hidden in the following way, people say: "The EZLN radicalized and became more left-wing." Excuse us, but our approach remains the same: we do not seek to take power, we think that things are built from the bottom up. And what happened is that those sectors, the solidarity intermediaries, the internationalist coyotes—or the coyote international—has run toward the right. Because power does not let you access it scot-free.

Power is an exclusive club that has certain requisites for entry. What we Zapatistas call the "society of power" has rules. And it can only be accessed if certain rules are followed. Anyone who seeks justice, freedom, democracy, or respect for difference has no possibilities of accessing it unless they surrender those ideas.

When we began to see this rush to the right by the sector that apparently was the most Zapatista sector, we began to ask ourselves what was beneath this, what was behind this. To be honest, we began the other way around: we began in the world, internationally, and then we asked ourselves about Mexico.

For reasons that you may be able to explain, Zapatismo's connection was stronger with other countries than with Mexico. And it was stronger in Mexico than with people from Chiapas. As if there were an inverse relationship in geography: those who lived farther away were closer to us, and those who lived closer were farther away from us.

Then came the idea to look for you, with the intuition and desire for you to exist: you, others like you. Along came the Sixth Declaration, the

---

4   The Spanish word *incómodo* can mean either "uncomfortable" or "inconvenient."
5   The General Confederation of Labor (Confederación General del Trabajo) is an anarcho-syndicalist trade union.

definitive split with this sector of solidarity coyotes. And the search, in Mexico and the world, for others who were like us, but who were different.

In addition to this position toward power, there is an essential characteristic in Zapatismo—and you are going to see it soon while you're here in these coming days, or if you talk to the Autonomous Councils and the Good Government Committees, with the autonomous authorities—the refusal to hegemonize and homogenize society. We do not work toward a Zapatista Mexico, nor a Zapatista world. We do not intend for everyone to become indigenous. We want a place, here, ours, to be left alone, where no one commands us. That is freedom: us deciding what we want to do.

And we think that it is only possible if others like us want and fight for the same thing. And if a relationship between compañeros is established, we say. That is what the Other Campaign wants to build. That is what the International Sixth Declaration wants to build. A gathering of rebellions, an exchange of learnings, and a more direct relationship—not media-based, but real—of support between organizations.

Several months ago, compañeros came here from Korea, from Thailand, from Malaysia, India, Brazil, Spain—and I don't remember where else—with Vía Campesina. We saw them in La Realidad, we were there with them. And when we spoke, we told them: a meeting between leaders is worth nothing to us. Not even the picture that gets taken. If two movements' leaderships aren't good enough for the movements to meet and get to know each other, their leaderships are no good.

We say the same now, to anyone who comes to propose that. What we are interested in is what's behind: you, others like you. We cannot go to Greece, but we can take a guess and say that of those who wanted to come, not everyone is here. How can we talk to those others? And tell them that we do not want charity, that we do not want pity. That we do not want them to save our lives. That we want a compañero, a compañera, and a compañeroa in Greece to fight for what's theirs. In Italy, in the Basque Country, in Spain, in France, in Germany, Denmark, Sweden; I'm not going to say all the countries, because what if I forget one and in comes a complaint . . .

Where do we look? When I'm doing this quick run-through, I'm talking about a moral and ethical inheritance from those who founded us. Above all, it has to do with struggle and respect for life, for freedom, for justice, and for democracy. We owe a moral debt to our compañeros. Not to you, not to intellectuals who distanced themselves, not to artists or writers, not to social leaders who are now anti-Zapatista.

We owe a debt to those who died fighting. And we want the day to come when we can say to them, to our dead, just three things: we did not give up, we did not sell out, we did not surrender.

And now for Lieutenant Colonel Moisés . . .

Words of Lieutenant Colonel Moisés for the National and International Caravan for Observation and Solidarity with Zapatista Communities

La Garrucha Caracol, August 2, 2008

Good evening, compañeros, compañeras. I want to explain, talk to you, about how autonomy is being built in the various caracols and in the Good Government Committees.

But before beginning this, it is like compañero Subcommander Marcos told you, before the arrival of the insurgent compañeros from the Zapatista Army of National Liberation, in all the communities life was very difficult: exploited, humiliated, trampled, pillaged.

I am talking to you now about the recovered land, which belonged to the estate owners. There, our grandparents lived there. And many more years beforehand. They saw that the employers were the bosses. And our grandparents saw that the evil governments[1] are the same.

So, when the Zapatista Army of National Liberation arrived—as compañero Subcommander Marcos said—the work in the communities began: talking about exploitation. So, our compañeros and compañeras,

---

1   This is what the Zapatistas call official government institutions.

our grandfathers and grandmothers, our fathers and mothers, understood the need to organize. Because they already saw what was happening, what was occurring.

So, then there was already the idea that we need to organize, that we need to unite, that like that we are strong. But in those times it could not be done, because the bosses and the evil government did not allow it. And there were other long stories there in that. Because then the evil government told us that we must join official organizations, like CNC,[2] and then CTM, National Confederation of Workers, something like that.

So, our parents and our grandparents participated in those legal organizations, which the evil government says that there, needs and demands are going to be resolved. They tried them and nothing was resolved.

Then came the idea that we must organize independently, independent organizations; they tried them and nothing was resolved. Just persecution, imprisonment, disappearance.

That is why, when the Zapatista Army of National Liberation arrived, our communities began to organize like that. So, the public appearance was done—as compañero Subcommander Marcos said—there it was decided, in '94, that we have to govern ourselves.

Thanks to the idea from before, it was seen that we do in fact have to unite and organize. Because it was seen before that the evil government did not respect us. So we organized, in the beginning, the autonomous municipalities. That's what it was called, "autonomous." Well, for us, peasants, indigenous people, Tzeltales, Tojolabales, Choles, Zoques, Mames, we did not understand what it meant, what the word "autonomy" means.

Little by little we understood that autonomy was exactly what we were doing. That we were asking ourselves what we are going to do. That we were discussing in meetings and in assemblies and then, well, the communities decide. Now we can explain about the autonomy that is being done with our Zapatista Autonomous Rebel Municipalities.

Right now, well, we feel it as indigenous people, that our indigenous brothers and sisters experienced this too in other states in Mexico. And, moreover, it was confirmed in the Other Campaign tour.

What we thought, what we imagined before, now is confirmed. That we indigenous are the most forgotten. But, also, we know that freedom and justice and democracy also need those who are not indigenous.

So, well, the autonomous municipalities' work has been consolidated more now. Our compañeros and compañeras have understood more, and now they realize that it should be this way throughout Mexico. Where the

---

2   The National Peasant Confederation (Confederación Nacional Campesina).

people command and the one who is governing must obey. That is how our compañeras and compañeros work now.

In all the areas of what is being built. Talking about health, talking about education, and about other collective work, it is discussed, analyzed, in the communities, and then the general decision on what comes next to build what needs to be built.

So our compañeros and compañeras have realized that it can be done. They have learned more with the compañeros and compañeras of the Good Government Committees. And a very important thing that our compañeros are also discovering, more each day, with the compañeras' participation in various positions in building autonomy, is that the compañeras cannot be left alone.

Of course, it has been very difficult for us. Because there is a problem from before, that our compañeras had ended up as if they were an object that is put aside. There we discovered, in that time of bosses—well, as the compañeras talked about in the women's gathering—the bosses in that time were mistreating, raping our compañeras, our grandmothers and grandfathers.

So, our grandfathers tried to protect our grandmothers, so they do not see them in front of them, of the bosses, what they are doing on top of them. And, unfortunately, it came about that only the men met, discussed, and the compañeras were left aside.

With this autonomy building that we are doing now, well, that is what we have discovered: we can no longer go on like before, where the compañeras were put aside. It is like now: the compañeras in the communities, with the compañeros, help resolve various problems, plan and discuss, make proposals for the autonomous municipalities' assemblies or the general assemblies that the Good Government Committee holds.

Where is the school, where is the learning? Right here, inside the communities. They are improving what we men do well. And what the compañeras see that men are not doing well, they push it aside now.

So, that type of autonomy building, our communities, men and women, are demanding that the seven principles of command by obeying must be fulfilled. So where our compañeros and compañeras say: well, if there were a government that obeys in Mexico, Mexico would be different.

When we discuss with our authority compañeros—the commissioners and agents—they talk, for example, in Mexico what is talked about and called the Congress of the Union, which are the congresspeople and senators that say they are representatives of the Mexican people, and those authority compañeras and compañeros ask the question: when have they consulted us about the laws that they make? They asked the question, for example, when Carlos Salinas de Gortari changed Article 27, what the great general[3] Emiliano Zapata was able to put into constitutional law that the land cannot be sold or rented. Carlos Salinas, along with the senators and congresspeople, changed that article where it says that owners are going to be made for the land, and that they can decide what they want to do with the land. That, saying it like that, now it can be sold and rented.

So, the question that our authority compañeros and compañeras ask: when did they ask us that? So, there is where they say: those congresspeople and senators who are there are good for nothing. They do not represent the Mexican people because they never asked us, they never consulted us. We do not believe that they consulted the workers either for the law that they need.

So, when general assemblies are held in the municipalities, the general assemblies that the Good Government Committees hold, this gets talked about. What would happen if, in Mexico, all the millions of indigenous people, all the millions of workers, all the millions of students were asked to say the law they want?

Because, for example, they say Diego de Cevallos, who already was a senator—I think—or congressman, he is a landowner. He does not feel what an indigenous person suffers; he does not feel what a worker suffers. So, he does not know how to think what type of law workers in the country and the city need.

Compañeros, compañeras, it seems very simple to talk about autonomy, but it is not true. The speeches sound very pretty, in practice it is something else. It is like, for example, there are many writers, intellectuals as they say; there are books that, well, they have things about autonomy written down. Who knows, maybe there is 2 or 5 percent of what approximately is covered there about autonomy. Ninety-five percent is missing.

To be able to talk about autonomy, one must live where it is being done. To discover, to see, and to know more what it's like. Because, for example, you are going to see how things come and go with the way how democracy is done in practice, the decision that is made.

In this case, the highest authoritative body is the compañeros and compañeras of the Good Government Committee. They meet to discuss the work plans. And then, they propose things to the MAREZ[4] authorities, and the authority compañeros and compañeras from the

3   In Spanish, "my general" (*mi general*) is a title of respect and admiration given to generals. Here Moisés is using that phrase in the plural: "our general."
4   Zapatista Autonomous Rebel Municipalities (Municipios Autónomos Rebeldes Zapatistas).

MAREZ—that is, from the autonomous municipalities—meet with the authority compañeros and compañeras—in other words, the commissioners and agents from the communities. There they bring the proposal on what is proposed by the Good Government Committee. And those commissioners and agents bring the proposal to their communities to present it to them.

The decisions are issued in the communities, the municipal assembly is held. There a majority decision is achieved on what the Good Government Committee proposed. And from there, the general assembly is held, which includes the Good Government Committee, until the people's mandate is decided there. Then it is sent to the Good Government Committee.

And then, the opposite. That is, the other way: the communities may propose work or laws that need to be done. That is, to give an example, in this zone, all the communities that are Zapatista right now are deciding how the recovered lands are going to be worked. In all the communities right now, in this zone, they are working on that. All the communities. This zone's general assembly still needs to be held, so that there the mandate is issued on how the land is going to be cared for.

So, what happens when there is a general assembly? Pretend that you are the commissioners, agents, who are here right now. Sometimes the majority, the decision, emerges, and a minority remains. One of the compañeros or compañeras again states that the agreement has problems—it has consequences later. So, the majority gives the compañero or the compañera the right to argue what the consequence would be for what the compañero or compañera suggests. According to the argument that the compañero or the compañera gives, the assembly listens, it pays attention.

If it is work that has not been put into practice, the majority says, "we are going to put it into practice, and if it does not go well, we are the ones who command, we are going to have to correct it again." In other words, they tell the minority that it isn't because what the minority says is worthless, but things are going to be practiced, are going to be improved.

So, autonomy building in all the Zapatista zones is varied. They work in different ways. That is why, upon your return, you will see that the compañeros and compañeras who went to the various caracols are going to talk about it, because it is not just one model for how things work. Because of the situation that is experienced in each zone.

For example, in the Oventik, Morelia, and Roberto Barrios Caracols there are many paramilitaries. That is what forces us to see how autonomy works with a lot of security. Because there is a lot of provocation from the paramilitaries. And, in other caracols, because of the distances there are from one community to another, that is what forces us then for our steps to go differently, how to go about building our autonomy.

But under one principle that we have to bring, practicing what our seven principles say. Which is that our government has to obey and the people command. That our autonomous governments have to go down to the communities and not go up above to command, not consult, not propose things to the people.

Our autonomous authorities, the MAREZ and the Good Government Committees, have to propose things to the people. And they are not going to impose. Our autonomous authorities have to work to convince the people, and not defeat them by force. Our authorities have to build what is needed, what is good, and not destroy.

Our authorities have to represent; in other words, what they say truly is the people's word, thought. And not just act like they say it is the people's word and have not consulted the people. In other words, we do not want the autonomous authorities to supersede. We want our autonomous authorities to serve the people. And not to serve themselves, because they are an autonomous government.

So, our communities, our authorities that there are in all the communities, that is what they are guided by to fulfill those principles. And here, in the Good Government Committees, they take turns governing their zone. Men and women. So that's where the participation of men and women is being achieved.

And that's why, compañeros, compañeras, this type of practice, our communities see that this, I hope it is useful to you, our brothers and sisters from outside, from Mexico and from other countries. Because when the people command, nobody can destroy them. But also, we have to think that the people, the people can also fail, they can make mistakes. But from there, there is no one they can blame.

It is not like how things are right now, we can blame the congresspeople and senators, the governors, the municipal presidents. But the day that the Mexican people—workers, teachers, students, indigenous people, peasants, everyone, the Mexican people—if they decide, then we are not going to find anyone to accuse.

So if one day we are going to make a mistake, just as we were good at deciding we were going to do that, we must be good at cleaning up the shit we are going to make. Something like this is where the people truly decide that. But this must be taken away from the one who is commanding right now, the evil government. They are the ones who have that power.

And that's why we say that taking the land from the landowners, or the estate owners, made us practice this autonomy here more. When it is seen that the means of production are taken there. It is not achieved just like that. That is why organization is needed.

So, compañeros, compañeras—well, that is how we work this. So let's hope that the way how we work has been useful to you, and the fact that we have lots of work to do, lots of improvement. But you are going to see it, because you are going to visit some communities. There more can be explained, directly, how they experience it. And how it was that, then, they gained where they are living now. That's all, compañeros and compañeras.

3.

Seven Winds in the Calendars and Geographies of Below

January 2–5, 2009

First Global Festival of Dignified Rage

Indigenous Center for Integral Training–University of the Earth
(CIDECI–UniTierra)

San Cristóbal de las Casas, Chiapas, Mexico

First Wind:
A Dignified Enraged Youth

Good evening.

Sintrófisa, síntrofe, Ekseyerméni Eláda. Emís, i pió mikrí, apó aftí ti goniá tu kósmu se jeretáme.

Déksu ton sevasmó mas ke ton zavmasmó mas giaftó pu skéftese ke kánis. Apó makriá mazménume apó séna. Efjaristúme.

(I hope I didn't say any bad words, what I wanted to say was: "Compañera, compañero, rebellious Greece. We, the smallest, salute you from this corner of the world. Receive our respect and admiration for what you think and do. From afar we learn from you. Thank you.")

I

On Violence and Other Things

For a long time, the problem of calendars and geographies has kept Power restless and exposed. In some calendars and geographies, it has seen (and shall see) how its shiny gear of domination gets stuck and breaks. That is why it tries to be very careful when handling them.

In geographies it may be more apparent: in Power's clumsy trick, which this festival has revealed, Greece is very far from Chiapas. And in schools they teach that Mexico is separated by an ocean from France, the Basque Country, Spain, Italy. And if we look at a map, we can see that New York is very far north of indigenous-Mexican Chiapas. This was refuted a few hours ago by the compañeras and compañeros from the Movement for Justice in El Barrio. And Argentina is very far south of this land, something challenged by compañero Solano, who just finished speaking.

But neither above nor below does this separation exist. Brutal neoliberal globalization—World War IV, as we Zapatistas call it—put the farthest-away places into spatial and temporal simultaneity for wealth to flow . . . and be appropriated.

No more fanciful stories about supposedly heroic discoverers/conquerors who defeated the weakness of those who were later "civilized" with the sword and the cross. Instead of three caravels,[1] a fast computer. Instead of Hernán Cortés, a puppet-made-government on every corner of the planet. Instead of swords and crosses, a massive machinery of destruction and a culture that is similar to fast food not only because it is omnipresent (McDonald's, like God, is everywhere), but also because it is difficult to digest and has no nutritional value.

And that same globalization makes the Israeli and American governments' bombs fall on Gaza while the whole world cringes.

With globalization, the whole world above put us in their hands . . . or, rather, in their gazes and their consciousness. The bombs that murder Palestinian civilians are also a warning that must be learned from and absorbed. And the shoe thrown at Bush in Iraq can be reproduced on almost any corner of the planet.[2]

And everything goes from the hand of the enlightened to the individual. The excitement created among the well-behaved by the shoe thrown at Bush (which only is proof of the journalist's poor aim) exists to put at the forefront an act that was brave but is fundamentally useless and inconsequential, demonstrated weeks later by the Bush administration's support for the crime perpetrated by the Israeli government in Palestinian territory . . . and—pardon me if I disappoint anyone who has lit a candle underneath Barack Obama's photo—that Bush's successor supports.

And while bad aim in Iraq leads to applause, the insurrection in Greece leads to worries: "There is the danger," people warn and exorcize, "of the rebellion in Greece spreading to the rest of Europe."

We have already heard and read what the rebellious Greek youth tell us about their fight and about what they are up against. The same for those in Italy who prepare to resist the government's strength. And the daily struggle of our compas north of the Rio Grande.

---

1   A type of ship used by Columbus and other explorers of the period. "Three caravels" is a reference to the ships used during Columbus's first voyage to the Americas.

2   During a December 2008 press conference in Baghdad, Iraqi journalist Muntadhar al-Zaidi threw his shoe at President George W. Bush, shouting, "This is a farewell kiss from the Iraqi people, you dog," as he did so. The shoe missed its target and sailed over the president's head.

And in light of this, up above everyone takes out their dictionaries and finds the word "violence" and counterposes it with "institutionalism." And without putting it in context—that is, social class—they accuse, judge, and condemn.

And they tell us that Greek youth who make the Hellenic peninsula burn are violent. Of course, the fact that the police murdered a young man is edited, cut out, erased.

In Mexico, in the geography marked by a city of the same name, an institutional-left government murdered a group of young people, mostly teenagers.[3] A sector of progressive intellectuality complicitly kept silent, arguing that this was to distract the public's attention, which supposedly was focused on the carnival that resulted from the so-called defense of the oil sector.[4] The subsequent sexual assault of women in police holding cells was lost in the hoopla announcing a consultation that later was a failure. And, in contrast, the police's violence was not condemned; contrary to what was said, they did not behave in a disorderly manner. Those police have been preparing for years to repress, harass, and abuse young people, street vendors, sex workers, tenants, and all those who take issue with the government of ice rinks, Fujimori-style megaspectacles, and recipes for making cookies. And it must not be forgotten that the doctrine that inspires these police was imported to Mexico City by the current "legitimate" president of Mexico when he was mayor of Mexico City.

In Mexico City and in Greece, governments murder young people.

The US-Israel governmental yoke in Gaza now indicates the rule of thumb: it is more effective to kill them when they are children.

Even before, in Mexico—in this calendar ten years will have passed—young students from UNAM built a movement that brought despair to the well-behaved Left that, hysterical like now, ferociously slandered and discredited them.[5] And back then it was also called a violent movement to distract attention from the gray electoral campaign of the gray

---

3   Here Marcos is referring to the New's Divine disco tragedy in Mexico City on June 20, 2008, in which a stampede resulted from a police raid designed to crack down on underage drinking. The police blocked the exit, causing panic and a stampede that killed nine teenagers and young adults, as well as three police officers. To make matters worse, the police are also accused of having beaten and stripped naked some of those arrested and of having denied medical assistance to some of the injured.

4   In Mexico, oil was a government-owned industry until a constitutional reform was passed in 2013, allowing privatization. For many years before, left-wing and center-left sectors of society fought against this change. Here Marcos is mocking what he views as the PRD's flawed attempts at protesting oil privatization.

5   In 1999, students at the National Autonomous University of Mexico (UNAM) went on strike to keep the university tuition-free. Their demands were met, and the strike ended in February 2000, shortly before campaigning began for the 2000 presidential elections.

presidential candidate from the gray Party of the Democratic Revolution. Now, ten years later, it must be remembered that UNAM is still public and tuition-free thanks to the determination of those young men and women we salute today.

But in our pained Mexico, the people who take first place in uses and abuses for tampering with the word "violence" are Felipe Calderón Hinojosa and media outlets that are with him (fewer each day, by the way).[6] Mr. Calderón, a fan of real-time strategy computer games (his favorite game, he once claimed, is "Age of Empires"), decided that instead of bread and circuses, the people must be given blood. Since professional politicians already put on a circus and bread is very expensive, Calderón—supported by a group of drug traffickers—decided to declare war against another group. In violation of the Constitution, he brought out the army to do the work of the police, prosecutor, court, jailer, and executioner. Anyone who is not part of his cabinet knows that he is losing that war, and it is also known that the death of his soulmate was an assassination, even if this does not get published.[7]

And in his war, Calderón's government forces can be credited with murdering more than a few people who did nothing wrong, of murdering children and the unborn.

With Calderón at the forefront, the government of Mexico is a step ahead of the US and Israeli governments; it kills them while they are in the womb.

But it has been said, and newscasters and columnists still repeat it, that the state was going to use force to combat the violence of organized crime.

And it is ever more apparent that organized crime is what directs the state's force.

Although perhaps it is all a clever ploy of Calderón's and his objective is to distract people's attention. As busy as the public is with the violent failure of the War on Drug Trafficking, they may not notice Calderón's failure with political economy.

But let's go back to condemnations of violence made from above.

There is a tricky transmutation, a false tautology: they say they condemn violence, but they really condemn action.

For them, those above, nonconformity is a calendarial evil or—when it also defies the calendar—a cerebral pathology that, according to some, can

---

6   Calderón's War on Drug Trafficking was beginning to lose popularity at the time.
7   Referring to Secretary of the Interior Juan Camilo Mouriño, whose jet crashed in Mexico City on November 4, 2008. He enjoyed a close relationship with Calderón, having coordinated his election campaign and having subsequently served as chief of the president's office, and he played an active and integral role in the War on Drug Trafficking.

be cured with enough mental concentration, bringing oneself into harmony with the universe and then we are all humans . . . or citizens.

For these violent pacifists, everyone is a human being: the young Greek woman who lifts her hand with a Molotov cocktail in it and the police officer who murders the Alexises[8] of the world who have existed and will exist; the Palestinian boy who cries at the funeral of his little brothers killed by Israeli bombs and the pilot of a combat plane with the Star of David on the fuselage; Mr. George W. Bush and the undocumented immigrant murdered by the Border Patrol in Arizona; the multimillionaire Carlos Slim and the Sanborns waitress who must travel three or four hours to get to work and go home, and is fired if she arrives late; Mr. Calderón, who calls himself head of the Mexican executive branch, and the peasant stripped of his land; Mr. López Obrador and the indigenous people murdered in Chiapas who he did not see or hear; Mr. Peña Nieto, predator of Mexico State,[9] and the peasant Ignacio Del Valle, of the FPDT,[10] in prison for defending the poor; in a nutshell, men and women who have wealth and power are human beings, as are women and men who have nothing more than their dignified rage.

And up above they demand and insist: "We must say no to violence, wherever it comes from" . . . making sure to emphasize it if the violence comes from below.

According to them, everyone must bring themselves into harmony for their differences and contradictions to be resolved and must chant: "armed people are also exploited," making reference to soldiers and police officers.

Our position as Zapatistas is clear. We do not support pacifist flags that are raised for someone else to turn the other cheek, nor violence that is encouraged when others provide the dead.

We are who we are, with all the good and all the bad that we carry and is our responsibility.

But it would be naive to think that all the good things we have accomplished—including the privilege of listening to and learning from you—would have been possible without preparing a full decade for the sun to rise as it rose on January 1, fifteen years ago.[11]

---

8   Alexis Grigoropoulos, a fifteen-year-old killed by Greek police in 2008, triggering weeks of widespread rioting over economic and social issues.

9   At the time, Enrique Peña Nieto was governor of Mexico State; he is currently serving a presidential term that began in 2012 and will end in 2018.

10   The People's Front in Defense of Land (Frente del Pueblo en Defensa de La Tierra, or FPDT) is an organization in Atenco, Mexico State that was initially established in 2002 to oppose the construction of an new international airport; it continues to work to protect farmland from expropriation and development.

11   January 1, 1994, when the Zapatistas declared war on the Mexican government and rose up in arms.

We did not make ourselves known with a march or a we-the-under-signed document. We made ourselves known to the world with an army, with battles against the federal troops, with armed resistance.

And our fallen, dead, and disappeared compañeros and compañeras have been in a violent war that did not begin fifteen years ago, but five hundred years ago, two hundred years ago, one hundred years ago.

I am not apologizing for violence, I am pointing out a verifiable fact: you met us at war, we have remained at war during these fifteen years, and we shall remain at war until this corner of the world called Mexico takes ownership of its own destiny, no tricks, no impersonations, no simulations.

Power has violence as a resource for domination, but it also has arts and culture, knowledge, information, the justice system, education, institutional politics, and, of course, the economy.

Each struggle, each movement—in its very-specific geographies and calendars—must resort to different ways of fighting. It isn't the only way and probably isn't the best, but violence is one way.

It is a beautiful gesture to confront gun barrels with flowers—why, there are even photos eternalizing the act. But sometimes it is necessary to make those barrels change target and point up.

The Accuser and the Accused

We have been accused of many things, it is true. And we are probably guilty of some of those things, but now I want to dwell upon one:

We did not shoot at the clock of time on that January 1, nor do we turn it into a nostalgic celebration of defeat, as some from that generation worldwide have done with '68, as is done in Mexico with '88 and now even with 2006.[12] I will come back to this sickly cult of rigged calendars later.

Nor do we edit history to rename it, indicating that we are or were the only ones or the best ones, or both (like that group hysteria that is the López Obrador movement, but I will come back to this later).

There was and there are people who criticize us for not having made the jump "to realpolitik" when our political bonds—that is, our media ratings—offered a good price for our dignity in the market of electoral

---

12   In 1968 there was a massive student movement in Mexico as well as many other such movements worldwide. In 1988 and 2006, center-left presidential candidates Cuauhtémoc Cárdenas and Andrés Manuel López Obrador, respectively, won elections but were deprived of the presidency through electoral fraud.

options (not political options).[13]

Specifically, we are accused of not having succumbed to Power's seduction, the seduction that has made very bright left-wing people say and do things that anyone else would be ashamed of.

We were also accused of "super-delirium" or "radicalism" because in the Sixth Declaration we point at the capitalist system as the cause of the principal evils that afflict humanity. Today we no longer insist on that point, because even the spokespeople for big financial capital on Wall Street say it.

Incidentally, now that the entire world talks and keeps talking about the global crisis, we must remember that thirteen years ago, in 1996, a dignified and enraged beetle warned us about it. Don Durito of the Lacandon Jungle, in the shortest speech I have heard at my young age, said that "the problem with globalization is that *globos*[14] pop."

We are accused of not constraining ourselves to the survival that we have built on these Indian lands with sacrifice and support from those below in all corners of the planet, and of not shutting ourselves off in what the "clear-minded" (that's what they call themselves) call "the Zapatista laboratory" or "the Lacandon commune."

We are accused of going out, again and again, to confront Power and to look for others, you, people who confront it without false comforts or conformism.

We are accused of having survived.

And people do not talk about the resistance that, fifteen years later, allows us to say that we keep fighting, not just living.

What bothers them is that we have survived like any other point of reference for struggle, for critical reflection, for political ethics.

We are accused, who would dare to say it, of not having given up, of not having sold out, of not having surrendered.

We are accused, in a word, of being Zapatistas from the Zapatista Army of National Liberation.

Today, 515 years later, 200 years later, 100 years later, 25 years later, 15 years later, 5 years later, 3 years later, we declare: we are guilty.

And, given that it is the Neozapatista way, we not only confess to it, we also celebrate it.

---

13   At various points in time, people have publicly encouraged the Zapatistas to form a political party or join one, because of their popularity and ability to unite disparate sectors of the population. However, the Zapatistas have insisted that elections in Mexico are not an effective means of change.

14   Durito is making a pun that cannot be translated into English; globos is a word that can be translated as "globes" or "balloons."

We did not imagine that this was going to hurt some people up above who simulate progressivism or who dress up in an off-yellow or colorless left,[15] but it must be said:

The EZLN lives on. Long live the EZLN!

Thank you very much.

Insurgent Subcommander Marcos
Mexico, January 2, 2009

P.S. Seven Stories for Nobody

Story 1: It Was Like This . . .

We have already heard Lieutenant Colonel Moisés introduce me as part of Zapatista childhood. Perhaps to defy the calendar, we Zapatistas have a tendency to age backward, and instead of being 515 years old like my birth certificate says, I turned 5 and am going on 6; in other words, I am 7 years old. Maybe, after all is said and done, if Zapatismo has shown us anything, it's that many things that appeared impossible are made possible with imagination, ingenuity, and audacity.

In defense of my absurd calendar, I could say that, like children, I am afraid of getting my shots and I like stories and fables.

Some time ago, when talking with a compañera from the city, I told her about some things that happened here in our mountains. She told me she didn't believe it. I told her I understood, that it was because it was unbelievable that I told them like fables.

In our mountains things happen that may seem unbelievable to you. So I'll tell you about them accordingly, as if they were fables.

Because it seems unbelievable that, in fact, in our mountains there lives a beetle with airs of being a knight errant; that there is a nonconformist stone training to be a cloud; that Marcos is making an alliance with Zapatista children to write a part of the National Platform of Struggle that strictly prohibits the production, trafficking, and getting of shots; that Old Antonio appears every now and then with stories and legends told to him by the very first gods, those who birthed the world; that Elías Contreras, EZLN Investigation Commission, had already passed away when he went to the city to fight against evil and evildoers, and that a homosexual sex worker saved his life—paradoxically so, because he was already deceased—one cold predawn morning in the capital, and that he sometimes talked with skater lingo;

---

15   A reference to the PRD, whose colors are yellow and white.

that Toñita carries three generations and six years on her shoulders and that she comes into the EZLN General Command without permission; that the moon sometimes drinks away its lack of love; that children think and act like Marcos is just another kid who hasn't put down that strange pacifier that gives off smoke; that Insurgent Erika refounded Marxism with downright feminist tendencies; that the other day a bomb went off in a Zapatista barrack and nobody died; that Shadow the Warrior was cursed by a grudging and resentful moon, and that he nonetheless continues looking to get lost; that there is an owl who studies not Greek and Latin but women's lingerie catalogs; that there is a girl named December who, as her name suggests, was born in November; that Moisés knows that when Marcos is nowhere to be found in the General Command, he must look at the top of the ceiba tree.

So, instead of arguing about the accuracy of such commonplace things in our mountains, I—a plain-old subcommander—come and tell them as if they were fables.

A few moments ago we gave a painting to the compañera who talked about insurrectionary Greece, painted by a compañera from the city, Beatriz Aurora. The painting depicts this city—San Cristóbal de las Casas, Chiapas—in many colors, and points out the places where people work who fight like us, albeit without weapons or balaclavas.

The meaning of this gift may be better understood with what I am now going to tell you:

Fifteen years ago seven municipal seats were taken by our troops: Las Margaritas, Ocosingo, Altamirano, San Cristóbal de las Casas, Oxchuc, and Chanal. So the governmental forces that protected them were overwhelmed or caught by surprise.

Perhaps it may be said that taking this city where we are now—San Cristóbal de las Casas, ladino[16] bastion of racism—was what made us known to the world. Maybe.

What I do know is that taking Ocosingo, Las Margaritas, and Altamirano was what gave us territorial control and allowed us to take and recover the good farmland after hundreds of years of dispossession.[17] This land grab was the economic foundation for building Zapatista autonomy.

I already talked about this one year ago, and those who want to delve into it must look online or get a secondary edition, because we have seen that everything that isn't for or against the López Obrador movement does not get published.

---

16   In indigenous regions of Chiapas, this is another word for *mestizo*, which refers to Mexicans who are not indigenous.

17   After the 1994 uprising, the Zapatistas began to seize farmland that was in the hands of cattle ranchers and administer it for collective agricultural projects.

Speaking of imagination, ingenuity, and audacity to make the impossible possible, the stories I am going to tell you now are not fables and they are not Zapatista stories. But they are about what happened fifteen years ago and shook the indigenous world and—as you shall soon see—the indigenous underworld too.

One is about a progovernment Tzotzil indigenous person, and the other is about a non-Zapatista indigenous person who survives by selling his products at the market here in San Cristóbal. It is a translation into Spanish of a translation into English of a translation into Spanish of some stories in Tzotzil, which is why you will be listening to something with very smooth writing and word choice.[18]

Translated by Jan Rus, in the book by Marián Peres Tzu, "Indigenous Revolts," Gosner & Ouweneel, Cedla, Amsterdam, 1996. Pp. 122–128.[19] Compiled in "Antigua y nueva palabra. Antología de la literatura meso-americana desde los tiempos precolombinos hasta el presente." Miguel León-Portilla and Earl Shorris, with Sylvia S. Shorris and Ascensión H. de León-Portilla. Ed Aguilar. Mexico, October 2004. Pps. 732–733.

Here goes:

Early January: Preparations and Visits.

Before the invasion of San Cristóbal, everyone always talked about how the soldiers at the army base overlooking the southern approach to the city had spread booby traps all around their land, how they had fixed it so no one would ever dare attack them. If the poor Indians ever came to make trouble, everyone said, the soldiers would finish them off right there, before they even got out of the forest. The army officers are *maestros* of killing, they said, and all they have to do every day, their only chore, is teach the young soldiers to kill too. And as if all of that weren't enough to scare away a bunch of raggedy peasants, they said, the soldiers also have mounds of bombs stored behind their fort. Nothing but special bombs for killing Indians!

---

18   The stories in this chapter were originally written in Tzotzil by Marián Peres Tzu, the pen name of Chamula writer Salvador Guzmán Bakbolom / Xalik Kusman Bakbolom, who passed away in 2011. The first published version was an English translation of his work by Jan Rus. So, Marcos is reading a Spanish translation of Rus's English translation of the Tzotzil original. The version presented here is Rus's English translation from Tzotzil and not a direct translation of what Marcos presented. Used with permission.

19   Marián Peres Tzu's stories are an excerpt of a testimonial whose title is "The First Two Months of the Zapatistas: A Tzotzil Chronicle," in *Indigenous Revolts in Chiapas and the Andean Highlands,* ed. Kevin Gosner and Arij Ouweneel, 122–28 (Amsterdam: Centro de Estudios y Documentación Latinoamericanos, 1996).

K'elevil, look here. According to what people said, the soldiers had strung a special wire around their barracks that was connected to a bomb every few steps. If the damn Indians ever did come around, they said, all the soldiers would have to do was lean out of their beds and touch the wire with a piece of metal—like, say, a beer can—and the bombs would all blow up. And if the Indians tried to cut the wire, it would also blow up. But of course, the soldiers are famous for never sleeping, so the Indians would never even get close to the bombs in the first place. No one, the soldiers figured, would ever get past them.

But after all those preparations, what happened? On January first, the soldiers were asleep when the Zapatistas arrived in San Cristóbal! But snoring! They didn't see the Zapatistas go by their check-points with the other passengers on the second-class buses! They didn't notice the Zapatistas get out of their buses at the station and walk into the center of town! They didn't see anything! And when the soldiers woke up, the Zapatistas had already seized the *Palacio de Gobierno*[20] and set up their own guards around the city! After all, it was the Army that was left outside of town, safely holed up in its barracks! The Zapatistas won by just ignoring them! Not until two days later, when they had finished their business in town, did the Zapatistas finally go to pay a visit on the soldiers![21]

The Zapatistas are only Indians, but what the army officers forgot is that Indians too are men. And since they are men, they also could be armed and trained, just like the army. All they needed was the idea. And as it turned out, their thinking was better than the army's! They fooled the officers, who are *maestros* of killing! Since that day, all of us, even those who are not enemies of the government, feel like smiling down into our shirts.

If there is a sad part to all of this, it is that even though the Zapatistas are men, they will have to live in hiding from now on. They won't be able to sleep in their own beds in their own houses, but will have to stay at all times in caves in the jungle. If they want to make babies like everyone else, they'll even have to screw in the caves. Like *armadillos*!

End of this story.

And since we are talking about the calendars of above and of below, let's remember that it has also been fifteen years since NAFTA took effect. So now something about free trade . . .

---

20   "Government Palace"—in this case, San Cristóbal's town hall. [Nick Henck]
21   The Zapatistas attacked the army post at Rancho Nuevo on January 2 as they were re-
      treating from San Cristóbal. [Jan Rus]

Late January: Toward a Free Market

For the first two weeks or so after the seizure of San Cristóbal, not a single *kaxlan*[22] official showed his face in public—not a policeman, not a parking officer, not a collector of market fees. Not one. They disappeared! They were so terrified of the Zapatistas that they hid. But the moment they were sure the Zapatista Army was gone and wasn't coming back, Ha!, immediately the parking officers were back unscrewing license plates,[23] the municipal police beating up drunks, and the market collectors chasing away poor women trying to sell tomatoes and lemons on street corners. With the Zapatistas gone, suddenly they were fearless again. But when the Zapatistas were here, they stayed in their bedrooms with the shades closed, quaking with fear. They couldn't even get it up with their wives they were so scared.

You see what that means? They were afraid of *Indians* because that's what the Zapatistas were, Indians. When we other Indians realized that, we felt strong as well. Strong like the Zapatistas. The *kaxlanetik* of San Cristóbal have always pushed us around just because we don't speak Spanish correctly. But now everything has begun to change.

One example of this is that in mid-January, when the *kaxlan* officials were all still hidden, the Indian charcoal sellers got together and formed the "Zapatista Organization of Charcoal Sellers." Then, without asking anybody's permission, they moved from the vacant field where they had always been forced to sell in the past to the street right next to the main market. The thing is, *ak'al* is really dirty—everything around it gets covered with black dust—so the market officials had always kept it far away from the part of the market frequented by "decent people" and tourists. With no one to stop them, however, the charcoal sellers came to be near everyone else.

But there are a lot of other Indians who have always been relegated to the edges of the market, too. When these people saw that the charcoal sellers had changed their location without asking anyone's permission, they started coming around and asking if they could change as well. *Híjole!* Suddenly there were a couple of hundred people sitting in orderly rows selling vegetables and fruit and charcoal in what used to be the parking lot where rich people left their cars! The first day they gathered there, the leader of the charcoal sellers gave a speech.

22   The word *kaxlan*, pronounced "kashlan," is a corruption of the Spanish word *castellano* and is the Tzotzil word for non-Indians. [Jan Rus]

23   The transit police would allegedly remove license plates from vehicles so as to charge the owner a penalty for the infraction. [Nick Henck]

"Brothers and sisters!" he cried, "Don't be afraid! There are too many of us selling here in this street now! Let all of those who have been forced to sell out of the backs of trucks, all of those who have been driven to the edges of the market, come sell right here in the center with us! Let them come and take a place here in these rows we have made, and then we'll see if the kaxlan officials dare say anything! Only one thing to all of those who join us: I don't want to hear anyone talking about being afraid! If we remain united and firm, we have nothing to fear!"

All the Indian peddlers jumped to their feet. "We're with you!" they responded joyfully.

So every morning early all of these people came and formed themselves into neat rows and spread their goods out on the ground. But then the day finally came when the Market Administrator returned. Since he's the boss of the market and all the surrounding streets, he stomped up to the first charcoal seller he saw and demanded, "Who gave you permission to sell here?"

"No one had to give us permission because we belong to an organization."

"What fucking organization? Pick up all this shit and get the hell out of here before I lose my temper," the Administrator screamed, "I don't want to hear another word from any of you assholes. Are you going to fucking obey or not?"

Mother of God! He seemed pretty mad.

"No, we're not going to move. We're poor and hungry, and we have to sell to eat," the Indian said stubbornly.

Then the leader of the charcoal sellers spoke, "You sound brave now," he said evenly to the Administrator, "but when the Zapatistas were here you didn't say anything because you were hiding behind your wife's skirts. Not until now have you had the balls to talk. So who's the asshole? Maybe it would be better for you if you kept quiet, because if you run us off we're going to make sure the sub-comandante of the Zapatistas gets your name, and then we'll find out how much of a man you are. You might win today, but maybe you ought to think about what it's going to cost you in the long run."

Hijo! The Administrator had never been talked to like that by an Indian before! He started to tremble, who knows whether from fear or rage, and then he turned and fled without saying another word, taking all of his fee collectors with him.

And that's where things remain at the beginning of March. Thanks to the Zapatistas, the Indians are learning to stand up for themselves . . .

The end.

Thank you very much and see you tomorrow.

Insurgent Subcommander Marcos
Mexico, January 2, 2009

Second Wind:
A Dignified and Enraged Endeavor

On Ceremonies and Regards (A Little Bit of Past and Present History and Hysteria)

Earlier we pointed out the geographic trick that Power uses to adjust non-existent distances between, on the one hand, its forms of domination and, on the other, the resistances that it encounters.

Power also uses calendars to neutralize movements that attack or have attacked its essence, its existence, or its normality.

That's what its commemorative dates are for. With them it narrows, limits, defines, and stops. With each day of the calendar that Above admits into its timeline, a takeover of history occurs. With these days, movements are stopped, they are terminated in all senses. There will be nothing above, in that calendarization of history, to account for the processes and movements that are then reduced to one day.

And so those dates are turned into statues. In Mexico, September 16 and November 20 have been mummified since the beginning of the long PRI era.[1] Each year, the clique of criminals on duty—that is, in the government—goes to monuments and parades only to ensure that Miguel Hidalgo, José María Morelos, Vicente Guerrero, Francisco Villa, and Emiliano Zapata remain dead.

---

1   September 16 is Mexico's Independence Day, and November 20 is the anniversary of the Mexican Revolution. The PRI has always promoted celebration of these holidays to solidify its position of political power, though in reality it is beholden to foreign interests and works to reverse the achievements of the Mexican Revolution.

And not only were there exorcism dates for the uncomfortable dead on the calendar of above, there were also dates where control was affirmed, like PRI May Days in Mexico.

Maybe that's why the PRD Mexico City government, asserting its deep PRI roots, has tried to formalize October 2[2] hand in hand with some of the ancients of participatory ideas from the 1968 student movement. As if they wanted to take control of a dignified and enraged capital-city youth.

And I am almost certain that, in all corners of mottled global geography, Power has built statues and points of control on its calendar.

From recurrent Greece, once again we received word that the government made the vacation period earlier to try to stave off the youth's mobilized rage.

But the liberal breeze turned into a neoliberal hurricane and globalization came. And with it came a creaking in the political classes' old foundations . . . and their customs and traditions.

In Mexico, May Day was never again the same—that is, a lengthy Thank-You-Mister-President—when the union-control apparatus cracked and the workers turned the march that should have been servile caravans into a march with demands and grievances. So a Molotov cocktail hit the doors of the National Palace. The year on the calendar? 1984. Several months later, I would have one of my deaths and one of my births in the mountains of the Mexican Southeast.[3]

The intermittent challenge by workers of the city, previously circumscribed to the left, then reached the great union centers. The shout turned into a murmur, true, but it is still latent. A Fidel Velázquez who died many years before being buried was the warning for them to look for new figures of control,[4] new transmission belts, so that the designs of above would go from dominant to dominated. And the Neocharros,[5] who were not and are not all that new, emerged. Well, if you see a progovernment union leader

---

2 On October 2, 1968, hundreds of students were massacred in the Plaza of Three Cultures in Mexico City. Ten days later, Mexico City began hosting the Summer Olympics.

3 In August 1984, Rafael Guillén left behind a comparatively comfortable life in Mexico City to become a rural guerrilla in Chiapas. In doing so he abandoned his former identity and was reborn as Marcos.

4 Velázquez, who passed away in 1997 at age ninety-seven, was a labor union leader who headed the pro-PRI and corrupt Confederation of Mexican Workers. He was extremely conservative and had been thoroughly co-opted by the government, going so far as to help it eliminate independent unions or at least their leadership. At the outset of their uprising, Velázquez stated that the EZLN had no legitimate grievances against the government and therefore should be "exterminated."

5 Leaders of officially recognized unions who are often perceived to be as corrupt and as co-opted by the state as their predecessors, the notoriously antidemocratic government-appointed union bosses such as Velázquez (see note 4 above).

now and see a photo of one from before, you will be alarmed and ask if the dates aren't wrong.

Power's control apparatus over the workers of the countryside and the city appeared to exist in a picture of Dorian Grey (I'm not really sure if that's spelled right) that, in spite of its decrepitude, always appeared bright, fresh, effective.

But the mirror broke and the aging was evident.

So the new figures of control in the countryside and in the city, the Neocharros of trade unionism and peasant unions, found that their task was no longer to dampen—sorry, I'm going to say a bad word—dampen the class struggle by acting as a cushion and manager of working-class and peasant demands (in Mexico, the impossible dream of the UNT and National Dialogue that accompanied it).[6] No, now it was about implanting savage capitalism's new strategies and tactics in the factories, in the businesses and banks, and in the countryside. I am not going to go into more detail about this process of workforce reorganization, there are several excellent texts in our country that provide an account of it.

In the countryside, the neoliberal crown jewel was the reactionary reform to Article 27 of the Constitution, implemented by the now-regular contributor to a progressive newspaper and an eternal criminal: Carlos Salinas de Gortari.

Although always with the dreams of a grandeur that his memorable place has in the calendar of ceremonies, Carlos Salinas de Gortari has never ceased to be an employee of international capital's large forces, a manager who first came to power through scandalous electoral fraud (although not as scandalous as Felipe Calderón's fraud) and then wanted to impose a virtual first-world country on his subalterns, his governed.

And he was successful . . . until, one January first fifteen years ago, an indigenous rifle made of wood[7] broke his computer screen, his keyboard, and his Mauser,[8] I mean, his mouse, and—judging by the incoherencies he writes nowadays—also ruined his hard drive. And not even Bill Gates can save him from that.

The criminal counterreform to Article 27 of the Constitution—perpetrated with the legislative approval of several people who today are "champions" of democracy and "defenders" of the people within López

---

6   The National Union of Workers (Unión Nacional de Trabajadores, UNT). The National Dialogue, which the UNT promoted, was a failed attempt at forging a united front among independent unions.

7   During the armed uprising, many Zapatistas were armed only with machetes or replica wooden rifles.

8   A German brand of firearms.

Obrador's ranks—in these indigenous lands became a detonator for the quantitative and qualitative growth, in troops and in territory, of what the world now knows as the Zapatista Army of National Liberation.

But we have already talked about that before.

The ways and methods of Salinas de Gortari and of the transnational corporations' employee—Zedillo Ponce de León—were closer to those of the ignorant hacienda overseer than the sleek sales manager, so great capital decided to try someone just as mediocre as his predecessors, but who had made his managerial career at Coca-Cola, a certain Vicente Fox who had shown his mental problems since the electoral campaign and who attacked the PRI's exorcizing calendar, bringing to the Patriotic Holidays[9] the already-customary ignorance of national history flaunted by members of the National Action Party.

His performance as executive was so clumsy that the PAN and its friends had to resort to colossal electoral fraud to take the presidency from an already agonized Mexico.

Incidentally, Felipe Calderón's administration recently launched a media campaign where it urges the citizenry to indicate which government paperwork is most useless.

We Zapatistas have our proposal: the presidential elections are the most useless government paperwork. In addition to being expensive and all of us having to put up with the stupidities that the candidates say and repeat, the person who sits in the presidential chair is decided elsewhere.

But if the National Action Party displays its historical ignorance as a flag, the López Obrador movement raises its hysterical conviction. They edit their history and the history of those who accompany them (to mark the death of Gustavo Iruegas—so-called head of the "legitimate government's" nonexistent foreign policy—a brief description of him was written, in which his biography was edited so that nothing was said about the fact that he was a member of the Zedillo administration's sabotaged dialogue with the EZLN, during which time he said that phrase, now a classic in government media: "You have to hit the Zapatistas for them to engage in dialogue." Perhaps like this, by mutilating his own story, it is possible to avoid having the congregants know well who they support and follow). And thanks to that mutilation of history, they can obviate the fact that the great majority of those at the head of their movement used to let and continue to let the so-called enemy play footsie, politically speaking.

---

9   These are five national holidays that celebrate Mexico's history: Anniversary of the Constitution (February 5), Benito Juárez's Birthday (March 21), Labor Day (May 1), Independence Day (September 16), and Revolution Day (November 20).

We are accused of being sectarian and intolerant, but, truth be told (ha!), no movement in Mexico has shown such sectarianism, intolerance, and hysteria as that which today, led by Andrés Manuel López Obrador, threatens to save Mexico.[10]

And hysteria turns into blunt schizophrenia when, looking at themselves in the mirror, these intellectuals say: "We are really the only ones doing something for this country, we don't see anybody else." And in their events and marches they find each other and say: "Listen, my dear, I think that my guidance is very good for this movement. My presence alone makes it historical." Indeed, the historical thing is the number of times that movement has conferred the appellation "historical" upon what it does.

If these National Palace widowers and widows do everything they do without having federal power, imagine what they would do if the illustrious one had gotten to the presidential chair.

Anyway, the Mexican political class's ways, methods, customs, and traditions are already in full-blown crisis. Although there are still specialists for that professional-politics specialty. We will come back to this later.

In recent times we have seen how, with ceremonies, Power of one color or another has managed to domesticate some of those people who may be critical of it. With the neutralization ("My God! How can I criticize the person who gave me this medal and/or this check?") of these figures, who were once critics of the system and its governments, they then become simple transmission belts of the day's truth.

Before, an embassy would have been required to achieve this, or at least a consulate.[11] Today not as much is needed, a little courtship is enough: luncheons and meetings, a ceremony charged to government coffers, cutting the ribbon for a public project, a few newspaper articles, and voilà! We now have a new spokesperson for the two governments that we currently suffer from in Mexico.[12]

Ceremonies are so seductive for intellectuals that some cannot resist the temptation, and faced with a lack of followers to organize one for them, they organize a ceremony for themselves, as did that other cretin,

---

10   One of López Obrador's campaign slogans was "We have to save Mexico."

11   Quite possibly a reference to Carlos Fuentes, who had been a staunch supporter of President Luis Echeverría (1970–1976) and who was made ambassador to France (1975–1977), and also to Octavio Paz, who was appointed ambassador to India (1962–1968). Thus, Marcos is accusing these authors of selling out in exchange for an ambassadorship.

12   By "two governments" Marcos is referring to that of the PAN, headed by President Felipe Calderón, and also that of PRD candidate Andrés Manuel López Obrador, who, believing Calderón's electoral victory to have been fraudulent, formed what he dubbed the "legitimate government," which never held political power but featured a number of "cabinet appointments."

alleged defrauder of the university where he works, who—inspired by alcohol—gives himself the right to slander, criticize, and give orders to the movements of Mexico and the world—from the comfort of a newspaper page—and in order to obtain congregants, went to the extreme of using the word "heroic" to describe the "Adelitas" and "Adelitos" of López Obrador's movement to defend oil.[13]

But corporate transmission belts are not the only ones that wear out. Mediation and management is not only economic. The now-agonized state also created its mediators and managers in arts and culture, communication, knowledge. First it courted them with ceremonies and praise, then it seduced them with prizes and grants, and then turned them into its employees for them to act as mediators for people in those fields who refused and refuse to be domesticated.

All institutions in charge of mediation and management are already or will be in crisis. The centerline between sides has become so fine that one must pick a side. So we have managerial peasant organizations resorting to the police and judges to repress and persecute other landless peasants, and intellectuals and societal leaders applauding the police repression against street barricades that the Other Campaign put up in Mexico City in May 2006 to support Atenco. These critics were later protected by those same police during López Obrador's encampment in Mexico City in August and September of that same year.

So put away your medals, save your checks, and make videos of your ceremonies, because the world is no longer the world, and the people are no longer the same.

Because if I am not mistaken, this festival has gone against those calendars. And there are, on that other path, other calendars that are drawn below.

Going into this year, 2009, we have been told ad nauseam that globalization is in crisis and that all of us shall pay the costs. That's what happens: in times of crisis capitalism becomes deeply "democratic."

But there are many things to celebrate. For example: twenty-five years of Botellita de Jerez,[14] ten years since the beginning of the student movement that defended a public and free university in Mexico, the lessons given by adolescents in Greece, the teachings of the unemployed

---

13   Supporters of López Obrador who protested oil privatization (see above, p. 135, n. 4.) dressed as "Adelitas" (female soldiers in the Mexican Revolution) and "Adelitos" (a masculinization of the term). The "cretin" to whom Marcos is referring here is quite possibly Guillermo Almeyra, who wrote about "the heroic resistance of the Adelitas and Adelitos" in a piece in *La Jornada* on November 16, 2008.

14   A band formed in Mexico City in 1982 that blends rock with cumbia and traditional Mexican genres of music. Their lyrics were often satirical and depicted everyday life and pop culture in the capital.

in Argentina, the endeavor for justice by others on New York soils, the rebellious steadfastness in the France of below, the stark hope and fight of indigenous Bolivia in that beautiful seminar that Oscar Oliveira gave us, the pleiad of resistances in Latin America that Don Raúl Zibechi told us about, the healthy and urgent task of rescuing the great general[15] Sandino sought by the Sandinista (as far as we're concerned) commander Mónica Baltodano, the fifty years of lessons in dignity given by the Cuban people.

We have talked about how ceremonies tame and domesticate oppositional criticism and the vulnerability of intellectuals and journalists to those siren songs.

Nonetheless, there are some who resist those ceremonies with their stubborn consistency.

Compañero Adolfo Gilly is here with us today. And I dare to call him "compañero" not because he is part of the EZLN or the Other Campaign, but because of his long history of struggle alongside those below and to the left.

We Zapatistas do not hold ceremonies unless they are for our dead and do not court people with luncheons, prizes, and medals, or invite people to ribbon cuttings for double-decker expressways.

We simply send our regards.

And today we want to send our regards to this man.

We have always considered him to be a consistent left-wing man, although sometimes—like with Okupache[16]—we have not agreed with his analysis or positions.

We send him our regards not only because in the times when the enlightened López Obrador movement's intellectual hysteria attacked and slandered us, he knew how to make us know—in his own way—that not only did he not share the disparaging remarks that were so joyously poured on us up above, he also saw the same dangers that we warned about.

Not only because in one of our barracks can you find—ragged and worn, as are books that get read again and again—his book, *The Interrupted Revolution*, whose foreword to the first edition—written in the Lecumberri prison, where he was a political prisoner—ends like this: "Today more than ever there is truth in the phrase Lenin put on the last page of *The State and Revolution* when October 1917 prevented him from

---

15   *Mi general*: title of respect given to generals.
16   Okupache is the "Occupy the Che" anarchist collective that has occupied UNAM's Che Guevara Auditorium since the strike there in 1999. Gilly had accused the collective of having "taken" the auditorium and called on them to return it for use by everyone, an interpretation not shared by Marcos and the EZLN.

finishing his text: 'It is more pleasant and useful to go through the *experience of the revolution* than to write about it.'"

Also, and above all, we send him our regards because of his life, which is a way of saying his struggle.

Cheers, Don Adolfo. Safe travels, and know that here and there you have a place in our heart, in our history. Burden whoever it may, hurt whoever it may, even compas of the Other Campaign who have done here what we did not do when—defying all the criticisms and threats we received—we were in the Okupache supporting the movement. And what compañeros must not do is disrespect each other. We do not disown you as compañeros. And we also do not disown Don Adolfo Gilly as the compañero he is to us.

And cheers to all those rebellious people who shall lift up their dignified and enraged endeavor this year.

Thank you very much.

Insurgent Subcommander Marcos
Mexico, January 3, 2009

P.S. Seven Stories for Nobody

Story 2: Marxism According to Insurgent Erika

After several hills and climbing a mountain range between farmland and abandoned fields, I got to the barrack of one of our insurgent battalions. I felt "absolutely screwed" (an expression used by our leader twenty-four years ago), but satisfied from having finished the workday, in spite of what seemed like more of an April sun than a November sun. During the entire trip, landscapes and situations brought my thoughts back to those first years of the EZLN, to our pains of then, to our dreams of always. Except for the past rains, what we call "November summer" appeared to want to extend its stay and defy the calendar . . . and the geography. Because the other North had leaned out for the sun that lengthened the day. Maybe that's why I was remembering our first trip through that part of Mexico during the Other Campaign.

I remembered then the arduous ascent through Nayarit, Sinaloa, crossing the Sea of Cortés toward Baja California Sur, the renewed ascent to Baja California, skirting the border with the stars-and-stripes empire, entering Sonora. Yes, my difficult battle to reach the heights of the Zapatista mountains had brought to mind a double, mixed memory.

The faraway North, of the Wixaritari, of the Yaqui, of the Mayo Yoreme, of the Tohono O'odham, of the Comca'c, of the Pima, of the Trique-Zapoteco-Mixteco (because we must understand how immense Oaxaca is), of the Kumiai, of the Kiliwa, of the Cucapá, of the Rarámuri, of the Tepehuano, of the Caxcán, of the Pame, of the Kikapú, of maquiladora workers, of local and out-of-state migrants, of young people, of students and teachers, of small businesspeople, of peasants who have no land or are currently being stripped of their land.

In the news from above, they talk about Northern Mexico, true, but about kidnappings, abductions, murders, confrontations between so-called drug traffickers and federal forces, police and military operations, environmental destruction, governmental corruption, abuses of authority.

As if the North of our country were nothing more than a cave of hungry wolves eating their fill of a ripe victim.

As if there were nothing else.

And the thing is that the entire country can be synthesized in each state and region in Mexico.

Above, little or nothing changes. If anything, the name of the person who commands destruction and the brand name of the person who sponsors it. Up above, they repeat methods of exploitation, dispossession, repression, and discrimination from two hundred years ago, when the Spanish crown sunk its thousand fangs into Indian lands that would later be Mexico, just as one hundred years ago the powers of Europe and the United States washed the bloodied body of the Porfirio Díaz regime with riches.

And below? Will it be the same as two hundred years ago, as one hundred years ago?

Anyway, back to the hill; I got there, which at my old age . . . sorry, I meant to say, which at my young age can be considered an accomplishment.

After washing my arms and making myself uncomfortable in a corner of the barrack, I went to the celebration that the insurgent troops gathered there had organized for the EZLN's twenty-fifth anniversary.

The cultural program went on as usual: songs with a perplexing rhythm and without any rhyming, choral and individual poetry, bulletin boards, etc.

Suddenly a Tzeltal recruit got her turn; she had arrived a few days ago and was just learning a bit of Spanish. So the compañera, addressing the audience, declared unhesitatingly:

"Compañeros and compañeras, I am going to be very pleased to throw a bomb at you."[17]

---

17   In some indigenous Maya cultures, a "bomb" is a short poem that is often satirical or

The mess it caused was one for the history books (the truth is that it was a shit show, but I am watching my language): the new ones ran who knows where, and us veterans laid on the ground and sought what little cover we could find within the benches that were trunks tied with vines.

The compañera was unfazed, perhaps thinking that this was the insurgent way, and continued:

"Here goes," she said, and we all buried our heads in the dirt and, instead of hearing the explosion, heard:

"Bomb, bomb, Felipe Calderón has an underwear face."[18]

Of course, we got back on our feet however we could and, while we tried to clean off the mud, applauded wildly.

With coffee and animal crackers (no offense to the animals out there) we tried to move past the bitter pill when Insurgent Erika sat next to me and said:

"Hey, Marcos, I want you are going to teach me poetry. Because I may get the bombs, and I concentrate hard but I can't get the tons right."

I choked on a giraffe that was in my throat and did not respond quickly, so Insurgent Erika thought that I was having doubts and had arguments galore:

"Come on, Marcos, if you teach me then I'll tell you a story that I read."

The Zapatistas' stories are very different, as you will realize when Lupita and Toñita tell you what they have prepared, so I was still unable to swallow the giraffe-shaped cracker. So Insurgent Erika thought that my silence meant yes and started up with a story that I'll reproduce below, respecting her way of telling it as much as possible:

"Well then, so once upon a time so there was a girl. So this girl was about fourteen years old, in other words she was going on fifteen, in other words she was sixteen. [Insurgent Erika does not say it, but she is giving the protagonist the same age that she was when she joined the EZLN and is using the same trick of calendar counting that she used then to be accepted into our ranks]. Well, so this girl studied what is philosophy with her teacher that she had and I don't remember where the teacher came from but that's how the story goes. And then well she was called to her teacher to study philosophy and the girl says that yeah, OK, and goes to look for her teacher who lives in a cabin in his woods. But the girl did not tell her mom, in other words as they say she went without the boss's orders. Well, then the girl started to walk and so then she went into the woods and so

---

carries a double meaning.

18 In Spanish, this rhymes, so it packs a bit more of a punch. The Spanish reads: "Bomba, bomba, el Felipe Calderón tiene cara de calzón."

she found an elderly man, an old man with a computer just looking, and so the damn old man doesn't look away from the computer, and so the girl says hi to him, and the damn old man doesn't answer, he just looks at his computer with his eye. Well, then the girl says hi again and again the damn old man just doesn't answer. Well, so then the girl got pissed off and says it louder, which would be like if she is scolding him.

"Well, then he answered and the girl asks what the damn old man is doing, but she doesn't call him damn old man but just says it to him, I'm saying damn old man you're going to see later why.

"Well, then the damn old man doesn't tell her right away what he's doing, but he takes a while. Well, then the damn old man doesn't say what he is reading on his computer, but, well, finally he tells her: 'I don't want to lose one cent and I am counting.' 'Ah, so you are as they say a rich man,' says the girl. 'Yes,' says the man. That's how the old man answered. Well then, 'All right,' said the girl and she said goodbye, in other words she was not interested in what the damn old man is doing counting his monies. Well then, the girl went and a few yards away she found another girl. She said hi and the other girl offered her a box of matches. Well, then the girl asked how much it costs and the other girl told her that one peso. Well, then the girl looked in her pocket to see if she has money and she does. Well, then the other girl almost cries with joy and says that it has been many years since someone bought something from her. 'That's not fair, but if there's a rich man here,' said the girl. Well, then the girl told her that she is going to take her there. Well, then they get there and find the rich man and the damn old man doesn't answer the girls. And they are there talking to him for a while, until the girl gets pissed off again and scolds the damn old man and he pays attention to her. Well, then the girl explains to the damn old man that he has to help the other girl who sells matches. And the rich man doesn't answer at all. So the girl gets pissed off and scolds the damn old man again and the rich man answers that he is not going to help, that it costs a lot of money to maintain and he already said that he doesn't want to lose one cent. Well, then they begin to argue about the fact that they have to help the other girl and the rich man says that he is not going to do it. And so the girl says that what he does is not fair, because you are very rich. 'Yes,' said the damn old man, 'but I worked with my own hands, I began with very little and then got rich. If you want to do that you will also get rich.' That's what the damn old man said. Well, then they continue to argue about the fact that he has to help her and that is where they were fighting. Well, so then the girl has to talk about justice. And the rich man answers that justice is made with one's own hands, I did not understand what that means but it must be a bunch of crap.

"Well, then they start to argue again that it is unbelievable that the rich man doesn't understand, and so the girl gets all pissed off. Well, then the girl tells the damn old man: 'If you are not going to help her I am going to burn you and you are going to die along with your useless idea.' And they say that they are going to light a match, because the two girls had already joined the revolutionary fight, in other words they were already in the organization. Well, then the rich man sees that the situation is fucked up because they are going to burn him and he says that he is going to help and he jumps, but they are already burning the computer and the damn old man disappears. Well, then with some difficulty the girl puts out the fire and goes to where her teacher and tells him and the subject that they are going to work on is Marxism because the girl's name was Karla Marx. Well, then they start to study what Marx's idea on the rich and poor is. And he put it on three rungs, something about society's superstructure, but I don't remember well. But I say that that idea is good because there it wakes people up how they are exploited and how capitalism is growing and the workers don't see any of that and they are only working and what they get paid is barely enough. So it wakes up people who are screwed over.

"And then the workers and peasants realized what is happening in this country. But I think that idea is not enough. We have to do what comes next."

Insurgent Erika had told her story in one go, almost without pausing, as if afraid to forget what she had read.

While I was listening to her, I had already choked on a cow, an elephant, a cat, and a dog—all of them were crackers.

Insurgent Erika waited patiently for me to finish swallowing the complex mouthful (made of animal crackers and the theoretical, historical, and gender hypothesis that she had raised).

When I got back my breath, I told her:

"It's good, but I thought that he was a man and that his name was Karl Marx."

Insurgent Erika responded without hesitation: "Ah, but that's a damn old husbands' tale, it came to my thoughts that she was a woman."

Insurgent Erika left for her shift at the barrack guard post. Of course, I promised her a book that explained how to write poetry . . . or Yucatecan bombs, what else could I do? By the way, if anyone knows of a book about poetry, let me know.

The end.

Insurgent Subcommander Marcos
Mexico, January 3, 2009

Third Wind: A Dignified and Enraged Earth-Colored Brown

Good evening. We are going to try to be brief, because it has been a long day and because afterward Lupita and Toñita are going to read some stories that they prepared just for you.

Here goes:

On Specialists and Specialties

A serious historian could certainly pinpoint the moment in human society when specialists and specialties appeared. And maybe that historian could explain to us what came first: the specialty or the specialist.

Because, in our looking out at and being astonished by the world, we Zapatistas have seen that oftentimes people define their ignorance or shortsightedness as a specialty and call themselves specialists. And they are praised and respected and paid well and ceremonies are held in their honor.

We do not understand. For us, someone with limited knowledge is someone who should push themself to learn more. But it turns out that in academia, the less you know, the more research funding you receive.

Old Antonio, on one of those mornings that surprised us walking downhill, laughed about this when I told him and said that back then the first gods, those who birthed the world, were specialists in specialties.

Anyway, it is well-known that our limits with intellectual production are encyclopedic, so now we would like to briefly talk about a special species of specialists: professional politicians.

Later on in this festival, tomorrow I believe, we will have the opportunity to listen to—in the voice of Insurgent Lieutenant Colonel Moisés—some portrayals of internal political tasks in Zapatista communities.

One of these political tasks, not the only one, is governmental work. There is also, for example, political work of the Zapatista women—which Commander Hortensia will tell us about—and much more.

And it turns out that this work not only is unpaid, it is also not considered a specialty. In other words, someone who is autonomous municipal president one day was in the fields the day before, or on the coffee plantation, planting or harvesting. Many of our Zapatista leaders did not even go to school or do not even know how to speak Spanish; in other words, they are not specialists in anything, much less in politics.

And, nonetheless, our autonomous municipalities have more advances in health, education, housing, and nutrition than the official municipalities that are governed by professional politicians, by political specialists.

Anyway, we'll wait for those talks by my compañeros to try to understand us. Right now, I only want to point out some of our inabilities to understand the political tasks of above, at least in Mexico.

For example, we do not understand how it gets decided, accepted, and made law for congresspeople to make more than construction workers. Because construction workers do something: they work, they build houses, walls, buildings. And they know how to make the mixture, how to place bricks or blocks.

Here, for example, you have this auditorium that we are in. More people can fit right here than in the City Theater here in San Cristóbal de las Casas, and they tell me it was built—from its design to its completion—by indigenous hands. The floor, the levels, the walls, doors and windows, roof, metalwork, and electrical installation were done by nonspecialists, indigenous people, who are compañeros of the Other Campaign.

Well, going back to construction' workers, they work. But congresspeople . . . congresspeople . . . well, could someone maybe tell us what congresspeople do? Or senators? Or secretaries of state?

Not long ago we heard a secretary of state say that the economic crisis, which had been dragging on for several years, was nothing more than a common cold.

Oh, we thought. A secretary of state is like a doctor who diagnoses a disease. But, we were left thinking, why would someone with the least bit of sense pay a doctor who says that someone has a cold and it turns out that they have pneumonia and the doctor gives them hot tea with lemon leaves to feel good as new. But it looks like the secretary of state in question gets paid well, and there is a law that says that he has to make a lot of money.

Someone will tell us that congresspeople and senators make laws and that secretaries of state make plans for those laws to be implemented. OK. How much did it cost the nation to do, for example, the indigenous counterreform that violated the San Andrés Accords?

And several months ago, a PRD lawmaker, questioned about why he voted in favor of an absurd and unjust law (like the majority of laws in Mexico), said in his defense . . . that he had not read it!

And when there was a debate about oil in the country's nerve center (that is, in the media), did the Calderón administration not say that people should not be consulted because it was something that only specialists understood? And did the so-called oil-sector defense movement not act the same way when it entrusted a group of specialists with crafting its proposal?

Specialization is, according to us, a form of private property for knowledge.

Those who know something treasure it and—complicating it to the point of making it look like something extraordinary and impossible, something that only a few can access—refuse to share it. And their pretext is specialization.

They are like sorcerers of knowledge, like the old priests who specialized in talking with the gods. And people believe everything they say.

And this happens in modern society, which tells us indigenous people that we are the backward, the uneducated, the uncivilized.

In our lengthy tour through the Mexico of below, we had the opportunity to directly meet other native peoples on this continent. From the Mayas on the Yucatán Peninsula to the Kumiai in Baja California, from the Purépechas, Nahuas, and Wixaritari on the Pacific coast to the Kikapus in Coahuila.

Part of what we see will be better explained by our compañeros from the Indigenous National Congress, Carlos González and Juan Chávez, when they accompany us at this table. I only want to note a few reflections on this issue of knowledge and Indian peoples.

– In the meetings prior to the Indian Peoples of the Americas Continental Gathering,[1] the different cultures of Indian leaders did not vie for supremacy or hierarchy. With no apparent difficulty, they recognized difference and established a type of deal or agreement within which they respect one another.

---

1   This event was held in Vícam, Sonora, from October 11 to 14, 2007, and brought together more than 570 indigenous delegates representing sixty-six indigenous peoples from twelve countries.

On the other hand, when two different conceptions of reality—two cultures, that is—confront each other in modern society, the issue of one's supremacy over the other is usually brought up, a question that is not infrequently resolved with violence.

But they say that we Indian peoples are the savages.

– When the ladino or mestizo world encounters the indigenous world within the latter's territory, the former develops what we Zapatistas call "evangelizer syndrome." I do not know if it was inherited from the first Spanish conquerors and missionaries, but the ladino or mestizo naturally tends to take the position of teacher and helper. Due to some strange logic that we do not understand, it is held as self-evident that ladino or mestizo culture is superior to indigenous culture in breadth and depth of wisdom and knowledge. In contrast, if this contact between cultures takes place in urban territory, the ladino or mestizo assumes a defensive and distrustful position or a position of contempt and disgust when around indigenous people. The indigenous are backward or peculiar.

On the contrary, when the indigenous come across or encounter a different culture outside of their territory, they naturally try to understand it and do not attempt to establish a dominant/dominated relationship. And when it is within their territory, the indigenous assume a position of curious distrust and a zealous defense of their independence.

"I've come to see what I can help with," mestizos tend to say when they get to an indigenous community. And it may come as a surprise for them when, instead of having them teach or lead or command, they are sent to go get wood, or carry water, or clean the pasture. Or wouldn't it be very strange for the indigenous to respond, "And who told you that we need you to help us?"

There may be cases, but as of now we do not know if anyone has gone to an indigenous community and has said, "I've come so you can help me."

– In collectives that support indigenous communities, on numerous occasions we have come across a type of zeal for their own knowledge, a constant affirmation that they are the owners of the knowledge they horde, it is their private property.

Autonomous authorities know well how unwilling groups that work with technology are to teach—that is, share—what they know. With the Internet, for example. Every time equipment stops working in the caracols, you have to wait for the person who knows, wait for them to get there and know that, when you ask them to teach someone else so you're not depending on them, they claim that they don't have time or that it's something for "specialists." And don't even mention community-radio equipment.

And sometimes something else happens.

There is an anecdote that the commanders in the Tojolabal Zone, or Border Jungle Zone, told me:

It turns out that, with all those well-intentioned people who come to Zapatista communities to help, an agricultural engineer once came to teach a course on improving coffee plantations. After his talk, the engineer went with the Zapatista compas to a coffee plantation to show them how they should make a cut on the tree. The engineer asked them to give him space, all right, now "behind the line I'm going to work." He took out all his scientific equipment and began to take measurements to determine the exact angle to cut the branch at. After many complicated calculations, determining the angle to cut at, the engineer took out a pretty little saw and began to saw very carefully. He took a while, so they tell me, and contradicting the supposedly ancestral indigenous patience, they took him aside and asked him: "OK, where exactly do you want the cut?" "There," responded the flashy agricultural engineer, and pointed. The compa unsheathed his double-blade Acapulco Collins machete and voilà! He made a perfect cut in the branch. "OK, now measure it," the compa asked, practically ordered. The agricultural engineer, with a university specialization, took out his apparatus for measuring angles. He measured again and again, and each time he just scratched his head. "So?" they asked him. "So yes," he responded ashamedly, "it is the exact cut you need, in the place you need, and at the angle you need." "And by golly, Marcos, then the engineer just began to ask us more and more things and just took notes and more notes and filled I don't know how many pages of the notebook he had."

So we make a plea to those who horde wisdom and knowledge and are compañeros and compañeras: say no to private property of knowledge, say yes to piracy among the compañeros that we are.

Some other points:

– In both indigenous people and urbanites from below and to the left, we find a human civility that we do not find in those above. In both, if someone in need arrives, they give that person the best they have. Those above do not give, or, if they do, it's what they have left over.

The sense of community that is notable in indigenous communities is no longer exclusively theirs. It also appears in sectors of below. And it is most developed in those who fight and resist.

– The brutal and ferocious advance of the neoliberal territorial reconquest war is doing something that I don't know if was in the great international financial centers' plans: rages are coming together, in depth, extent, and common history.

– These feelings coming together in what El Ruso[2] called "the gut" are still not accompanied by wisdom and knowledge coming together. There may be cases, but, believe me, in Indian peoples I have not encountered feelings of greed for the knowledge they possess.

Finally, we do not idealize ourselves as Indian peoples: we are not perfect and, of course, we do not intend for everyone to become indigenous. We have knowledge and we have shortcomings. I believe we can share the former to resolve the latter, without any one of you losing the opportunity to get rich because one of us gets the patent for your knowledge.

Now, since promises must be kept, we are going to listen to some stories by Lupita and Toñita.[3] And after them, I'll tell you another.

Lupita first:

"Once upon a time there was a cat who was very hungry, and he didn't know where to find his food. And he went to look for his food and so he found a bunny. And the cat ran until he got the bunny and ate him, and left a little piece. And another cat came and took the piece of bunny meat.

"And the other cat, when he woke up, went to eat the bunny meat. And when he looked for it, the bunny meat wasn't there anymore. The other cat was very angry and sad. That's all. Thank you very much."

Now it's Toñita's turn:

"Good evening, compañeros and compañeras. I want to tell you a story:

"One day the mouse went in to eat the bread, because the cat did not put the bread away. He left it on top of the fridge. And the mouse went in to eat the bread.

"And the next day, the cat looked for his bread and did not find it. And the day after that, the mouse found it and fled so he wouldn't get caught, and the cat was very pissed off.

"That's all, compañeros and compañeras."

Toñita is going to read another story:

"Well, compañeros and compañeras, I'm going to tell you how rich people treat us. Rich people treat us like animals. But that's what they are, because they have animal faces. But, united we will always defeat the rich people who want to do away with us. That's all, compañeros and compañeras."

---

2 The nickname of Ángel Luis Lara, a sociologist, TV screenplay writer, former vocalist with the Spanish rock group Hecho contra el Decoro, and longtime supporter of the Zapatistas. He gave a presentation at the Festival of Dignified Rage's roundtable "Other Media, Other Culture," which preceded by a couple of hours the roundtable in which Marcos delivered his presentation. The Spanish audio of Ángel Luis Lara's presentation is available at "Mesa de la Otra Comunicación, la Otra Cultura," Enlace Zapatista, January 3, 2009, http://bit.ly/2jnSeRE.

3 The following stories were in fact read during the presentation by two young girls, not by Marcos. In the text below, paragraphs in italics were read by Lupita or Toñita.

Well, now you'll have reason to complain about my stories.[4]
Thank you very much.

Insurgent Subcommander Marcos
Mexico, January 3, 2009

P.S. Seven Stories for Nobody

Story 3: The Pedagogy of the Machete

The other day, for a change, Toñita, without permission, went into the ee-zee-el-en General Command, a supposedly impenetrable fortress (actually it's a hut).

I was thinking about what the most appropriate topics would be for these supposedly round tables at the Festival of Dignified Rage when I realized that Toñita was next to me and telling me:

"Hey Marcos, there's no need for you to do this," while she pointed at a life-size photo of a scantily clad Angelina Jolie.

"There's no need for me to do what?" I asked while I inspected the "anti-Toñita" barriers that I had arranged for to stop what was already happening from happening.

"Well, this thing that you're doing now," says Toña and adds: "Why do you have that naked lady with you?"

I lit my pipe and responded: "Firstly, she's not naked, I want nothing more than for that to be so. And secondly, I don't have her with me, I re-want nothing more than for that to be so."

Toñita, as is her custom, stays in a part of the movie because she asks me: "And the third?"

"What third?" I asked her.

"Well if there's a first and a second, then there's a third. And I got third place at school." Toñita has left out a small detail: in that class there were only three students.

Since I don't want to get into an argument, I suggest that if I tell her a story, then she'll leave to go tell it to other people.

"All right," says Toñita and sits on the ground.

I clear my throat and begin with, "Once upon a future time . . ."

Toña interrupts: "And is there gonna be popcorn?"

"What do you mean popcorn?" I ask her, bewildered.

"Well yeah, popcorn, like when we watch a movie," says Toñita.

---

4 At this point, the audience is wildly applauding and cheering for Lupita and Toñita.

"No," I tell her, "this is a story, not a movie, and there's no popcorn here."

"All right," says Toñita.

I continue:

"Once upon a future time, a subcommander who was veeeeeery bad got very pissed off at girls who would go into the command building without permission and cause trouble."

Toñita pays attention. I take advantage to give the story a pedagogic spin, with a style and method that leaves Paulo Freire and Anton Makarenko[5] in the dust.

"So, when a little girl went into the command building without permission, that subcommander took out his machete and whoosh! He cut off the girl's head."

Toñita opened her eyes wide, terrorized.

Noticing that the essential educational concept was being absorbed, I decided to reinforce the story with that Marconian pedagogic technique that has given me so much fame in psychology symposiums where there is a lot of Freud, a lot of Fromm, a lot of Luria,[6] and a lot of everything:

"And the machete had a dull blade, so it would take longer to cut. And it was all rusty, so the wound would get infected."

Toña, horrified, waits for a happy ending.

"And then?"

"And then what?"

"Well, and what's the rest of the story."

"Ah, well, it turns out that then they gave the girl a lot of shots so she wouldn't get infected. The end."

"The end? Err, Marcos, your stories are all useless now."

"Of course they're useful," I tell her while I urge her to leave the hut.

"You have that naked lady there for nothing, if there's no popcorn," says Toñita while leaving.

It wasn't over yet. The meeting I had with the Clandestine Committee finished. While getting my backpack ready to go to the barracks, I realize that my machete isn't there.

"Toña," I thought, and I sent for her.

"Hey Toñita, I can't find my machete, have you seen it around?"

"No, but I'm going to tell you a story," responded Toñita.

"Once upon a time there was a very pretty girl, like me, and whose

---

5   Freire and Makarenko are influential pedagogues known for developing effective teaching methods that break with educational tradition.

6   Sigmund Freud, Erich Fromm, and Alexander Luria are influential thinkers in the field of psychology.

name was Toñita, like me. And then there was a veeery bad subcommander who wanted to cut off her head with a machete."

"And why did he want to cut off her head?" I interrupted, in a futile attempt to regain control of the situation.

"Who knows," Toñita responded, "I think it just popped into his head. And so then the girl sneaked into that subcommander's house. And then she took that subcommander's machete and went and threw it in the outhouse. The end."

Toñita said "the end" far out of my reach.

So I think I know where my machete is. Someone just has to go get it. Any volunteers?

The end.

Insurgent Subcommander Marcos
Mexico, January 3, 2009

Fourth Wind:
An Organized Dignified Rage

(Words of Lieutenant Colonel Moisés)

Good afternoon compañeros, compañeras.

Compañeros, I want to talk to you about, convey what our compañeros from the various authorities in the five caracols do. What compañero Villoro said, it seems to the Zapatista compañeros that he is reading well about what our autonomous authority compañeros and compañeras are doing. I only want to complete a bit of what he already mentioned: political work on democracy.

There are three levels in what they are practicing now. Fifteen years ago, there wasn't what the compañeros and compañeras from the authorities are practicing now, and the authorities in the communities and Good Government Committees. What are these three? They are three collectives, and one of these is divided into hundreds of collectives. In other words, the first entity is the communities, a collective composed of hundreds of communities that make up each caracol. And then, the other collective is the MAREZ,[1] which are men and women, authorities selected by those hundreds of collectives that I already told you about. And within those two collectives, the other collective—the Good Government Committee compañeros and compañeras—is chosen.

So, they again form a collective from those three collectives to put into practice, in their long fifteen-year journey, the seven principles of

---

1   Zapatista Autonomous Rebel Municipalities (Municipios Autónomos Rebeldes Zapatistas).

command by obeying.[2] But not just that, here are my political leader compañeros, the commander compañeras and compañeros who read by listening, who read by looking, and who also read by doing.

I'm going to tell you about some achievements made by the compañeros and compañeras from those three collectives that I already mentioned. For example, the Good Government Committee in Caracol I, which is La Realidad, has invented what they call BANPAZ, which means "Zapatista Popular Bank." If you ask us or think, imagine, wanting to ask where the resources from. Another is the tax that is charged to the evil government[3] because it is putting in the highway so its police and army can arrive easy to dispossess our compañeros and compañeras, and other brothers and sisters, in Montes Azules. And they are charged a tax and that is what they invest in the Zapatista Popular Bank.

What for? Because the compañeros from those three levels of authorities—that is, the commissioners, agents, and the MAREZ and the Committee—form a collective to listen to each other, to look at what there is within their work. Once seen, read, these two begin to also look at how to do what that collective thinks. And then afterward it goes to consultation in the communities, if what the compañeros and compañeras think is accepted.

There are, for example, also collectives of authorities in Caracol II, Oventik. Before there was never a secondary school, which they now have, they prepare there. And it is showing the compañeros who learned there, because their teacher came from there, the teacher of compañera Lupita, who read you the story yesterday.

There is also the example of the compañeros and compañeras from Caracol III, the Good Government Committee for La Garrucha. Now, those three collectives, they are seeing the best way to work Mother Earth. Before they did not know, they did not understand what being an engineer is. Now they understand because they themselves are practicing it.

There is also the example of the compañeros from Caracol IV, what the compañeros and compañeras from the Committee are doing, at the three levels, which are also doing the how to improve.

Compañeros and compañeras, we can give you an example of what I have seen, because I work with the compañeros and compañeras, I accompany them. That is where what I am telling you comes from, it is not mine, it belongs to the compañeros and compañeras. For example, also, because

---

2   The seven principles are (1) serve and not be served, (2) represent and not supersede, (3) build and not destroy, (4) obey and not command, (5) propose and not impose, (6) convince and not defeat, and (7) come down and not go up.

3   This is what the Zapatistas call official government institutions.

maybe there are some people here who are compañeros and compañeras who have given their solidarity as supportive people[4] for some projects. We want you to listen to it, to understand what sometimes has happened, what sometimes occurs.

When a project comes from a supportive compañero or compañera, the compañeros of the Good Government Committee receive it as a proposal, because they cannot accept, because the people are going to be the ones who approve if yes or no. Because they are going to be the ones who work, not the Committee, it is not the compañeros and compañeras of the MAREZ.

The authority compañeros and compañeras understand that the supportive compañeros and compañeras, who also made an effort to get where they are from where they live, demand that there be reports. It's understandable, but also, from our side, we hope that they do not get offended, but from where our compañeros and compañeras live there are no planes, no helicopters, no trains or metro or I don't know what it's called. The only thing is bipod: two feet. You have to walk and some horses that are in the resistance too.[5]

So, that takes a while, it takes a while for the projects to be approved, and then, when the message arrives from the supportive compañeros and compañeras, for them to receive that it is approved.

I hope that, from here forward, the authority compañeros and compañeras have a lot of work, because what I am telling you is just mentioning a few things. Really though, in the Committees, in the five Committees, they have a lot of work that you can't imagine, because they don't only just see that, each point that I told you about. There are problems to resolve regarding justice and many more other things.

And then, the method is that the people have to be informed, the people have to know; in other words, they have to be consulted. That is where the work gets delayed, but delaying the work isn't bad for us, it's the opposite, it's good for us because then it's the people who accepted the good. Only because then there are delays, that is.

And also, what I want to tell you about is that the compañeros . . . democracy, as they are saying or as we are listening to the compañeros, those who are working as authorities, they are also now realizing that they have a great responsibility that they had never seen before. And so the method that they use is discussing, listening, looking, doing once they are

---

4   *Solidarios*: people who demonstrate solidarity.
5   Many Zapatista communities have no road access and are accessible only by foot or horseback; however, many communities have few or no horses.

done thinking, and so, those authorities, men and women, already learned that then they are not just going to dictate how to do things, like being a leader. The word itself is to lead, I think that that's where its continuation comes from: leader. And so the compañeros say: "No, here we are going to discuss, here we are going to take the proposal to the general assembly."

And when I say general assembly, it's that all the authorities from all the communities are here, which are men and women. And the authorities, men and women, from the MAREZ are also here; the compañeros and compañeras have a sense right away. They say: "We are not going to approve this here, we have to bring it to our communities because they are going to be the ones who decide if yes or no."

And the proposals of the compañeros in the Good Government Committees, for what they see that has to be done, or for what they see that is wrong, that general assembly of authorities there are things that are dictated about how it has to be corrected, and there are things that they have to take to the communities for all of them, men and women, to find out what their authority is doing wrong or what the failures of their authority are.

There the compañeros are demonstrating that they are putting into practice the idea of not superseding, because they do not decide, they feel that they cannot decide, that their community has to decide.

And when it is a work proposal, or proposal for a project, the proposal is taken to the communities. Each collective of communities begins to discuss, and in the general assembly, as if it were like this where we are now, the communities begin to propose, the authorities from each community perceived well, because there hundreds of men and women are listening to which proposal is for the best idea on how they intend to do the work.

Then, as a mutual community there is already that, the agreement is immediately made, I think they say unanimous, I think that's what it's called, because then there are some compañeras or compañeros in the communities that the majority convinces them right away. Then, the practice that the compañeros are carrying out, we did not imagine before '94, but when it is put into practice, when it is carried out like this in actions, things change and improve.

And if you ask me or imagine, because certainly then you would want to ask questions, it would be about how if everything that they are doing is good . . . if the compañero's or compañera's failure or error is serious, they are simply thanked and go off to the side. They go off to the side, but do not leave. In other words, they don't leave from the support base, they leave from their position as public servant because they are not doing as the people command. And all this, what I am telling you, the compañeros and compañeras say: "Why didn't the evil governments let us do this back then?" And they themselves say: "No, because if they had let us, Mexico would not be like this," the compañeros and compañeras respond.

The compañeros and compañeras have put into practice, made completely real, and have invented, have created a way to look after their authority. And they have seen now that it does work. Because, as I'm telling you, they have support, which they call the Supervision Commission. They are the ones that report to their communities in the municipal assemblies about what is happening. And when there is a general assembly, where they ask the Good Government Committees for reports, it has worked. Because that is how errors and faults that the compañeros and compañeras have had have been corrected.

And what we have also seen that the compañeros and compañeras do, above all the compañeras, their participation—the compañeras are already participating in the three levels of authorities because there are compañeras in the Good Government Committees, and there are compañeras in the MAREZ, and there are compañeras as authorities, commissioners, and agents in the communities.

And that, the compañeros are already recognized, because then they also assume the responsibility that is the maximum authority. So, but that maximum authority also understands that they are the authority for all three collectives, they say: "We are not the ones who command, we are here as representatives, the people are the ones who command."

Here I want to tell you something: when the compañeros are able to understand what the thing is that says it is the people who command, we have to be careful. Why? Because the compañeros . . . Sometimes when there is a proposal from the collective that is the Autonomous Municipality, something has happened, for example, a community that doesn't want to, the great majority doesn't accept, then the solution (that is where intelligence is needed) . . . that work already has a purpose, whether it is to support the various authorities, the shifts of the MAREZ authorities; in other words, it isn't for it to be divided up in the communities, but is for the communities not to contribute, it is so what little is left does not leave their pockets, that is why collective work is done.

So, instead of them grabbing each other for the compañeros to start fighting with the majority and with the minority, because it is a community that does not accept, that does not want to, the compañeros simply say: "No problem compañero, compañera, we are going to work in the collective, just know that that's where what our authorities spend is going to come from, and we are going to ask our authorities for records on how it is being spent, on how it is being used. And if you as a community don't want to, no problem. That person will continue being the authority for you, our compañeros. Just that when there is a municipal collective, they'll tell you: but there is another way to do it. There in your community, do collective work. So that it doesn't really come out of each of your pockets. Do collective work so that what you need to give to the compañeros and compañeras from the Autonomous Municipality comes from the collective.

So, division is not found, to put it one way. That's why I was telling you that the authority compañeros and compañeras read by listening; they read by looking at what needs to be done, from what they see. And they read by doing. Because there it is going to be demonstrated, in practice: from what was seen and what was heard.

There is, for example, like the authority compañeros in La Garrucha, what I am telling you about is the Agrarian Law. Right now they are seeing how they are going to take care of the earth. They already improved the Zapatista Agrarian Law, from what was already there, they are devoting themselves to caring for the earth. They added more, what is needed, what needs to be done to take care of Mother Earth.

So, when the compañeros were discussing there, there was an autonomous municipality and it said this: "Why doesn't the evil government, and why don't the congresspeople and senators do what we are doing?" Because we have to change the law that is made. How often? When necessary, when they see, when they hear that it isn't working anymore.

And the compañeros, because Insurgent Radio[6] works there, the compañeros responded: "Have you not heard on Insurgent Radio how the congresspeople and senators and the evil government live? They write laws to make money." Well, where are they going to do what we are doing?

I tell you about that law, how they thought about how they're going to take care of the land that has been recovered.

There are many things that the compañeros have invented for health, for education, for trade. Even for transportation. The compañeros do not have vehicles, but they are obligated to see how to control them. Because the compañeros and compañeras realized that owners of passenger vehicles were becoming like a landowner, like it was before. Because only those who are owners entered and left. Only they wanted to occupy, take possession of the road. While they did not allow others to.

So, the compañeros said: "No, this is over, it's just like a landowner. They have to organize themselves as a cooperative, or as a collective."

6   Radio Insurgente is the Zapatistas' radio station, broadcasting in Chiapas in Spanish and various indigenous languages.

Because just as we all want to eat bread . . . looking at what there is, listening to what happens, and they are putting it into practice.

Compañeros and compañeras: There is a lot to say about the compañeros, about how they do it. But, with time, you are going to discover it. And I hope that you don't get tired, when visiting them, meeting them, to understand much more better than giving a talk, an explanation.

Because they are there, and they are going to stay there. And the authority compañeros and compañeras and the Zapatista communities will stay there.

That's all, compañeros and compañeras.

Fifth Wind:
A Dignified and Feminine Rage

(Words of Commander Hortensia)

Good evening to all.

Compañeros and compañeras of the Other Campaign and the International Sixth Declaration:

Brothers and sisters of Mexico and the world:

Compañeros and compañeras, brothers and sisters, people who are at this First Global Festival of Dignified Rage:

On behalf of my support-base compañeras and compañeros, of the insurgents and militia members, of the local and regional leaders from the Indigenous Revolutionary Clandestine Committee, of the Good Government Committees, of the Zapatista Autonomous Rebel Municipalities, of the compañeros and compañeras who are providing their services in different work areas in Zapatista territory.

On their behalf I make use of the word. I am going to talk a little about the work, participation, and organization of women in Zapatista territory.

As we already know, ever since our Zapatista organization was founded, women's participation has been promoted. They are given a place equal to men for them to participate in all levels of work, such as in political, economic, social, and military work.

But when women were given a place, for them to do work in our organization, from the beginning it was difficult for both men and women. Because we had it in our heads and in our hearts that it wasn't our work, that women's work was only being at home, having children, taking care of their husbands, and other things that we have to do.

But thanks to those who gave beginning and life to our organization, who took women into account, we were selected as compañeras in the struggle. In this way, women were given a name, a life, and a face. But above all, for indigenous women, because we suffer the most from exploitation, contempt, humiliation, and oblivion at all levels of life.

That is why we thank the Zapatista organization, which gave us a rebirth, both men and women. They gave us light, gave us hope, and gave us life. So that one day what we wish for so much will flourish: for women to have rights and be taken into account as equals.

That is why there have been dignified and rebellious women who gave their lives, their work, to make our organization grow. But, during those fifteen years of struggle and resistance, there have been women who have tried to give their work and participation at each level of government.

For example, in politics, there have been women in our organization's leadership, part of the Indigenous Revolutionary Clandestine Committee. As local and regional leaders, and also compañeras have been chosen to be CCRI substitutes. Women already participate in the community assemblies. Whether it is in political studies or general assemblies, to choose their authorities, like, for example, municipal authorities, Good Government Committees, municipal agents, ejido commissioners, and education committees. And also to choose their political leaders in the communities, like local leaders.

That is why there are compañeras who are already part of this level of authorities. Additionally, there are compañeras who have organized to look for a way to resist in the struggle. And also, to look for a solution to their problems. That is why they have organized to work in collectives. Whether it is in a bakery, raising animals, producing crafts to sell, or having their gardens for collective consumption.

That is the work that women are trying to do in Zapatista territory. In addition, there are women who are preparing to be autonomous health and education promoters. So that they themselves can share their knowledge and provide their services to the communities for free.

There are women who are preparing to learn about and save medicinal plants. And the compañeras are also preparing to be midwives and healers, since this is the way our elders healed. That is why it is important and necessary for us to rescue what our ancestors left.

For these two levels of work—in health and education—there are compañeras who have been able to hold positions as general coordinators of these two levels of work.

There are also women who have tried to do work in the Zapatista communities, such as communication-radio operators, FM radio presenters, and there are young women who are preparing to be photographers and camera operators.

In addition to all this, there are compañeras who have been able to be militia members and insurgents. And who have been able to be military leaders in our Zapatista Army of National Liberation.

But all this work that we women are doing in the five Zapatista zones is to try to exercise our rights, our obligation as Zapatistas. Although it has not been easy for us, but we are and we will continue making an effort and a sacrifice to try to fulfill what the Revolutionary Women's Law indicates.

But also, we thank the compañeros[1] who have already understood the importance of women's participation. But above all, for the compañeros who now let their compañeras leave to do their work. Although, also, it is not easy for the compañeros, but they are doing what the organization asks. That is why we women must no longer step to the side. We must prepare ourselves more and more. To be able to continue forward and advance as much as possible in all levels of work.

Because if we do not do it, those of us who are already in this world, which is a world where we women still do not have a face, a name, or a voice for the capitalists and neoliberals. That is why it is time to exercise and assert our rights. But, to do all that, all one needs is resolve, determination, strength, and rebellion. And we do not need to ask anyone for permission.

But everything that we are doing and that I am saying is not made up, or imaginary. It is reality. We showed it there in the Third Gathering, which was held in the La Garrucha Caracol one year ago.[2] There we talked about and explained our work as women.

But I also would like to be honest by telling you, brothers and sisters, compañeros and compañeras, that there are still some communities and regions in Zapatista territory where work and participation are lacking at some levels of work. The thing is that the compañeros and compañeras have still not clearly understood the importance of women's participation.[3] But we are going to make a struggle to be able to fulfill what being a Zapatista and being revolutionary means.

---

1   In this instance, and many instances below, Hortensia is using *compañero* to refer only to men.

2   Zapatista Women's Gathering with Women of the World (Encuentro de las Mujeres Zapatistas con las Mujeres del Mundo), which was the third gathering held by the Zapatistas in 2007 and featured presentations by Zapatista women and other invited guests.

3   This is discussed in-depth in EZLN, *Participation of Women in Autonomous Government: First-Grade Textbook for the Course "Freedom according to the Zapatistas,"* trans. Henry Gales, available at escuelitabooks.blogspot.com.

But, during these twenty-five years since the beginning of the Zapatista Army of National Liberation, and fifteen years since our armed uprising, we have already achieved very important advances. But above all, women's participation at almost all levels. The thing is that more than twenty-five years ago, there were no Zapatista communities. It was only full of ignorance, of slavery, and oblivion.

But fifteen years ago, there were no more women who were in the political leadership. But over the course of these fifteen years of struggle and resistance, we have been incorporating ourselves little by little into the different levels of work.

There we realized that it is true that we can think and decide. We can hold a position just like the compañeros. And also, we women can do the work. But everything, what little we could do over the course of these fifteen years is not enough. There is a lot left to do.

Now, our peoples, our homeland which is Mexico, and our planet earth need men, women, boys, girls, young people, elderly people to rebel, to fight, and to have dignity and rage.

But, when we have these two important things in our mind and in our heart it is what carries us forward until we achieve what we want.

Lastly, we want to make a call to all the women of Mexico and the world, to unite our forces, our voice, our rebellion, and our rage. To fight for our rights, for our autonomy, and to build a world with room for everyone.

Democracy, freedom, and justice
For the Indigenous Revolutionary Clandestine Committee, General
Command of the Zapatista Army of National Liberation
Chiapas, Mexico, January 4, 2009
Thank you very much

Sixth Wind:
An Other Dignified Rage

Good evening.

Thank you to Don Eduardo Almeida for helping us with the moderation. It is an honor to have you with us.

Since the beginning of our uprising, it has caught our attention that we received, and fortunately continue to receive, support from four sectors of the population: from indigenous people, from women, from young people, and from gays, lesbians, transgender people, transsexuals—principally, although not always, sex workers.

And since then we have made an effort to find the reasons or causes that gave us this privilege.

Little by little we have been understanding, I still don't know if we are right, that it is because we have in common the status of being "others," excluded, discriminated against, feared.

As if a norm or a standard had been imposed, with its classifications and shelves, and everything that did not fit into those classifications was put in a filing cabinet that becomes bulkier every day, labeled with a sign: The Other.

Of course, these classifications are also descriptions, and with them comes a series of cultural codes and behavioral guidelines that must be followed.

A type of survival manual that human beings do not receive in a bound copy, but assimilate in doses—brutal doses most of the time—over the long or short course of their maturation—that is, their domestication.

Think about it like a "What to Do When . . ." brochure.

And like this, unwritten but evident and omnipresent, there would be brochures for "What to Do When around Indigenous People," or "What to Do When around Women," or "What to Do When around Young People," or "What to Do When around Gays, Lesbians, Transgender People, or Transsexuals."

Of course, these are not an editorial project, but they are so widely disseminated that their publication would make anyone a millionaire. The collection could be called "Be a Normal Person" and be released in collectible installments.

One could think that each of these "education" or "survival in normalcy" manuals has its particularities, and each does. But they also have things in common:

"Distrust!" "Despise!" "Discriminate!" "Assault!" "Mock!" These would be a few.

And in their particularities we could find the following:

The "What to Do When around Indigenous People" brochure could give details. For example, it would say: "Look down from above, so that this thing you have in front of you knows who is in charge and knows that we are not all equal, smile mockingly, make jokes about the way they talk or dress in that thing. Their value? Less than a chicken."

And "What to Do When around Women" would say: "If you are a man, look at her like what she is, like an object, like a whore with an owner or still without an owner. If you are a woman, do the same. Value her based on her potential for sexual use, her labor power, or as a decorative element. Assault her. If she's good, grope her, take her, make her yours, or at least try. If the use of force is necessary, don't hesitate, use it. Let that object you have know who's in charge and know that we are not all equal."

We must not be afraid to say it; this manual is extremely widespread and is practiced enthusiastically among the sector of men or males who say that we are below and to the left. Silencing it, hiding it, does not absolve us of guilt or exorcize the specter: sometimes we look too much like what we claim to fight against.

And the "What to Do When around Young People" brochure would say: "For starters, assume that you are with an active or potential criminal. In addition to pimples and blackheads, that thing has natural tendencies toward vandalism and violence. Also assume the advantage that you have in calendars, something that thing should understand. Do not worry about their rebelliousness, it will pass when the calendar, with help from the police, does its work."

And in the brochure on "What to Do When around Gays, Lesbians, Transgender People, or Transsexuals" one would read: "Assume that you are with a diseased criminal, so back away (we have not ruled out the possibility that whoredom may be contagious). If you have children, keep them at a distance. In extreme cases, go to your chief confessor (note: in their absence, a member of the PAN, or of any right-wing party, will do)."

Let's say it: not only with women, also with different sexual preferences, the Left is deeply sexist.

And the Zapatistas?

Maybe we are the same or worse. In the best-case scenario, we have a long way to go.

But with a determination to learn and, above all, with the spaces that make that learning possible and with the teachers: you.

In the stories that we have been unleashing all these years, we have tried to show our reality, our failures and shortcomings, but also our "ways" to try to overcome the former and the latter.

With sexual differences, it has been easier. Maybe because we arrived less domesticated.

On one of the Other Campaign's tours, we came across compañeros and compañeras from the Brigada Callejera[1] (who have taught us, even without knowing it, for a very long time). We asked them about the @ issue.[2] It is politically correct, but it only includes masculine and feminine and that's it, as if they were the only sexual options—it leaves out the other. The compañeros and compañeras of the Brigada Callejera told us that they used "compañeric" or "compañerotic," I'm not entirely sure.

We looked for our way, and we settled on what we call "compañeroa."

Well, the first story tells of an encounter between Elías Contreras and Magdalena. Magdalena was a "compañeroa." Anyone who thinks that they[3] are a literary character is mistaken. Magdalena existed and was real, locatable in Zapatista calendar and geographies, as locatable as the time when they saved Elías Contreras's life, an indigenous Zapatista who went out to the city with an ability for amazement and a determination to understand that few people have.

In things related to women, we are still very behind. A while ago, in the afternoon, we heard in the voice of Commander Hortensia about the advances women have had in the struggle.

What she left out is that they have achieved this in spite of our

---

1   An organization in Mexico City that specializes in defending sex workers' human rights and labor rights.

2   With gendered nouns and adjectives, people sometimes use the @ sign to symbolize both the masculine *o* and the feminine *a*.

3   That is, Magdalena; see above, p. 88, n. 3.

staunch opposition. If we men do not talk about it much, it's because it would be a long and painful story of defeats.

We have many problems. For example, in our barracks the hygiene conditions are not optimal, and it is common for female insurgents to get diseases like urinary-tract infections. Health-Captain Elena will not let me lie: it is a big struggle to get their male partners to also take the treatment they receive, and the men reinfect them again and again.

And not just that. We also struggle with condom use. Our insurgent compañeras tend to be very young, and they have health problems with using contraceptives. The pill or the patch or the implant are bad for them, and the IUD too. Since they are very young, they insist that their male partners use a condom. But, as you may understand, it is very difficult to check if that is being done, since we cannot go to each house to see if they are using condoms or not. I have offered my "pedagogy of the machete," and I threaten to give them a vasectomy with my surgical abilities.

And we also have a ways to go with respect to women. There is an anecdote that I want to tell you:

Several days ago we met to talk about how the Sandinista commander Mónica Baltodano was going to come. One of the female commanders brought up that phrase that the Sandinista women used to say that goes: "Revolution cannot be made without the participation of women." I jokingly told her that I was going to make a phrase that went: "Revolution can be made in spite of women." The commander looked down at me from above, just like it says in the manual, and told me: "Err, Marcos, we are waging a war for liberation. If it's taking us a while, it's because of the goddamn men."

Here go the pending stories:

Seven Stories for Nobody.

Story 4: The Encounter between Elías Contreras and Magdalena.

Elías Contreras, EZLN Investigation Commission, talks:

"Sometimes like God also makes mistakes. The other day I was meandering around near the Monument to the Revolution in Mexico City, that is, I was surveying the area. That is, to know where to run, that is, in case things got rough. Well, so I was walking around those parts and for a while I had been in a little park called San Fernando, there is a cemetery right there. And for a while I was in front of the statue of the great general Vicente Guerrero, the one where the EZLN's motto is written in stone, 'Live for the Homeland or Die for Freedom.'

"And so it got late and it was already nighttime. And so I set off walking down that street called Puente de Alvarado and right there I got stopped by the law, that is, by police officers. And so they say who am I, what am I doing, give us what you're carrying, and other things I didn't understand well because those officers talk real different. And then they wanted to put me in the cop car, but up comes a girl with a real short skirt and a little blouse, that is, she was right-well naked and it was very cold. And so the girl talked to the officers and then they let me go. And so the girl came up to me and started talking to me and told me that her name was Magdalena. And so she asked me where I was from because I talked real different. And so, since I saw that she is a good person because she scared off the police officers for me, I told her that I was from Chiapas. And so she asked me if I was a Zapatista. And so I told her that I don't know what Zapatista means. And so she said it was obvious I was a Zapatista, because the Zapatistas don't go around saying they're Zapatistas. And so she told me that she's not a she but a he. And then, since I didn't understand her well, she lifted up her skirt and there was her whatever-it's-called making a bulge in her underwear. And so I asked her how she was a he and dresses like a she. And so she, or he, told me that she is a woman but has a man's body. And so she invited me to her room, because there were no customers, she said. And so in her room she told me everything and that she, that is, he, wants to save money to operate on her man's body and make it a woman's body and that's why she was going around in heels. And so I didn't understand well what 'going around in heels' means and she explained it to me. And then she, or he, fell asleep.

"And so I got comfortable in a corner with my jacket and Magdalena's blanket that she lent me. And I didn't sleep because I was thinking that sometimes God also makes mistakes, because God put Magdalena, who is a woman, in a man's body.

"And then the next day we drank some coffee, it was already late because Magdalena didn't get up right away. And so I told her about the Zapatista struggle and about how the communities are organized in resistance and she was very happy to listen. And then I didn't tell her that I was with the Investigation Commission and she didn't ask what I was doing here in The Monster, that is, in Mexico City.[4] And so I saw that she is a good compañera, or compañero, because she, or he, is discreet and doesn't ask me what I'm doing. And so she told me that if I needed I could stay in her room for as long as I want. And so I thanked her and then went out and bought her a bouquet of red roses and gave it to her and told her that when we win the war we are going to build a hospital to straighten out

---

4   One common nickname for Mexico City is "El Monstruo."

everything that God didn't get right. And so she started to shriek, which is because no one had ever given her flowers, I think. And so she was shrieking for a while and then left to go around in heels. And so I went to keep looking for evil and evildoers."

The end.

Story 5: The Women's Movie

I was eating a vegetable soup with mushy squash (yuck!), and I was doing it with great pleasure, great joy, and overwhelming enthusiasm, when outside of the ee-zee-el-en General Command hut, I heard the voice of Insurgent Erika asking for permission to enter (did you hear that, Toñita?). In the doorway of the hut, Insurgent Erika asks:

"What do the compañeros say about if they can watch a movie."

"Which one are they going to watch?" I asked.

Insurgent Erika doubted herself, she did not answer right away.

"Well, of course I'll tell you, compañero Subcommander Marcos, that I don't know how I'm going to tell you," she finally responds while her brown face turns red.

"Hmm . . . well, but it wants that you are going to make popcorn," I said to save her from trouble whose reasons I ignored, and to counter any harmful effect that the squash might have on my delicate body (ha!). Because you must know that we subcommanders are allergic to vegetables, especially squash. I think it's genetic.

"All right, then," Insurgent Erika said, and ran off.

Having collapsed belly up, like the boa in Saint Exupery's *The Little Prince*, I very much regretted having eaten so many vegetables, and I started thinking and reflecting if it might be good to prohibit squash soup in Zapatista territory.

Insurgent Erika returned with the medicine, I mean, with the popcorn and ran off again. I waited for her to be out of sight to be able to eat with the elegance and good manners that I am known for; in other words, I shoved fistfuls of popcorn into my mouth.

A while later, once again in the same position as the boa in *The Little Prince*, I again had major regrets, trying to digest my popcorn overdose. Then, like a lightning bolt, something came to mind: "Wait a second! Why couldn't Erika tell me what movie they were going to watch? It must be one with naked ladies and that's why she was ashamed to tell me."

Not without some difficulty, I sat up and made my way toward the barracks, which is a ways from where my hut is.

A bluish glow emanated from the hut that serves as a dining area, armory, and meeting place for the political-studies and cultural-activities cadre. No insurgent voices could be heard, only the humming of a small generator and the dull sound of a few moans. Hot tamales!

"Aha!" I thought, "So they are watching a movie with naked ladies and they didn't invite me! Now I'll arrest them all and stay to watch the movie alone."

I snuck up to catch them in their crime, as the saying goes, and entered without them noticing.

What a disappointment! They were watching a Jean-Claude Van Damme movie, and the moans that I heard were those of a poor man, with the look of a citizen who is part of the Other Campaign, getting karate kicks from the film's protagonist.

"Mother 'ucker," I said out loud, "that was really the movie you were going to watch?"

When they heard me, the insurgents quickly stood at attention, paused the movie, and turned on the light.

I turned toward Insurgent Erika and asked: "And why couldn't you tell me that you were going to watch a movie about karate?"

"It wasn't exactly this movie, Marcos," Insurgent Erika responded and turned toward the other compañeras, as if asking for help.

The public health insurgent came to the rescue and she declared: "No compañero Subcommander, the thing is that the movie we were going to watch is one about sexual health, about diseases and hygiene and those things."

"Yes, about AIDS," said Erika, now feeling supported by the other women, but still red with shame.

It isn't the first time that I hadn't understood anything about my troops, so I lit my pipe and waited for the explanation to continue, which was the following:

It turns out that the female insurgents wanted to watch the movie "about AIDS," to use Erika's words, and the men wanted to watch *Lionheart*, which, by the way, they had already seen like 365 times. They couldn't agree and they argued and, as it should not be, the women won and they watched the movie "about AIDS." The men, too, because the women promised that if they watched the movie "about AIDS," they would watch Van Damme afterward. And they kept their word.

The end.

Story 6: Four Notes from a Beetle. Taken from Don Durito of the Lacandon Jungle's notebook.

One. One of the reasons that women are superior to men is that, with orgasms, the man's brief party is over. And the woman's party still has a lot of celebrating left.

Two. When women rebel, they rebel several times. Men, on the other hand, only rebel once and do so pushing and shoving. But the statues are for them. Women? Maybe the statues' shadows.

Three. Not infrequently, feminism from fashionable magazines or international conferences has served as a pretext for crimes and abuse. And gender equality is achieved thanks to the social class's alchemy. "People criticize me because I'm a woman," says the woman from above when she issues orders to defraud, imprison, and kill, with the same cynicism as men from above.

Four. Love often follows the ancestral path of the species' reproduction. It has a lot of routine and has learned and repeated lessons. But sometimes, rarely, almost never, love is a flash of light and shade that defies calendars, geographies, and sexology manuals. So it again teaches—for a small audience of naked skins and hearts—a terrifying, unique, and wonderful lesson. And the students never learn.

The end.

Thank you very much.

Insurgent Subcommander Marcos
Mexico, January 4, 2009

Seventh Wind: Some Dignified and Enraged Deceased

Good evening.

Compañero Don Pablo González Casanova is with us today, at our side, as he has been for fifteen years.

We are not going to talk about his intellectual capacity, about the brilliance of his analysis, about his position alongside those who struggle. Anyone who has a bit of memory or who looks in the past knows about this. We know about it.

His simplicity and modesty with us Zapatistas has never ceased to amaze us. I hope I'm not offending anyone, but he doesn't seem like an intellectual.

This compañero has been with us during the good, the bad, and the ugly. He was part of the National Intermediary Commission (CONAI), then led by Don Samuel Ruiz García, and in it he was able to give a first-hand account of the contempt and racism that the government delegation demonstrated in the San Andrés Dialogues. He, I believe, could also attest to the steadfastness and dignity of my compañeros and compañeras who were part of our delegation to those dialogues ruined by the government.

We'll tell you clearly: for us, this man is a scholar. And as such he has shown, at least with us, a humility and a simplicity that make him more like the knowers that are found among Indian peoples than the arrogant "specialists" that—from the comfort and privilege of academia—judge and condemn a reality that they have always been foreign to.

Unlike many "big heads"—which is what our Commander Tacho calls people with big ideas—Pablo González Casanova, Don Pablo, as we call him, has never tried to tell us what we must do, "keep us in line," give us orders, or direct us.

He has told us—sometimes in person, sometimes in writing—what he thinks of this or that thing. We have agreed on many things, and his word has enriched our heart. And I hope our word has been of some use for his wisdom.

We have differed on other things and argued about them. And even then, we have been amazed by the simplicity and sense of humor, sometimes as acidic as ours, with which he accepts our criticisms and remarks, and those of others.

Maybe because one of the things that we agreed on is that thought must not be one, alone, singular, and unanimous, and that criticism, dissent, and discussion do not mean, most of the time, crossing over to the opposing side.

I have said before that Don Pablo is a scholar. As I explained a few days ago, wisdom—according to us Zapatistas—does not consist of a specialization in thought, of knowing a lot about a small part of reality. Nor is it knowing a little of everything. According to our thought, wisdom consists of knowing how to read what is coming and interpret what has gone by, to understand what is happening. And thus knowing and respecting the worlds that there are in the world.

This—which looks like one of those word games typical of the Zapatistas—is what, as Old Antonio will tell in the seventh story, our dead taught us. This is how they train us.

We do not intend to say that this way of thinking about the world and acting in it and with it is the best. It probably is not. What we do know is that it is not the only way. And that, just as we have regulated our steps and our stumbles with that thought, others have and shall have other thoughts and, in consequence, other steps and other stumbles.

Cheers, Don Pablo. Believe us when we say we are not going to give you a balaclava because we know, better than anyone, how uncomfortable they have been and are . . . and will be. And know that more than a few times your words and thoughts have become words on our lips, and your heart has always been.

Cheers, Neozapatista compañero Don Pablo González Casanova.

In these days, we have respectfully asked three thinkers—from those who have come to share with us, here and in Mexico, their ear and their words—to sit among us to emphasize our calling them "compañeros." We wanted to say that they are not the only ones, there are others. Sometimes timidly, as if asking for permission, sometimes with the ease and impertinence that tends to occur between comrades in the struggle, we know, recognize, and call thinkers "compañero," "compañera."

Nor are they the only ones with whom there have been, or are, differences or outright disagreements. We have asked them, and they have accepted, to help us give this message that the world we Zapatistas fight for is not one, singular, and indivisible. That truth is not one, but many. And, in spite of them all, we have never discarded the possibility of being mistaken about something, about several things, or about everything.

We are not in EZLN territory. I was going to say that we are not in Zapatista territory, but after seeing the CIDECI compañeras and compañeros' new and great effort, I'm not sure that I am not in Zapatista territory. Thank you to these compañeros and compañeras. And I hope Doctor Raymundo can convey what we feel to everyone who works here.

I was saying we are not in EZLN territory. CIDECI has offered us this space for the events, generously and unconditionally. Also, the compañeros and compañeras of the Francisco Villa Independent Popular Front–UNOPII and the compañeros and compañeras from the Los Reyes de Iztapalapa Charros[1] Association—who we call "the other charros" to distinguish them from the corrupt leaders that plague worker and peasant movements—have provided us with the same generosity and unconditionality, and we express our gratitude and recognition to them.

In the calendar that convenes us, we must not forget the geography in which our rages found each other: thank you Lienzo Charro in Iztapalapa, thank you CIDECI.

You have been our invitees. And in this festival, at the same time, we have been guests in the Lienzo and CIDECI. As such, as guests, we owe those who receive us and attend to us not only thanks and admiration, but also, and above all, respect. And therefore we could not and should not act as if we were on home turf.

One of the spirits that enlivens the Sixth Declaration and the Other Campaign is respect for the "ways" of each struggle in its territory. When we went out on our tours to places we got to, we did not do so to criticize or judge those who gave us not only shelter and food, but also the medicine of their struggle. We offered respect and we followed through.

And we have also received respect from our compañeros and compañeras of the Other Campaign. Those of you who were in the caravan and those of you who accompanied us during the most ominous days of repression in Atenco know that we were yelled at and attacked in public events and meetings by the López Obrador movement, even in our delegation's movements within Mexico City. And you know that the "way" that we—our compañeros and compañeras—were criticized and talked to was

---

1   Traditional type of horseback riding in many Mexican states.

not always measured, but instead rough and caustic more often than not, and a few times like outright provocation.

Last night, Commander Zebedeo was telling a compañero about the López Obrador supporters' attacks (he and Commander Miriam personally experienced some) and distinguished them from the "ways" that compañeros and compañeras of the Other Campaign criticize. He said that the Zapatistas have thick skin. Not only from fifteen years of war and resistance, but also, and above all, from an over five-hundred-year-long war of oblivion. He said that we listened to everything we were told and that, inside ourselves, the good remained in our heart and the rest went out the other ear.

As if the wounds received all this time had scarred and had thickened our skin, making it leathery, hard, resistant. And yes, if we have resisted five hundred years of domination and annihilation attempts, if we have resisted twenty-five years in the mountains, if we have resisted fifteen years of military siege, we don't see why we couldn't resist hysterical cries, slander, lies, condemnations, and journalistic vetoes from the López Obrador movement.

And very different are the criticisms that have been made, are made, and will be made by our compañeros and compañeras of the Other Campaign in Mexico and the world.

Because it turns out that with the Sixth Declaration, we do not call on them to follow us or obey us, or to be like us, or to import our "ways," or to subordinate their struggles, projects, dreams, to ours.

We call on them to get to know us and get to know each other, to know that neither we nor they are alone, to respect us, to make a deal to support each other, so that the silence in the face of our pains is not unanimous, we invite them to be others.

We do not agree with a few of them . . . well, with more than a few . . . well, with many . . . well, in reality we do not agree with any one of them. Because if that were so, we would no longer be the EZLN and we would be part of them. But we recognize them as being on our side, and we believe they too recognize us.

And we are very proud and amazed that they are our compañeros, compañeras, and compañeroas.

And those of us who are with the Sixth Declaration have this advantage, or disadvantage: knowing that there is a place, work, a space, a struggle, where one can check if what is preached is also practiced.

In these days, and also throughout these fifteen years, what we have said about ourselves can be verified. You can still go, maybe not for much longer, to Zapatista indigenous communities (if you do, ask for permission first in the Good Government Committee, it is our way) and see if it is true that there are women in governmental positions or who are educators or health promoters or local and regional leaders. For female commanders it may not be necessary, because unless it is a virtual effect achieved with laser beams or male commanders have repeated the marvelous transformation that Krishna taught us about yesterday,[2] some of the female commanders are here.

You can go and see if it is true that there are schools and health clinics, if the Good Government Committees really do look for an agreement between parties when there are conflicts and disputes, if it is true that the teachers who teach classes to Lupita and Toñita were trained in the autonomous education systems. In a nutshell, you can see if we practice what we preach.

And the same thing happens with our compañeros, compañeras, and compañeroas of the Other Campaign. You can go to Brigada Callejera's office and verify if they do what they told us about yesterday; you can go to the small offices where people work who—in truly harrowing conditions—do alternative communication, or say they have informative round-tables, or organize tenants, peasants, urban workers, Indian peoples, or paint, or sing, or what each says they do.

Some time ago, before coming to die and be reborn in these mountains in the Mexican Southeast, I was at the National Autonomous University of Mexico and several times was in the auditorium of the School of Philosophy and Letters, in the auditorium known as "El Che." Back then, the president's office and its administrative authorities were in charge of "El Che." I won't lie to you: it was a dunghill. And a neglected dunghill at that, because there are dunghills that are well taken care of.

Sometime later, being who we are now, as part of our work for the Other Campaign, I had the opportunity to be in El Che two times. The first without knowing the scale of the dispute. The second, knowing and taking a position. I won't lie to you: it was impeccable, clean, ordered, functioning. The only thing that was missing were seats, which I believe were taken out by the president's office. Several workshops were given there, there was a cafeteria—vegetarian unfortunately for those of us who are hopeless carnivores and taco eaters. There was work, struggle, life. El Che was not the gray building that only opened for film clubs, assemblies, and very rare cultural events.

---

2   During a performance the previous day, Krishna, one of the speakers from Brigada Callejera, transformed from a guerrilla dressed in combat gear to a negligee-clad diva.

Maybe, it is a suppository, the compañeros and compañeras of Ok-upache only cleaned and organized it because I was going to come, and they put on a show to make it look like they practice what they preach. I don't think so. We believe that it is true that they practice what they preach, but, in any case, it is something that you can verify by visiting our compañeros and compañeras of Okupache. We have certainly verified that they have "ways" and positions that we do not share. And certainly there are others, compañeros and noncompañeros, who think the opposite or have an image that is diametrically opposed to what we see. That's OK, it is the National Autonomous University of Mexico. And people are right when they say it is that university—that is, universal—community that must discuss, analyze, dissent, take a position, decide. And we believe that maybe it can be done without shouting and easy condemnation, but also without threats of eviction or confrontations. Anyway, there you have it. But have no doubt, we will be on the side of our compañeros and compañeras, on the side of the attacked, as we were here several days ago.

The political parties of above may say one thing and do the opposite. One can verify this anywhere they have power. And it isn't because their criteria for consistency are different. For them, the number of people they can mobilize in an election or a march is their thermometer for whether they're doing good or bad or all right, without regard for the methods that they resort to.

We have different criteria: we are doing well if what we say coincides with what we do, whether that is good or bad for other people.

Two people we love and respect, perhaps to their chagrin, asked us what the Zapatistas get out of Marcos criticizing the López Obrador movement. One asked why, when I am around the media, among other things, I always defame AMLO.

Well, I am not around the media, that time has long since passed. We are talking with and listening to our compañeros, compañeras, and compañeroas of the Other Campaign in Mexico and the world, and listening to the word of people who struggle and think in different corners of the planet.

I would like you to allow me to have a little time to explain how we organize our work in the CCRI-CG of the EZLN. Look, here in the EZLN, various Indian peoples come together: Tzeltales, Tzotziles, Tojolabales, Choles, Zoques, Mames, and mestizos.

These peoples have indigenous communities that form zones. Each zone has an organizational structure, now parallel to the autonomous authority's structure. And in each zone structure, there is an organizational collective leader. When I say "organizational collective leader," not only am I saying that it is a collective, I'm also saying that it is not military. This zone leader is what we call the zone CCRI. And each zone has its "way." The Tzotziles, Tzeltales, Tojolabales, Choles, Zoques, Mames, and mestizos have their own problems and own "ways" of confronting them or solving them. The EZLN is then in charge of being like a bridge: it comes and goes between zones. When the EZLN as a whole is going to do something, there must be an agreement between all the zones. When one zone is going to do something, it must communicate with the other zones, through the EZLN, so they know and see where help can be offered.

In addition to that, the EZLN is responsible for representing all the zones as a whole for the outside world, for those who are not Zapatistas. Although she is a commander in the Highlands, Hortensia does not talk to you about the Highlands; through her voice, the voice of the EZLN speaks. And what she tells you about women is not only what is happening in the Highlands, but the trend that she takes from all the Zapatista communities. The same is true when I talk or Lieutenant Colonel Moisés or Commander Zebedeo or Commander David or anyone who is part of the CCRI-General Command.

So, when Marcos or any of us speak in public like now, that person does it as the EZLN, not on their own behalf.

We think that everyone must be responsible for what they say and do, as an individual and as a collective. I believe that the EZLN has always held itself responsible for what it says and does, and dedicates its life to it. Individual life and collective life.

So, what does a movement get out of saying what it thinks and feels? Well, we rose up in arms for that too, to recover our word, to be able to say ourselves what we think and feel.

Let them tell us who among our "allies" are persecutors, discriminators, and murderers of indigenous people. We have told them which of their leaders and "allies" are just that. Those who persecute, harass, and shut off the water on our Zapatista compañeros in Zinacantán are people from the pro–López Obrador CND. Those who attack us inside and outside our territory are AMLO supporters, of course, in addition to the federal, state, and municipal governments, media outlets (all of them now), the army, the state police, the AFI, the CISEN,[3] the CIA, and friends who accompany them.

---

3   The Federal Investigative Agency (Agencia Federal de Investigación) is tasked with a role and duties similar to those of the FBI in the United States, and the Center for Investigation and National Security (Centro de Investigación y Seguridad Nacional) is Mexico's nonmilitary intelligence agency.

Those who put Zapatista compañeros evicted from the Montes Azules first in an abandoned brothel and then in a warehouse were supporters of López Obrador. Government officials from Mexico City and members of the AMLO movement went to Chiapas to carry out the eviction "operation," alongside the government that AMLO helped bring to power. I said in a warehouse. The indigenous have always pointed out that the dominators treat us like animals. They went further: they treated us like things, like packages. Not even animals are put in a warehouse. And there are more examples like this that we have denounced again and again.

I know that it may be an escape route or comforting to say to others or oneself that it's Marcos's thing and that the Zapatista bases are dying to be whisked away to an AMLO event, or are burning with desire to proselytize for the upcoming elections.

But no. This is the Festival of Dignified Rage, and, like everyone, we have come here to express our rage. Not Marcos's, or Moisés's, or Hortensia's, or Zebedeo's, or David's rage. No, the rage of the Zapatista communities that are no longer only attacked by the evil governments, but also by those who say they are left-wing and progressive.

And when we speak, we only express our rage. If they listened to the rage of others who are not from the EZLN, which they also cultivated with attacks and persecutions, maybe they would understand a few things.

On the other hand, why doesn't anyone ask AMLO why he preferred to ally himself with persecutors and murderers of indigenous people in general and indigenous Zapatistas in particular?

Who here came to tell us: "Compañeros, we are going to fuck you up but it is for an alternative national project. Don't mind the bludgeon and don't make a fuss because it is for the good of our homeland. You wait while we save the nation"?

And what does the López Obrador movement get out of allying with people like Nuñez, Monreal, Muñoz Ledo, Sabines, Albores, Kanter, Iruegas, Fox's indigenous former government officials; those who voted against the San Andrés Accords "to demonstrate governmental drive"; those who persecute street vendors, young people, sex workers, workers, peasants, indigenous people; those who—in places where they are the government—evict, dispossess, repress, exploit, discriminate, court the powerful, and give nature's riches to foreigners?

And what does the López Obrador movement get out of slandering us, misrepresenting us, blatantly lying, verbally attacking us in our events, closing pages on us, editing their history instead of responding to our criticisms with arguments?

What does the López Obrador movement get out of saying again and again that they are the only ones fighting in this country, that they are the only ones opposed to Calderón, that they have "the best writers and artists" on their side and that no other organization can say the same? What do they get out of that arrogance in the face of humble people and people from below?

What does the López Obrador movement get out of not seeing us or hearing us, and not seeing or hearing the dead that they are responsible for?

They may say that is not AMLO. It is. It has always been, and those who don't want to see it do not see it. And a leader must take responsibility for what they and their movement say and do. And the members of a movement too.

Just as the indigenous Zapatistas take responsibility for being indigenous and for being Zapatistas—and, for having taken responsibility for this, they are evicted, harassed, and attacked.

Several months ago an international caravan came to our lands to show its support for Zapatista communities faced with military incursions. As I remember, people came from Greece, Italy, France, and Spain, as well as other countries of the world. What caught our attention is that not a single Basque person came. Probably, we thought, they did not write their names down or the list did not include them. Lieutenant Colonel Moisés, who was in charge of the Intergalactic Commission, went to see, and Basques had in fact come but said, in more or less these words, "that they had written their names down along with the Spanish to not cause problems." We told them that we had not fought with half the world to make public our recognition of the Basques' right to independence just to go and put them along with the Spanish "to not cause problems." That we had fought with half the world to be able to say: ¡Gora Euskara! ¡Gora Euskal Herria!

If we took responsibility for our uprising, if we took responsibility for our word, if for it we challenged the strength of the government and its armies and police, if we took responsibility for our dead, I cannot see why we would not take responsibility for our rage.

Compañeras and compañeros:

Early this morning with a small group and this afternoon with the entire delegation, we gathered the compañeras and compañeros to decide what the principal message of this presentation should be.

We have heard many good words during these days here in San Cristóbal and before in Mexico City. Of course, we also heard some nonsense.

Almost all have been about the global and national crisis, and the ominous times that are ahead. There have been sincere worries. But there has also been joy. As if each person, individually and collectively, knew that they have something with which to act in the face of those fears and horrors. As if we had not stopped being afraid and ashamed, but those feelings were different. As if we took that fear and that shame and controlled it, gave it a path, destination. As if we could in fact do what Mariana, Italia, and Norma told us about. As if we knew that what's going to happen is going to happen.

Some of those who have spoken in this festival, in their positions or in their presentations, have shown concern for who, or how, or what is going to lead that movement. They venture structures, ways, forms, for that great movement that certainly is to rise up even against the darkest and most perverse of things. As the Palestinian people certainly shall rise up against the crime that is being committed today in their land and against their people.

As the Zapatistas that we are, of course we tell them that we are very pleased that the questions and concerns that keep them restless and exposed are no longer, "Can something be done?" "Is something going to happen?"

You and we have seen and felt that accumulated rage.

But we are not worried about who, or how, or what is going to direct that rage. Nor about what step, speed, rhythm, or company. We are not worried about the dream's speed.

We have learned to trust people, the people, our people. We know that you no longer need anyone to lead you, that you are equipped with your own structures to fight and to win. That you take your own destinies into your hands and that you do it better than governments that impose themselves from outside.

No, we are not worried about the movement's leadership. Listening now to compañero Carlos González of the Indigenous National Congress, we see that we have the same concern.

We are worried about the path and the destination. We are worried about what defines us, the way. We are worried that the world our rage is going to give birth to may be like the one we suffer from today.

Allow us to tell you: the EZLN had the temptation of hegemony and homogeneity. Not only after the uprising, but also before. There was the temptation to impose ways and identities. That Zapatismo was the only truth. And the communities were the ones who stopped this first, and then taught us that it's not like that, that isn't the way. That we could not substitute one dominion with another and that we must convince and not defeat those who were and are like us but are not us. They taught us that there are many worlds and that mutual respect is possible and necessary.

And we are not talking about the respect that is demanded of us for those who attack us, but for those who have other ways but the same determination for freedom, for justice, for democracy.

And so what we want to tell you is that this plurality, so similar in rage and so different in feeling, is the path and the destination that we want and propose to you.

Because some may make declarations against the parties and organizations that—they say—want to hegemonize and homogenize the Other Campaign, and when what they do is criticized or disagreed with, they then start with shouts and condemnations.

We are not all Zapatistas (something that we sometimes celebrate). Nor are we all communists, socialists, anarchists, punks, skaters, goths, or whatever each person calls their difference.

There must be a word for what we want to tell you. And it has occurred to us that the word that compañero Jean Robert used yesterday may work: "proportionality."

With the Sixth Declaration, we Zapatistas did not propose to organize and lead all of Mexico, much less the entire world. In it we said: here we are, this is what we are, this is what we want, and this is how we think we need to do it. And in it we recognize our limits, our possibilities, our proportionality.

In the Sixth Declaration, we do not tell all the Indian peoples to join the EZLN, nor do we say that we are going to lead workers, students, peasants, young people, women, others. We say that everyone has their space, their history, their struggle, their dream, their proportionality. And we say, then, let's make a deal to fight together for everything and for each person and each thing. By making a deal among our respective proportionalities and the country that results, the world that is achieved will be made up of the dreams of each and every dispossessed person.

May that world be so mottled that there is no room for the nightmares experienced by any one of us from below.

We are worried that in this world born from so much struggle and so much rage, women will continue to be seen with the same variants of contempt that patriarchal society has imposed; that different sexual preferences will continue to be seen as strange or diseased; that it will continue to be assumed that youth must be domesticated, forced to "mature"; that we indigenous will continue to be despised and humiliated or, in the best-case scenario, confronted as noble savages that must be civilized.

Well, we are worried about this world being a clone of the current world, or a GMO or a photocopy of the world that horrifies us today and that we repudiate. We are worried, in other words, about that world not having democracy, or justice, or freedom.

So we want to tell you, ask you, let us not turn our strength into a weakness. Being so many and so different will allow us to survive the catastrophe that is ahead, and will allow us to build something new. We want to tell you, ask you: may what is new also be different.

This is the message we wanted to give you. This is our word.

Thank you very much to everyone who spoke to us and listened to us and, as such, gave us the disease and got the disease of dignified rage.

Freedom and justice for Atenco! Freedom, justice, and appearance for political prisoners and disappeared persons!

For the men, women, children, and elderly of the Zapatista Army of National Liberation.

Insurgent Subcommander Marcos.
Mexico, January 5, 2009

P.S. Seven Stories for Nobody

Story 7: Old Antonio Tells . . .

One cold, frosty, and silent predawn morning finds us awake, like fifteen years ago. And like twenty-five years ago, Old Antonio draws a little light between the shadows that we are by lighting his cigarette made with a roller. We are silent. Nobody says anything. Wait. Old Antonio then summons the warmth of the word, which relieves, which comforts, which gives hope.

"The oldest of our old, our earliest knowers, used to say that the very first gods, those who birthed the world, it looked like they had made it without any order. That they had just gone around throwing pieces made wherever. That the world created was not one, but there were many and each one very different. In other words, as you say, there were many geographies. And our oldest knowers tell that then the times—which are the past, the present, and the future—met and went to the gods to protest. 'It just can't be done like this. I mean, we can't do our work with this shit show of worlds that there are. It wants that there is going to be just one, so that the times can walk our step on just one path.' That is what those times said. So the gods heard what the past, the present, and the future said and told them: 'Okeydokey, we'll see to it, then.' So the first gods, those who birthed the world, met and who knows what they talked about, but they sure did take a long time. And more later the first gods called the times and told them this: 'We were thinking about your words that you took out and we want to tell you that your thought is not right.' The times began to grumble, 'Mother 'ucker, we get screwed over because we're not gods, yada-yada.' The gods told them to wait, that they still had not finished saying their word. 'Okeydokey,' said the times and waited for what was next. So the very first gods explained that the time would come when the Boss was going to want to dominate the entire world and enslave everything the world had, that he was going to destroy and kill. That the Boss's strength was very great and there would be no equal force in the world. That the only way to resist and fight against the Boss was being many and different, so the Boss does not catch on to the way of just one and defeat everyone. That the gods understood it was real crappy for the times to make themselves many and different to do their work in each world that the world had, but what can you do, that's the way it was. And they told them that there was not going to be matching time for all the worlds there were in the world, but that there were going to be many times. In other words, as you say, many calendars. And the very first gods told the times: there is going to be in each of those many worlds that make up the world, some who know how to read the map and the calendars. And the time will come when the past, the present, and the future are going to get together and then all of the worlds are going to defeat the Boss. That's what the very first gods said. And the times, just to be butts because they already knew the answer, asked if when the Boss was defeated, are the worlds going to join into just one. And the very first gods told them that that is going to be decided by the men and women of those times, that there they are going to see if being different makes them weaker or makes them stronger for resisting and defeating the Bosses that are going to keep coming."

Old Antonio left. It stayed cold, but a little light remained, as if for the shade to not be alone.

The end.

Thank you very much compañeros and compañeras and compañeroas.

Insurgent Subcommander Marcos
Mexico, January 5, 2009

On Plantings and Harvests: Subcommander Marcos's Presentation in the January 4, 2009 Morning Session

Good afternoon.

Don Luis Villoro is with us today. If I may, compañero Luis Villoro.

His closeness to Indian peoples of this country is not post–1994, but precedes it by numerous calendars.

In our case, the Zapatistas', his support has been vital. I will say it plainly: more than one compañero, compañera in the indigenous communities is alive and fighting thanks to this man's support. And he has never, never even so much as insinuated that he expected something in return for his support, something that others have done.

In him we have found a generous ear, and ever since we went public, he has tried to understand us, and more than a few times his thoughts have been the fuel for our step. And you do not know how difficult it has been, in these fifteen years, to find someone who tries to understand us and not judge us.

With him, as with others, we have had and continue to have differences, and more than a few times our discussions have been bitter, like the one about the student movement that—ten years ago at UNAM[1]—amazed and taught us Zapatistas.

---

1   National Autonomous University of Mexico (Universidad Nacional Autónoma de México).

With all these differences, there has never been a single doubt in our heart about his convictions and commitments to our side, below and to the left.

Classifying those who think differently from us as "right-wing"—as a clumsy and dastardly banner declared yesterday—is a manifestation of an impositional trend created, paradoxically, by those who claim to have an anarchist ideology. I may not know much, but from what I gather, anarchism is not exempt from understanding. And you must understand before judging and condemning.

It is an honor, Don Luis, to have you at our side today, as it has been for the past fifteen years.

The world that we dream of is not one with unanimity of thought—even if it is ours, Zapatista thought—nor with the imposed hegemony that comes with it.

Cheers, Don Luis, we only wanted to tell you that, for many calendars, you have had a place in the brown-skinned heart that enlivens us.

After Lieutenant Colonel Moisés's presentation, I am supposed to read you a story. That will come later, now we have to say something different. Here goes:

On Plantings and Harvests

Maybe what I am going to say is off-topic given this table's focus, or maybe it isn't.

Two days ago, the same day on which our word made reference to violence, the ineffable Condoleezza Rice—a US government official—declared that what was happening in Gaza was the Palestinians' fault, due to their violent nature.

The underground rivers that run through the world may change geographies, but they sing the same song.

And the song we hear now is one of war and sorrow.

Not very far from here, in a place called Gaza, in Palestine, in the Middle East, right next to us, a heavily armed and trained army, the Israeli government's army, continues its advance of death and destruction.

The steps it has followed so far are those characteristic of a classic military war of conquest: first an intense and massive bombardment to destroy "neuralgic" military points (that's what military manuals call them) and "soften" resistance fortifications; then an iron grip on information: everything that is heard and seen "in the outside world"—that is, outside the theater of operations—must be selected with military criteria; next, intense artillery fire on enemy infantry to protect the troops' advance to new positions; then comes encirclement and siege to weaken the enemy garrison; then the assault that conquers the enemy's annihilated position; then "mopping up" probable "resistance nests."

The military manual of modern war, with some variations and additions, is being followed step-by-step by invading military forces.

We do not know much about this, and certainly there are specialists on the so-called Middle East conflict, but from this corner we have something to say:

According to the news agencies' photos, the "neuralgic" points destroyed by the Israeli government's aircraft are houses, shacks, civilian buildings. We have not seen a single bunker or military airport or gun battery among the destruction. So we, pardon our ignorance, think that the planes' gunners have bad aim or there are no such "neuralgic" military points in Gaza.

We have not had the honor of going to Palestine, but we suppose that people live or lived in those houses, shacks, and buildings: men, women, children, and elders, not soldiers.

Nor have we seen resistance fortifications, just rubble.

We have seen thus far the information blockade's vain attempt and various governments of the world vacillating between burying their heads in the sand and applauding the invasion, and a UN—useless for some time now—issuing tepid press releases.

But wait. Now it has occurred to us that for the Israeli government, maybe those men, women, children, and elderly are enemy soldiers and, as such, the shacks, houses, and buildings where they live are bunkers that must be destroyed.

So surely the artillery fire that fell on Gaza early this morning was to protect the Israeli Army infantry's advance from those men, women, children, and elderly.

And the enemy garrison that they want to weaken with the encirclement and siege taking place around Gaza is none other than the Palestinian population that lives there. And the assault will seek to annihilate that population. And any man, woman, child, or elderly person who manages to hide and escape from the predictably bloody assault will then be "hunted" to finish the mop-up, and the military commander in charge of the operation may report to his superiors, "we have completed the mission."

Pardon our ignorance again, maybe what we are saying is beside the point. And instead of repudiating or condemning the crime in progress, as the indigenous people and as the warriors that we are, we should be discussing and taking a position on "Zionism" or "anti-Semitism," or that in the beginning it was Hamas's bombs.

Maybe our thought is very simple and we lack the nuances and notes so eternally necessary in analyses, but for us Zapatistas, in Gaza there is a professional army murdering a defenseless population.

Who below and to the left can remain silent?

Does saying something work? Do our cries stop any bombs? Our word, does it save any Palestinian child's life?

We think that it does work, that perhaps we won't stop a bomb nor will our word turn into an armored shield stopping that 5.56 mm or 9 mm bullet—with the letters "IMI," "Israeli Military Industry," written on the bottom of the cartridge—from reaching the chest of a girl or boy, but perhaps our word will join other words in Mexico and the world and perhaps first turn into a murmur, then into a loud voice, and finally into a scream that is heard in Gaza.

We don't know about you, but we Zapatistas of the EZLN know how important it is to hear a few words of encouragement amid destruction and death.

I don't know how to explain it, but it turns out that words from far away may not be able to stop a bomb, but they are as if a crack opened in death's black room and a light filtered in.

As for the rest, what is going to happen will happen. The Israeli government will declare that it dealt a severe blow to terrorism, it will hide the scale of the massacre from its people, the great arms producers will have obtained an economic breath of fresh air to confront the crisis, and "global public opinion"—that malleable and eternally bought-and-paid-for entity—will turn to look the other way.

But not just that. Another thing that will happen is the Palestinian people are going to resist and survive and keep fighting, and continue having the sympathy of below for their cause.

And, maybe, a boy or a girl from Gaza will survive too. Maybe they will grow, and with them anger, indignation, and rage will grow. Maybe they will become soldiers or militants in one of the groups that fight in Palestine. Maybe they will confront Israel in combat. Maybe they will do it by firing a rifle. Maybe by immolating themselves with a belt of dynamite sticks around their waists.

And then, up above, people will write about Palestinians' violent nature and will make declarations condemning that violence and go back to discussing Zionism or anti-Semitism.

On Plantings and Harvests:

And then nobody will ask who planted what is being harvested.

For the men, women, children, and elderly of the Zapatista Army of National Liberation.

Insurgent Subcommander Marcos
Mexico, January 4, 2009

4.

Between Light and Shade

May 25, 2014

Ceremony for Compañero Galeano

Caracol I: La Realidad

San Pedro Michoacán Autonomous Municipality (Las Margaritas Municipality), Chiapas, Mexico

Between Light and Shade[1]

La Realidad, Planet Earth.
May 2014.

Compañera, compañeroa, compañero:

Good evening, afternoon, morning in whichever your geography, your time, and your way may be.

Good predawn.

I would like to ask the compañeras, compañeros, and compañeroas of the Sixth Declaration who come from other places, especially the free media compañeros,[2] to have patience, tolerance, and comprehension for what I am going to say, because these will be my last words in public before ceasing to exist.

I address you and those who listen to and watch us through you.

Maybe at the beginning of or during these words there will be a sensation growing in your heart that something is out of place, that something does not add up, as if you were missing one or several pieces that would give meaning to the puzzle being shown to you. As if what's missing is in fact missing.

Maybe later, days, weeks, months, years, decades later, what we are saying now will be understood.

I am not worried about my compañeras and compañeros at all levels of the EZLN, because that is just our way here: walking, fighting, always knowing that what needs to be done still needs to be done.

---

1   Another possible translation for the title is "Between Light and Shadow."
2   "Free media" is a term that the Zapatistas use to distinguish nonprofit (usually volunteer-based) media organizations from commercial media organizations, which they call the "paid media."

In addition to the fact that, no offense to anyone, the intelligence of Zapatista compas is well above average.

As for the rest, we are satisfied and proud that this collective decision is being made public before compañeras, compañeros, and compañeroas, both of the EZLN and the Sixth Declaration.

And how good indeed that this archipelago of pains, rages, and dignified struggle that calls ourselves "the Sixth Declaration" will be made aware of what I will tell you through the free, alternative, independent media, wherever they may be.

If anyone else is interested in knowing what happened on this day, they will have to go to the free media to find out.

All right then. Welcome to Zapatista reality.[3]

I. A Difficult Decision

When we irrupted and interrupted in 1994 with blood and fire, it was not the beginning of the war for us Zapatistas.

We had been suffering the war from above for centuries, with death and destruction, dispossession and humiliation, exploitation and silence imposed upon the conquered.

What began for us in 1994 is one of the many moments of war by those below against those above, against their world.

That war of resistance fought day by day in the streets everywhere on all five continents, in its fields and in its mountains.

Like many from below, ours was and is a war for humanity and against neoliberalism.

Against death, we demand life.

Against silence, we demand word and respect.

Against oblivion, memory.

Against humiliation and contempt, dignity.

Against oppression, rebellion.

Against slavery, freedom.

Against imposition, democracy.

Against crime, justice.

Who with a little humanity in their veins could or can question these demands?

And back then many listened.

---

3   In Spanish this is a pun because they are in a place called "La Realidad," which translates as "Reality." So this sentence could refer to their specific location or to "reality."

The war that we began gave us the privilege of reaching attentive and generous ears and hearts in geographies near and far.

What was needed was needed, and what's needed is needed, but we then obtained the other's gaze, ear, heart.

So we found ourselves with the need to answer a decisive question: "What's next?"

In the grim calculations on the eve of war, the possibility of asking ourselves any questions had been nonexistent. So that question took us to others:

Prepare those who are next on the road of death?

Train more and better soldiers?

Invest our efforts in improving our battered machinery of war?

Simulate dialogues and willingness for peace, but continue preparing new strikes?

Kill or be killed as our only fate?

Or did we have to rebuild the path of life, the path that had been broken and continues to be broken from above?

The path not only belonging to native peoples, but also to workers, students, teachers, young people, peasants, as well as all differences that are celebrated above and pursued and punished below.

Did we have to engrave our blood on the path that others direct toward Power? Or did we have to turn our hearts and our gaze toward ourselves and toward those who are what we are: native peoples, guardians of the earth and memory?

Nobody listened to it then, but in our first babblings that were our words, we warned that our dilemma was not between negotiation and fighting, but between life and death.

Those who would have warned then that this early dilemma was not an individual one perhaps would have understood better what has happened in Zapatista reality these past twenty years.

But I was telling you we had run into that question and that dilemma. And we chose.

And instead of devoting ourselves to training guerrilla warriors, soldiers, and squadrons, we trained health and education promoters, and the foundations were laid for the autonomy that amazes the world today.

Instead of building barracks, improving our weaponry, erecting walls and trenches, we built schools, hospitals, and health centers; we improved our living conditions.

Instead of fighting to have a place in the Parthenon of individualized deaths below, we chose to build life.

All this in the middle of a war whose quietness did not make it less lethal.

Because, compas, it is one thing to shout "you are not alone"[4] and another to confront an armor-clad column of federal troops with nothing more than one's body—as happened in the Chiapas Highlands Zone—and to see if you're lucky and someone finds out, and to see if you're even more lucky and those who find out are enraged, and even more lucky and those who are enraged do something.

In the meantime, the tanks are stopped by Zapatista women, and, lacking any ammunition, insults and rocks were what forced the steel serpent to retreat.

And in the Northern Chiapas Zone, suffering the founding and evolution of white guards, recycled then as paramilitaries; and in the Tzotz-Choj Zone, continuous attacks from peasant organizations that sometimes aren't even called "independent"; and in the Tzeltal Jungle Zone, the combination of paramilitaries and contras.

And it is one thing to shout "we are all Marcos" or "we are not all Marcos," as applicable, and another to be persecuted with all the machinery of war, the invasion of villages, the "combing" of mountains, the use of trained dogs, the blades of artillery helicopters whipping the tips of ceiba trees, the "dead or alive" that emerged in the first days of January 1994 and reached its most hysterical level in 1995[5] during the presidency of the man currently employed at a transnational corporation, and that this Border Jungle Zone has suffered since 1995 and was later compounded by the same sequence of attacks by peasant organizations, use of paramilitaries, militarization, harassment.

If there is any myth in all this, it is not the balaclava, but the lie that they have been repeating since those days and has even been taken up by people with advanced degrees: that the war against the Zapatistas only lasted twelve days.

I will not provide a detailed account. Someone with a bit of critical spirit and seriousness can reconstruct the story, and add and subtract to get the numbers, and say if there were and are more reporters than police and soldiers, if there were more flattering statements than threats and insults, if the reward offered was to see the balaclava or to capture him "dead or alive."

Under these conditions, sometimes only with our effort and other times with generous and unconditional support from good people all over

---

4   A common chant at political events: "No están solos."
5   When President Zedillo sent the federal army to capture Marcos and the Zapatista leadership, "dead or alive." See above, p. 95, n. 2.

the world, progress was made with building what we are; true, it is still incomplete, but it is already well-defined.

So then, "here we are, the dead of always, dying anew, but now to live" is not a fortunate or unfortunate phrase (depending on whether it is seen from above or from below). It is reality.

And almost twenty years later . . .

On December 21, 2012, when politics and esotericism—as on other occasions—agreed to predict disasters that, as always, are for those below, we repeated the surprise blow from January 1, 1994, and without firing a single shot, without weapons, with our silence alone, we again overwhelmed the arrogance of the cities, cradle and nest of racism and contempt.[6]

If on January 1, 1994, thousands of faceless men and women attacked and overcame the garrisons that protected the cities, then on December 21, 2012, without a word, tens of thousands took the buildings where our disappearance was celebrated.

The simple unquestionable fact that not only had the EZLN not become weaker, much less disappeared, but had instead grown quantitatively and qualitatively, would have been enough for any moderately intelligent mind to realize that, in these twenty years, something had changed inside the EZLN and the communities.

Perhaps more than a few people think that our choice was mistaken, that an army cannot and should not insist on peace.

For many reasons, true, but the main one was and is because, in doing so, we would end up disappearing.

Maybe it's true. Maybe we were mistaken when we chose to cultivate life instead of worshipping death.

But we chose without listening to those from outside, those who always demand and call for a fight to the death, as long as others provide the dead.

No. We chose looking at and listening to ourselves, being the collective Votán[7] that we are.

We chose rebellion—that is, life.

This does not mean that we did not know the war from above would try and does try to impose its domination over us once again.

We knew and know that we shall defend what we are and how we are, again and again.

We knew and know that there will continue to be death for there to be life.

---

6   On December 21, 2012, a new cycle began on the Mayan calendar; many falsely billed this event as the Mayan "end of the world." To commemorate this new cycle, thousands of Zapatistas marched silently through San Cristóbal de las Casas, and Marcos released the communique that is quoted immediately after this book's title page.

7   In Zapatista territory, *Votán* is used to refer to a collective guardian and heart.

We knew and know that in order to live, we die.

II. A Failure?

There are people out there who say that we have not achieved anything for ourselves.

It never ceases to be surprising that this opinion is expressed with such impudence.

These people think that the commanders' sons and daughters ought to enjoy international vacations, private educations, and then high-level positions in the company or in politics. That instead of working the land to pull up food with sweat and determination, they ought to shine on social networks, enjoying themselves in clubs, displaying their riches.

Maybe the subcommanders ought to procreate and pass on the positions, the perks, the stages to their descendants, like politicians do across the spectrum.

Maybe, like the leaders of the CIOAC-H and other peasant organizations, we ought to receive privileges and payment as projects and aid in exchange for carrying out the criminal orders that come from higher up, keep the bulk of it, and leave our bases with just a few crumbs.

But, it's true, we have not achieved any of this for ourselves.

Difficult to believe that, twenty years after that "nothing for us,"[8] it turned out not to be a catchphrase, something nice for posters and songs, but a reality, the reality.

If being consistent is a failure, then inconsistency is the path of success, the route to Power.

But we do not want to go that way.

We are not interested.

Within those parameters, we prefer failure over triumph.

III. The Hand-Off

In these twenty years, there has been a multiple and complex hand-off in the EZLN.

Some have only commented on the obvious one: the generational hand-off.

Now, those who were little or had not yet been born at the beginning

---

8   A saying used in Zapatista territory is "For everyone, everything. Nothing for us."

of the uprising are making the struggle and leading the resistance.

But some scholars have not noticed other hand-offs:

The class hand-off: from enlightened middle-class origins to indigenous peasants.

The race hand-off: from mestizo leadership to purely indigenous leadership.

And the most important one, the thought hand-off: from revolutionary vanguardism to command by obeying, from taking the Power of Above to creating the power of below, from professional politics to everyday politics, from leaders to peoples, from the marginalization of gender to the direct participation of women, from mocking the other to celebrating difference.

I will not elaborate on this, because the course "Freedom according to the Zapatistas"[9] has been precisely what provides the opportunity to determine if celebrity is worth more than community in organized territory.

Personally, I do not understand why thinking individuals who claim that history is made by peoples are so frightened by the existence of a government of the people where there are no "specialists" in governing.

Why are they so terrified by the fact that the peoples are those who command, those who direct their own steps?

Why do they shake their heads with disapproval at command by obeying?

The cult of individualism finds its most fanatical extreme in the cult of vanguardism.

And this—the fact that the indigenous command and that now an indigenous person is the spokesperson and leader—is exactly what has scared them, alienated them, and finally they need to keep looking for someone who needs vanguards, strongmen, and leaders. Because there is also racism within the Left, above all within that which aims to be revolutionary.

The ee-zee-el-en is not like that. That's why not just anyone can be a Zapatista.

IV. A Changing and Deceptive Hologram: What Shall Not Be

Before the sun rose on 1994, I spent ten years in these mountains. I personally knew and interacted with some in whose death we die a lot. Since then, I know and interact with others who are here today like us.

---

9   In August 2013, December 2013, and January 2014, the Zapatistas invited thousands of people to come to Zapatista communities and learn from them in the "Escuelita on Freedom according to the Zapatistas"; "escuelita" is an endearing way of saying "school."

Many predawn mornings I found myself trying to digest the stories they told me, the worlds they drew with silences, hands, and gazes, their insistence on pointing out something further away.

Was that world—so other, so distant, so foreign—a dream?

Sometimes I thought that they had gotten ahead, that the words that guided and guide us came from times for which there were still no calendars, lost as they were in indefinite geographies: the dignified south always omnipresent at all cardinal points.

Then I knew that they were not talking about an imprecise, and thus improbable, world.

That world was already walking with its step.

Didn't you see it? Don't you see it?

We have not deceived anyone from below. We do not hide the fact that we are an army, with its pyramidal structure, its command center, its top-down decisions. We do not deny who we are to curry favor with anarchists or in the name of style.

But anyone can now see if our army is one that supersedes or imposes.

And I must say this, since I have already requested authorization from compañero Insurgent Subcommander Moisés to do so:

Nothing that we have done, for better or for worse, would have been possible if an army, the Zapatista Army of National Liberation, had not risen up against the evil government, exercising the right to legitimate violence. The violence of those below against the violence of those above.

We are warriors, and as such we know what our role and our moment is.

In the predawn hours of the first day of the first month of the year 1994, an army of giants—that is, indigenous rebels—went down to the cities to shake up the world with their step.

Just a few days later, with the blood of our fallen still fresh in the city streets, we realized that those outside did not see us.

Used to looking at the indigenous from above, they did not look up to see us.

Used to seeing us humiliated, their heart did not understand our dignified rebellion.

Their gaze had stopped on the only mestizo that they saw with a balaclava; in other words, they did not look.

Our bosses then said:

"They only see how small they are, let's make someone as small as them, they'll see him and see us through him."

And so began a complex diversionary maneuver, a terrifying and wonderful magic trick, a mischievous move by the indigenous heart that we are; indigenous wisdom challenged modernity in one of its strongholds: the media.

And then the character named "Marcos" started to be constructed.

I ask you to follow me in this reasoning:

Let's suppose that there is another way to neutralize a criminal. For example, creating their murder weapon, making them believe it is effective, admonishing them to build their entire plan on this effectiveness, so that, when ready to be fired, the "weapon" goes back to being what it always was: an illusion.

The entire system, but above all its media, plays the game of constructing reputations to then destroy them if they do not fit its designs.

Its power lay (but no longer does, as it has been displaced by social networks in this regard) in deciding what and who existed when it chose what to say and what to silence.

Anyway, don't pay much attention to me. As has been demonstrated in the last twenty years, I don't know anything about the mass media.

The point is that Marcos went from being a spokesperson to being a distractor.

If the path of war—that is, of death—had taken ten years, the path of life took longer and required more effort, not to mention blood.

Because, believe it or not, it is easier to die than to live.

We needed time to be what we are and to find those who knew how to see us for what we are.

We needed time to find those who saw us not looking up, not looking down, but looking straight at us, looking at us with a compañero gaze.

I was telling you that the character started to be constructed.

One day Marcos had blue eyes, another day they were green, or brown, or yellow, or black, everything depending on who did the interview and took the photo. So he was a benchwarmer on professional soccer teams, a department-store employee, a driver, philosopher, filmmaker, and the etceteras that you can find in the paid media during those calendars and in different geographies. There was a Marcos for every occasion, for every interview. And it wasn't easy, believe me; back then there was no Wikipedia and if someone came from Spain, they had to research, for example, if El Corte Inglés[10] was a typical English suit cut, a convenience store, or a department store.

If you'll allow me to define Marcos the character, I would say without hesitation that he was a costume.[11]

---

10   A Spanish department store chain; its name literally translates as "The English Cut."
11   *Botarga*: a full-body costume used for fictional characters, brand symbols, and mascots. Marcos is likely referring to costumes like "Pollo Feliz" and "Dr. Simi," worn by people who dance around outside of their respective chain's stores as a form of brand promotion.

Let's say that, so you can understand me, Marcos was a Not-Free Media Outlet (note: this is not the same as being a paid media outlet).

When building and maintaining the character, we made a few mistakes. "To heir is human," said the heir.[12]

In the first year we depleted, as they say, the repertoire of possible "Marcoses." So in early 1995, we were in trouble and the communities' process was in its early stages.

So in 1995 we didn't know what to do anymore. But that was when Zedillo, hand in hand with the PAN, "discovered" Marcos with the same scientific method used to find skeletons: an esoteric informer.

The story of the man from Tampico allowed us to take a deep breath, although Paca de Lozano's subsequent fraud made us fear that the paid press would also question Marcos's "unmasking" and discover that he was just another fraud. Fortunately, this did not happen. As with that one, the media continued to swallow other similar millwheels.[13]

Sometime later the man from Tampico came to these parts. Subcommander Moisés and I spoke with him. We then offered to hold a joint press conference, that way he could free himself from persecution since it would be obvious that he and Marcos were not the same person. He did not want to. He came to live here. He left a few times, and his face can be found in the photographs from his parents' funerals. If you want, you can interview him. Now he lives in a community, in . . .[14] Ah, he doesn't want you to know exactly where he lives. We won't say anything else so that, if he wants to one day, he can tell the story of what he has experienced since February 9, 1995.[15] We only wish to thank him for having given us information that we use every so often to fuel the "certainty" that Marcos is not what he really is—that is, a costume or a hologram—but a university professor, native of the now-painful Tamaulipas.

In the meantime we kept looking, looking for you, those who are here now and those who are not here but are here.

We launched one initiative after another to find the other. Different initiatives, trying to find the look and the ear that we need and deserve.

In the meantime, the communities continued to advance, along with

---

See "Simi bailando el nene malo," posted by Emma Lopez Romero, September 17, 2014, http://youtu.be/zPNwH3uxePI.

12 The Spanish text uses a similar pun involving a blacksmith: "'Es de humanos el herrar,' dijo el herrero."

13 See above, p. 48, n. 15.

14 Here Marcos whispers to Subcommander Moisés, who is sitting next to him on the stage. Moisés responds by shaking his head no.

15 The date on which President Zedillo announced that Marcos was Rafael Sebastián Guillén Vicente, a former university professor born in the Mexican city of Tampico, Tamaulipas.

the hand-off that has been talked about a little or a lot, but which can be verified directly, without intermediaries.

In the search for the other, we failed again and again.

Those who we found wanted to lead us or wanted us to lead them.

There were those who reached out and did so in an attempt to use us, or to look back, whether with anthropological nostalgia or with activist nostalgia.

So for some we were communists, for others Trotskyists, for others anarchists, for others Maoists, for others millenarianists, and there you have several "ists" to which you may add others you've heard of.

That's the way it was until the Sixth Declaration of the Lacandon Jungle, the boldest and most Zapatista initiative we have launched so far.

With the Sixth Declaration we have finally found those who look straight at us and who greet and embrace us, and so are greeted and embraced.

With the Sixth Declaration we finally found you.

At last, someone who understood that we were not looking for shepherds to guide us nor herds to lead to the Promised Land. Neither masters nor slaves. Neither strongmen nor headless masses.

But it remained to be seen if it was possible for you to watch and listen to what we are by being.

Inside, the communities' progress has been impressive.

So then came the course, "Freedom according to the Zapatistas."

In three rounds, we realized that there was already a generation that could look straight at us, that could listen to us and talk to us without waiting for guidance or leadership, and without seeking submission or followership.

Marcos, the character, was no longer necessary.

The new era of Zapatista struggle was ready.

So what happened happened, and many of you, compañeras and compañeros of the Sixth Declaration, know this firsthand.

You may say later that the character was futile. But an honest review of these days will tell how many turned to look at us, with pleasure or displeasure, because of a costume's disfiguration.

So the change of command is not occurring because of illness or death, nor because of internal shifts, purges, or cleansing.

It is occurring logically according to internal changes that the EZLN has experienced before and now.

I know that this does not add up in the square diagrams that exist in the various aboves, but honestly we couldn't care less about that.

And if this ruins the sluggish and poor preparation done by Jovel's[16] rumorologists and Zapatologists, oh well.

I am not nor have I been sick; I am not nor have I been dead.[17]

Or yeah, even though I was killed so many times, died so many times, here I am again.

If we fueled those rumors, it was because doing so was in our best interest.

The final great trick of the hologram was to simulate terminal illness, and even all the deaths they say I have suffered.

By the way, "if his health permits it"—which Subcommander Moisés used in the communique announcing the exchange with the CNI—was equivalent to "if the people ask for it" or "if the polls are in my favor" or "God willing" or other cliches that have been taglines in the political class in recent times.

If you'll allow me to give a piece of advice: you ought to cultivate your sense of humor a bit, not only for your mental and physical health, but also because you're not going to understand Zapatismo without a sense of humor. And those who do not understand, judge; and those who judge, condemn.

In reality, that has been the simplest part of the character. To feed the rumor, it was only necessary to tell a few specific people: "I'm going to tell you a secret but promise me that you're not going to tell anyone else."

Of course they told.

The main involuntary contributors for the disease and death rumor have been the "Zapatology experts" in arrogant Jovel and chaotic Mexico City who boast of their close ties to Zapatismo and their profound knowledge of it, in addition to, of course, the police officers who also get paid to be journalists, the journalists who get paid to be police officers, and the journalists who only get paid, poorly, to be journalists.

Thanks to all of them. Thanks for their discretion. They did exactly what we figured they were going to do. The only bad thing about all this is that now I doubt anyone will trust them with any secret.

It is our conviction and our practice that neither leaders nor strongmen nor messiahs nor saviors are necessary to rebel and fight. To fight, the only things necessary are a little shame, a bit of dignity, and a lot of organization.

---

16   San Cristóbal de las Casas. See above, p. 98, n. 4.

17   Prior to this event, members of the Zapatista leadership leaked a false rumor to those who disingenuously presented themselves as Zapatista insiders or "experts" on the Zapatistas (Marcos calls these people "Zapatologists"). They told them that Marcos was very sick, dying, or dead, hoping (correctly) that these people would spread this false rumor and destroy their own credibility.

The rest is either useful to the collective or isn't.

It has been particularly comical to see what the cult of the individual has caused in political scientists and analysts from above. Yesterday they said that the future of this Mexican people depended on an alliance between two people. The day before they said that Peña Nieto had become independent of Salinas de Gortari, without realizing that then, if they criticized Peña Nieto, they were on Salinas de Gortari's side; and if they criticized the latter, they were supporting Peña Nieto. Now they say that we must pick sides in the fight above for control over telecommunications, so you're with Slim or you're with Azcárraga-Salinas.[18] And further above, with Obama or with Putin.

Those who yearn and look upward can keep looking for their leader; they can keep thinking that now the electoral results are going to be respected, that now Slim is going to support the left-wing electoral option, that now dragons and battles are going to show up in *Game of Thrones*; that now Kirkman is going to be faithful to the comic in his TV series *The Walking Dead*, that now tools made in China aren't going to break the first time you use them, that now soccer is going to be a sport and not a business.

And sure, perhaps in some of these cases they'll get what they want, but it must not be forgotten that in all they are mere spectators, passive consumers.

Those who loved and hated Marcos now know that they have hated and loved a hologram. Their loves and hatreds have then been useless, sterile, empty, hollow.

So there will not be a museum-house or metal plaques where I was born and grew up. Nor will there be anyone who makes a living from having been Subcommander Marcos. Neither his name nor his position will be inherited. There will be no all-expenses-paid trips to give speeches abroad. There will be no transfers to or treatment in luxury hospitals. There will be no widows or heirs. There will be no funerals, nor honors, nor statues, nor museums, nor prizes, nor anything that the system does to promote the cult of the individual and undervalue the collective.

The character was created and now we its creators, the Zapatistas, destroy it.

If someone can understand this lesson that our compañeras and compañeros teach, they will have understood one of Zapatismo's fundamentals.

18　Carlos Slim is a Mexican telecommunications mogul, the Azcárraga family is a media dynasty, and Ricardo Salinas is founder and chairman of Grupo Salinas, a group of corporations with interests in, among other things, the television and telecommunications industries.

So in recent years what happened has happened.

So we saw that the costume, the character, the hologram, was no longer necessary.

Again and again we planned, again and again we waited for the right time: the exact calendar and geography to show what we truly are to those who truly are.

So Galeano came with his death to indicate the geography and the calendar: "Here, in La Realidad; now: in the pain and the rage."

V. Pain and Rage: Whispers and Screams

When we got to the caracol here in La Realidad, without anyone telling us to, we started to speak in whispers.

Our pain spoke quietly, our rage very quietly.

As if we were trying to prevent Galeano from being driven away by noises, sounds unfamiliar to him.

As if our voices and steps called him.

"Wait compa," our silence said.

"Don't go," the words whispered.

But there are other pains and other rages.

Right now, in other corners of Mexico and the world, a man, a woman, *an other*,[19] a boy, a girl, an elder, a memory, is relentlessly beaten, surrounded by the heinous crime that is the system, clubbed, macheted, shot, finished off, dragged among taunts, abandoned, their body recovered and cared for, their life buried.

Just a few names:

Alexis Benhumea, murdered in Mexico State.
Francisco Javier Cortés, murdered in Mexico State.
Juan Vázquez Guzmán, murdered in Chiapas.
Juan Carlos Gómez Silvano, murdered in Chiapas.
El compa Kuy, murdered in Mexico City.
Carlo Giuliani, murdered in Italy.
Aléxis Grigoropoulos, murdered in Greece.
Wajih Wajdi al-Ramahi, murdered in a refugee camp in the West Bank city of Ramallah. Fourteen years old, murdered with one shot in the back from an Israeli Army observation post. There were no marches, nor protests, nor anything in the street.

---

19   *Otroa*: someone who is neither male nor female.

Matías Valentín Catrileo Quezada, Mapuche murdered in Chile.

Teodulfo Torres Soriano, Sixth Declaration compañero, disappeared[20] in Mexico City.

Guadalupe Jerónimo and Urbano Macías, Cherán communal farmers, murdered in Michoacán.

Francisco de Asís Manuel, disappeared in Santa María Ostula.

Javier Martínes Robles, disappeared in Santa María Ostula.

Gerardo Vera Orcino, disappeared in Santa María Ostula.

Enrique Domínguez Macías, disappeared in Santa María Ostula.

Martín Santos Luna, disappeared in Santa María Ostula.

Pedro Leyva Domínguez, murdered in Santa María Ostula.

Diego Ramírez Domínguez, murdered in Santa María Ostula.

Trinidad de la Cruz Crisóstomo, murdered in Santa María Ostula.

Crisóforo Sánchez Reyes, murdered in Santa María Ostula.

Teódulo Santos Girón, disappeared in Santa María Ostula.

Longino Vicente Morales, disappeared in Guerrero.

Víctor Ayala Tapia, disappeared in Guerrero.

Jacinto López Díaz "El Jazi," murdered in Puebla.

Bernardo Vázquez Sánchez, murdered in Oaxaca.

Jorge Alexis Herrera, murdered in Guerrero.

Gabriel Echeverría, murdered in Guerrero.

Edmundo Reyes Amaya, disappeared in Oaxaca.

Gabriel Alberto Cruz Sánchez, disappeared in Oaxaca.

Juan Francisco Sicilia Ortega, murdered in Morelos.

Ernesto Méndez Salinas, murdered in Morelos.

Alejandro Chao Barona, murdered in Morelos.

Sara Robledo, murdered in Morelos.

Juventina Villa Mojica, murdered in Guerrero.

Reynaldo Santana Villa, murdered in Guerrero.

Catarino Torres Pereda, murdered in Oaxaca.

Bety Cariño, murdered in Oaxaca.

Jyri Jaakkola, murdered in Oaxaca.

Sandra Luz Hernández, murdered in Sinaloa.

Marisela Escobedo Ortíz, murdered in Chihuahua.

Celedonio Monroy Prudencio, disappeared in Jalisco.

Nepomuceno Moreno Nuñez, murdered in Sonora.

---

20 Forced disappearance is a common strategy used by repressive governments in Latin America. The victims are not arrested or assassinated but rather are captured and moved to undisclosed locations. Sometimes these people are later released, but more often than not they are secretly murdered or end up in the hands of human trafficking rings.

The forcibly disappeared, and likely murdered, migrants in any corner of Mexican territory.[21]

The prisoners they are trying to kill while still alive: Mumia Abu-Jamal, Leonard Peltier, the Mapuche, Mario González, Juan Carlos Flores.

The continuous burial of voices that were life, silenced by dirt falling and bars closing.

And the greatest mockery is that, with each shovelful of dirt cast by the henchman on duty, the system is saying: "You are worthless, you do not matter, nobody cries for you, nobody is enraged by your death, nobody follows in your footsteps, nobody holds up your life."

And with the last shovelful, it proclaims: "Even if you catch and punish the people who killed you, I will always find someone else, others to ambush you and repeat the macabre dance that ended your life."

And it says, "Your small, runt justice, manufactured for the paid media to simulate and obtain a bit of calm to halt the chaos coming down upon them, it does not scare me, does not hurt me, does not punish me."

What do we tell the cadaver that, in some corner of the world of below, is buried in oblivion?

That only our pain and rage count?

That only our anger matters?

That while we whisper our history, we do not hear its scream, its howl?

Injustice has so many names and causes so many screams.

But our pain and our rage do not stop us from listening.

And our whispers are not only to lament the fall of our unjustly dead.

They allow us to listen to other pains, make other rages ours, and continue on the complicated, long, and torturous path of making from all this a howl that turns into a liberatory struggle.

And to not forget that whenever someone whispers, someone screams.

And only an attentive ear can listen.

While we talk and listen now, someone screams with pain, with rage.

And just as one must learn to direct one's gaze, one's listen must find the course that makes it fertile.

Because whenever someone rests, there is someone who continues uphill.

To look at that endeavor, all you need is to lower your gaze and raise your heart.

Can you do that?

---

21   Many Central American migrants die or disappear while migrating through Mexico in an attempt to reach the United States, falling victim to violent drug cartels, gangs, and immigration authorities.

Will you be able?

Petty justice looks so much like revenge. Petty justice is justice that hands out impunity; by punishing one person, it absolves others.

The justice that we want, that we fight for, does not end with finding compañero Galeano's murderers and seeing that they receive their punishment (that will happen, make no mistake).

A patient and obstinate search looks for the truth, not the relief of resignation.

Great justice has to do with the buried compañero Galeano.

Because we ask ourselves not what to do with his death, but what we must do with his life.

Pardon me if I'm entering the swamplands of cliche, but that compañero did not deserve to die, not like that.

His whole endeavor, his daily, punctual, invisible sacrifice for those who were not us, was for life.

And I can certainly tell you that he was an extraordinary human being and that, this is the amazing part, there are thousands of compañeras and compañeros like him in the Zapatista indigenous communities, with the same determination, same commitment, same clarity, and a single destination: freedom.

And now that we're doing macabre calculations: if anyone deserves death, it is someone who does not exist and has never existed, except in the paid media's fleetingness.

And our compañero Subcommander Moisés, leader and spokesperson of the EZLN, has told us that by murdering Galeano, or any of the Zapatistas, those above wanted to murder the EZLN.

Not as an army, but as a pig-headed rebel that builds and erects life where they, those above, wish for the wasteland of the mining, oil, and tourism industries, the death of the land and of those who inhabit and work it.

And he has said that we have come, as the General Command of the Zapatista Army of National Liberation, to unbury Galeano.

We think that it is necessary for one of us to die so that Galeano may live.

And for that impertinent being that is death to be satisfied, in Galeano's place we provide another name so that Galeano may live and death may take not a life, but just a name, a few letters empty of all meaning, without their own history, lifeless.

So we have decided that today Marcos ceases to exist.

Shadow the Warrior and Little Light will hold his hand so that he doesn't get lost on the way; Don Durito will go with him, as will Old Antonio.

He will not be missed by the children who used to get together to listen to his stories, since they are grown up now, have their wits about them, fight more than anyone for freedom, democracy, and justice, which are the task of any Zapatista.

The cat-dog, instead of a swan, will now sound the farewell song.

And at last, those who understand will know that someone who never was here cannot leave, and someone who has never lived cannot die.

And death will leave, cheated by an indigenous man named *Galeano* in the struggle,[22] and on those stones that have been placed on his tomb he will again walk and teach those who met him about the basics of Zapatismo: not selling out, not giving up, not surrendering.

Oh death! As if it were not evident that it frees those above of all shared responsibility, aside from the funeral prayer, the gray homage, the sterile statue, the controlling museum.

And us? Well, death commits us because of the life that it has.

So here we are, mocking death in reality.

Compas:

All that having been said, at 02:08 hours on May 25, 2014, in the EZLN southeastern combat front, I declare that he who is known as Insurgent Subcommander Marcos, the self-styled "stainless-steel subcommander," ceases to exist.

That's the way it is.

Through my voice, the voice of the Zapatista Army of National Liberation shall no longer speak.

All right. Cheers and see you never.[23] Those who understood will know that it no longer matters, that it has never mattered.

From Zapatista reality.

Insurgent Subcommander Marcos
Mexico, May 24, 2014

P.S. 1: Game over?

P.S. 2: Checkmate?

P.S. 3: Touche?

P.S. 4: There you have it, folks, and send tobacco.

P.S. 5: Hmm . . . so this is hell . . . Piporro! Pedro! José Alfredo! How?

---

22 Galeano's birth name was José Luis Solís López, and he chose to adopt the name Galeano when he joined the Zapatista movement.

23 "Salud y hasta nunca . . . o hasta siempre." "Hasta siempre" literally means "until forever," but in this context means "farewell"; "hasta nunca" literally means "until never" and is similar to saying "see you never" instead of "see you later."

For being machistas? Nah, I don't believe it, if I never . . .

P.S. 6: So, as they say, without the costume, can I walk around naked now?

P.S. 7: Hey, it's real dark here, I need a little light.

(. . .)[24]

(A voice is heard offstage.)

Good predawn, compañeras and compañeros. My name is Galeano, Insurgent Subcommander Galeano.

Is anyone else named Galeano?

(Voices and shouts are heard: "My name is Galeano. We are all Galeano.")

Ah, so that's why they told me that when I was reborn, it would be collectively.

All right then.

Have a nice trip. Take care of yourselves; take care of us.

From the mountains of the Mexican Southeast.

Insurgent Subcommander Galeano
Mexico, May 2014

---

24   At this point, Marcos walks off the stage. Moisés says, "Compañeros, compañeras, we're
      going to hear another compañero speak."

5.

Appendix: Relevant Communiques

November 2013–May 2014

Originally Published in Spanish on the Zapatistas' Website

(enlacezapatista.ezln.org.mx)

Rewind 3

Which explains the why of this strange title and those that follow, which tells of the exceptional encounter between a beetle and a perplexing being (more perplexing than the beetle, I mean), and of the irrelevant and unimportant reflections that took place in it, as well as the way that Marcos—taking advantage of an anniversary—tries to explain, unsuccessfully, how the Zapatistas see their own history.

November 2013.

To whom it may concern:

WARNING. As was warned in the text that called itself "Bad and Not-so-Bad News," the texts that preceded the aforementioned text were not made public. Ergo, what we are going to do is "rewind," to get to what was supposed to come out on Day of the Dead. Following which, you may proceed to read in reverse order of the reverse order that they will be coming out in and then you will have . . . hmm . . . forget about it, now even I'm confused as heck. The point is to understand the spirit of, as they say, "hindsight"; in other words, one goes over there but comes back to see how it is that one got the idea to go over there. That makes sense? Right?

WARNING TO THE WARNING. The following texts do not contain any reference to current, relevant, transcendental, or important situations, etc., nor do they have political implications or references, nor any of that. They are "innocent" texts, as are all the writings by he who calls himself "the stainless-steel subcommander" (me, in other words). Any appearance or similarity to real-life people or events is mere schizophrenia . . . yes, like the international and national situation where one can see that . . . OK, OK, OK, no politics.

WARNING CUBED. In the very unlikely event that you feel alluded to by what is said below, you are flat-out wrong . . . or you are a shameless fan of ad hoc conspiracy theories (which may be translated as "for every flaw, there is a conspiracy theory to explain everything and repeat the mistakes").

Here goes:

෨෫

P.S. Durito's First Encounter with the Cat-Dog.

Durito was stern. But not with the false imposture of any-old official from any-old government. He was stern like when a great sorrow slaps us in the face and there is nothing to be done, besides curse . . . or tell a story.

Don Durito of the Lacandon Jungle lights his pipe, wandering and erroneous gentleman that he is, the bereaved's comfort, the children's joy, women's and others' impossible longing, unreachable mirror for men, tyrants' and strongmen's unrest, discomforting thesis for ignorant pedants.

Looking with enrapture at the light of our concerns, he tells almost whispering, so that I may write it down:

The Story of The Cat-Dog
(On how Durito met the cat-dog and what they said about fanaticism on that predawn morning)

At first glance, the cat-dog looks like a dog . . . well, more like a cat . . . or a dog . . . until he meows . . . or a cat . . . until he barks.

The cat-dog is an unknown for biologists and marine biologists (what classification table of living things do we put this case in?), an irresolvable case for psychology (neural surgery cannot uncover the cerebral center that defines *dogness* or *catness*), a mystery for anthropology (customs and traditions are similar and antithetical at the same time?), a despair for jurisprudence (what rights and responsibilities emanate from being and not being?), the Holy Grail of genetic engineering (impossible to privatize that elusive DNA). In sum: the missing link that would bring down all Darwinism in laboratories, seminars, symposiums, reiterated scientific fashion.

But let me tell you what happened:

As is law, it was predawn. A glimmer was enough to make a shadow. Silent, I walked only with the steps of memory. Then I clearly heard someone say:

"A fanatic is someone who hides a doubt with shame."

Not without first giving him credence within my innermost being, I moved closer and found him. Without so much as an introduction, I asked:

"Ah, so you are . . . a dog."

"Meow," he responded.

" . . . Or, a cat," I said doubting myself.

"Woof," he replied.

"Well, a cat-dog," I said and told myself.

"That's it," he said . . . or I think he said.

"And life, how is it?" I asked (and I wrote this down without doubting, able to not let myself be surprised by anything, since it was a beetle who was telling this remarkable story).

"At times worth it," he responded with a type of purr. "At times like cats and dogs," he growled.

"Is it an identity issue?" I asked, lighting my pipe and taking out my multitouch tablet-smartphone to write (it's really a spiral-bound notebook, but Durito likes to make himself out to be very modern. –Scribe's note).

"Nah, one does not choose who they are but does choose who they may be," the cat-dog barked disdainfully. "And life is nothing more than that complicated transit, completed or cut short, from one thing to another," he added with a meow.

"So, cat or dog?" I asked.

"Cat-dog," he said as if pointing out the obvious.

"And what brings you to these lands?"

"A her, what else."

"Ah."

"I am going to sing to her, because some cats know how."

"Err . . . before your serenade, which I do not doubt will be a splendid song for the femme who troubles you so, could you clarify what you said at the beginning of your participation in this story?"

"The thing about fanaticism?"

"Yes, it was something like there are people who hide their doubts of faith behind irrational worship."

"That's it."

"But, how to avoid settling in to one of the gloomy rooms in that grim house of mirrors that is fanaticism? How to resist the cries and blackmail to settle in and serve in religious fanaticism or lay fanaticism, currently the oldest but not the only one?"

"Simple," says the cat-dog laconically, "by not going in."

"Building many houses," he continues, "each person their own. Abandoning fear of difference.

"Because there's something equal to or worse than a religious fanatic, and that is an antireligious fanatic: lay fanaticism. And I say that it may be worse because the latter goes to reason as an excuse.

"And of course, its equivalents: for the homophobe and machista, phobia of heterosexuality and hembrism. And add the long etcetera of humanity's history.

"Fanatics of race, color, creed, gender, politics, sports, etc., in the end are fanatics of themselves. And everyone shares the same fear of what is different. And they pigeonhole the entire world in a closed box of exclusive options: 'If you are not this, then you are the opposite.'"

"Do you mean, my dear sir," Durito interrupts, "that people who criticize sports fanatics are the same?"

"It's the same. You have, for example, politics and sports, both paid: in each one, fanatics think that the professional is what counts; in both, they are mere spectators applauding or booing the rival, celebrating victories that are not theirs and lamenting defeats that do not belong to them; in both, they blame the players, the referee, the field, the opponent; in both, they hope that 'next time we'll win'; both think that if they change techniques, strategies, or tactics, then everything will be resolved; in both, they pursue the opposing fanatics; in both, the fact that the problem is in the system gets ignored."

"Are you talking about soccer?" asks Durito while he takes out a ball autographed by himself.

"Not only about soccer. With everything, the problem is who's in charge, the owner, the one who makes the rules.

"Both sectors despise anything that is unpaid: sandlot or street soccer, politics that does not come together in electoral seasons. 'If no money is being made, for what then?' they ask themselves."

"Ah, are you talking about politics?"

"Not a chance. Although, for example, with each day that goes by it is more evident that what people call 'the modern nation-state' is a pile of ruins for sale secondhand and that the respective political classes again and again endeavor to remake the peak of a demolished house of cards, without realizing that the cards at the bottom are completely broken and worn, unable to stay upright, much less hold something up."

"Hmm . . . it will be difficult to put that in a tweet," says Durito while he counts to see if it can be adjusted to 140 characters.

"The modern political class vies for who will be the pilot of a plane that crashed into neoliberal reality some time ago," pronounces the cat-dog, and Durito thanks him with a nod.

"So what is to be done?" asks Durito while he carefully puts away his Los Jaguares de Chiapas pennant.

"Avoid the trap that claims that freedom is the power to choose between two imposed options.

"All strict options are a trap. There are not only two paths, in the same way that there are not two colors, two sexes, two beliefs. So neither there, nor there. Better instead to make a new path that does go where one wants to go."

"Conclusion?" asks Durito.

"Neither dog, nor cat. Cat-dog, not at your service.

"And may no one judge or condemn what they do not understand, because difference is a sign that not everything is lost, that there is still much to see and hear, that there are other worlds yet to be discovered . . ."

The cat-dog left; as his name indicates, he has the disadvantages of a dog and of a cat . . . and none of their advantages, if there are any.
The sun was already rising when I heard a sublime mixture of meowing and barking. It was the cat-dog singing, off-key, to the light of our best dreams.

And some predawn morning, perhaps distant still in the calendar and in an uncertain geography, she—the light that keeps me restless and exposed—will understand that there were hidden lines made for her, perhaps only then will they be revealed to her or perhaps she recognizes them now in these letters, and she will know in that moment that it did not matter what paths my steps walked: because she was, is, and shall be, always, the only destination that is worth it.

The end.

P.P.S. In which Marcos tries to explain, in a postmodern multimedia way, how the Zapatistas see, and see themselves in, their own history.

Well, first I must clarify that for us, our history is not only what we have been, what has happened to us, what we have done. It is also, above all, what we want to be and do.

Now then, in this avalanche of audiovisual media that ranges from 4D film and 4K LED televisions to polychrome and multitouch cell-phone screens (which show reality and colors that, allow me to digress, have nothing to do with reality), on an unlikely "timeline" we can locate our way of seeing our history with . . . the kinetoscope.

Yes, I know that I went way off track, to the origins of film, but with the Internet and the multiple wikis that abound and overflow, you will have no problem knowing what I am talking about.

Sometimes, it may seem that we are getting closer to 8-millimeter and super-8 formats, and even then 16-millimeter format is still far off.

I mean, our way of explaining our history looks like an image in continuous and repetitive movement, with some variations that create that sensation of mobile immobility. Always attacked and pursued, always resisting; always being annihilated, always reappearing. Maybe that is why the denunciations of the Zapatista support bases, made through their Good Government Committees, have so few reads. It is as if one had already read that before and only the names and geographies changed.

But here, too, we show ourselves. For example, in bit.ly/2kgTqEH.[1]

And yes, it is a bit like if in Edison's motion picture from 1894 ("Annie Oakley"), in his kinetoscope, we were the coin tossed into the air, while Ms. Civilization shoots at us again and again (yes, the government would be the servile employee who tosses the coin). Or as if in the Lumiere brothers' *Arrival of a Train at La Ciotat*, from 1895, we were the ones who stay on the platform while the train of progress comes and goes. At the end of this text, you will find some videos that will help you understand this.[2]

But the fact is that the collective we are takes and makes each frame, draws it and paints it seeing the reality that we were and are, many times with the blacks of persecution and prisons, with the grays of contempt, and with the red of dispossession and exploitation. But also with the brown and green that we are from the earth that we are.

When someone from outside stops to watch our "film," they usually comment: "What a sharpshooter!" or "What a daring employee who tosses the coin into the air unafraid of being wounded!" but nobody says anything about the coin.

Or, with the Lumiere brothers' train, they say: "How stupid, why do they stay on the platform and not get on the train?" Or, "Here is another example of why the indigenous are in this situation, because they do not want to progress." Someone else ventures, "Did you see how ridiculous their clothes were back then?" But if someone asked us why we do not get on that train, we would say, "Because the stations that follow are 'decay,' 'war,' 'destruction,' and the final destination is 'catastrophe.' The real question is not why we do not get on, but why you do not get off."

---

1   This is a communique from a Zapatista Good Government Committee that informs the public of attacks against Zapatista communities.
2   This communique was published online and included several videos at the end. The videos can be found at: rewindvideos.tumblr.com.

Those who come to be with us to watch us watching ourselves, to listen to us, to learn us in the Escuelita discovered that in each frame we Zapatistas have added an image that is imperceptible at first sight. As if the apparent movement of images shared the particulars of each frame. What cannot be seen in daily comings and goings is the history that we will be. And there is no smartphone that can capture those images. They are only discernible with a very big heart.

Of course, there is no lack of people who come and tell us that there are now tablets and cell phones with front and rear cameras, with colors more vivid than reality's, that there are now three-dimensional cameras and printers, that plasma, LCD, and LED, that representative democracy, that elections, that political parties, that modernity, that progress, that civilization.

They tell us to leave behind that whole collectivism thing (which also rhymes with primitivism): abandon that obsession with taking care of nature, the Mother Earth rhetoric, self-management, autonomy, rebellion, freedom.

They tell us all this while clumsily editing out the fact that it is in their modernity where the most atrocious crimes are committed, where infants are burned alive and the pyromaniacs are congresspeople and senators,[3] where ignorance pretends to rule a nation's destinies, where sources of employment are destroyed, where teachers are persecuted and slandered, where an enormous lie is obscured by another bigger one, where inhumanity is rewarded and exalted and any ethical or moral value is a symptom of "cultural backwardness."

For the major paid media outlets, they are the modern, we the archaic. They are the civilized, we the barbarians. They are the ones who work, we the idlers. They are the "well-to-do," we the outcasts. They the wise, we the ignorant. They are the clean, we the dirty. They are the beautiful, we the ugly. They are the good, we are the bad.

And they forget what is fundamental: this is our history, our way of seeing it and seeing ourselves, our way of thinking about ourselves, of making our path. It is ours, with our errors, our falls, our colors, our lives, our deaths. It is our freedom.

This is what our history is.

Because when we Zapatistas draw a key below and to the left in each frame of our film, we are not thinking about what door to open but about what house with what door must be built for that key to have reason

---

3   A reference to the fire at the ABC Day Care Center, in which forty-nine children died in an alleged attempt to destroy compromising government records.

and destiny. And if this movie's soundtrack has a polka-ballad-corrido-ranchera-cumbia-rock-ska-metal-reggae-trova-punk-hip-hop-rap-and-whatever-else-comes-along beat, it is not because we have no understanding of music. It is because that house will have all colors and all sounds. And there will then be new gazes and ears that will understand our endeavor . . . even if we are only silence and shadow in those worlds to come.

Ergo: we have imagination, they only have frameworks with strict options.

That is why their world collapses. That is why ours reemerges, just like the glimmer whose smallness is not what makes it lesser when it blankets the shade.

All right. Cheers and may we have a very happy birthday; fighting, I mean.

Marcos confusing the heck out of himself with the videos he has to add to, as they say, put the candle on the cake that does not say, but does taste thirty-something.

Mexico, November 17, 2013.

Thirtieth anniversary of the EZLN.

Rewind 2:
On Death and Other Pretexts

December 2013.

> You know that you've died when things around you
> have stopped dying.
> —Elías Contreras
> Profession: EZLN Investigation Commission
> Marital Status: Deceased
> Age: 521 years and counting

It is before dawn, and if I were asked, which I haven't been, I would say that the problem with the dead are the living.

Because sooner or later that absurd, futile, and infuriating debate over their absence tends to appear.

"I knew them / saw them / they told me" is only a pretext that hides the "I am the administrator of that life because I administrate its death."

Something like a copyright over death, then turned into a commodity that is held, exchanged, circulated, and consumed. Well, there are even establishments for it: historiography books, biographies, museums, calendars, theses, newspapers, magazines, and colloquiums.

And there's that trick of editing one's own history to polish errors.

So the dead are used to build a monument over them.

But, in my humble opinion, the problem with the dead is surviving them.

One dies with them, a little or a lot each time.

Or one declares oneself their spokesperson. After all, they cannot talk, and their story is not what gets told; instead, one's own is justified.

Or they can be used to pontificate with the boring "when I was your age." When the only honest way to complete that cheap and unoriginal blackmail (almost always directed toward young people and children) would be to finish with "I had made more mistakes than you."

And behind the kidnapping of these dead is the cult of historiography, so top-down, so incoherent, so useless. The idea that the only history that counts is what's in a book, a thesis, a museum, a monument, and their current and future equivalents, which are nothing but a childish way of domesticating the history of below.

Because there are those who live at the cost of others' dying, and over their absence construct theses, essays, writings, books, movies, ballads, songs, and other largely stylized ways of justifying their own inaction . . . or sterile action.

"You have not died" may be nothing more than a chant if nobody keeps walking.[1] Because from our modest and nonacademic point of view, the path is what matters, not the walker.

And taking advantage of the fact that I am rewinding this tape days, months, decades, I might ask, for example:

With Subcommander Pedro, Mr. Ik, Commander Ramona, do their family trees matter? Their DNA? Their birth certificates with first and last names?

Or is what matters the path that they walked with the nameless and faceless, those without family lineage or heraldic coats of arms?

With Subcommander Pedro, do his real name, his face, his way matter when collected in a thesis, a biography—in other words: in a conveniently documented lie?

Or is what matters the memory there is of him in the communities that he organized? Certainly, religious fanatics would have accused, judged, and condemned him for being an atheist, and race fanatics too, but for being mestizo and not having earth-colored skin, with that inverse racism that claims to be "indigenous."

But the decision to fight made by Subcommander Pedro, Commander Hugo, Commander Ramona, Insurgents Álvaro, Fredy, Rafael, does it matter because someone gives it a name, calendar, geography? Or because that decision is collective and there are those who follow?

When someone lives and dies fighting, in their absence do they tell us "remember me," "honor me," "carry me"? Or do they impose upon us a "continue," "don't give up," "don't surrender," "don't sell out"?

---

1   "You have not died" is a common chant at marches in Latin America.

I mean, I feel (and talking with other compas, I know that it is not only my feeling) that I am accountable to our dead for what has been done, what needs to be done, and what is being done to complete what motivated that struggle.

I am probably mistaken, and someone will tell me that the meaning of all struggle is to live on in historiography, written or spoken history, because the example of the dead—their managed biography—is what motivated people to fight, and not the conditions of injustice, slavery (which is the real name for a lack of freedom), authoritarianism.

I have spoken with some compañeras, compañeros, Zapatistas of the EZLN. True, not with everyone, but with those I can still see, those I can be with.

There was tobacco, coffee, words, silences, agreements.

It was not the urge to live on, but the feeling of duty that put us here, for better or for worse. The need for something to be done against age-old injustice, that anger we feel as the most resounding characteristic of "humanity." We do not intend to have any place in museums, theses, biographies, books.

So in our final breath, will we Zapatistas ask: "Will I be remembered?" Or will we ask: "Was a step taken on the path? Is there someone to keep walking it?"

When we go to Pedro's grave, do we say what we have done to remember him or do we tell him what has been done in the struggle, what needs to be done (what needs to be done always needs to be done), how small we still are?

Are we giving him good news if we take "Power" and if we build a statue for him?

Or if we can tell him, "Hey Pedrín, we are still here, we did not sell out, we did not surrender, we did not give up"?

And, well, now that we're questioning . . .

The thing where we use another name and hide our faces, is it to hide ourselves from the enemy or to defy its mausoleum ranking, its hierarchical nomenclature, its purchase-sale offers whether they're disguised as bureaucratic appointments, prizes, praise and commendations, large or small clubs of followers?

/ *Yes, my dear, times change, teachers—or the equivalent knowledge leader—used to be courted by carrying their books, taking delight in their words, blissfully staring at them. Now people post comments on their writings, like their web pages, add themselves to the number of followers that chaotically chirp . . .* /

I mean, do we care who we are? Or do we care what we have done?

The evaluation that interests and affects us, does it come from outside or from reality?

Is the measure of our success or failure found in how much of ourselves appears in the paid media, in theses, in comments, in "thumbs up," in history books, in museums?

Or in what was accomplished, what failed, what was correct, what remains to be done?

And rewinding more . . .

With Chapis, does it matter that she was a believer and a consistent Christian, or does it matter that she lived and fought, with and in her Christian being, for those who never knew her? Fanatics of atheism certainly would have accused, judged, and condemned her for not practicing the religion of *isms* that tries to monopolize the explanation and leadership of all struggles.

Once, after reading *The Gospel According to Jesus Christ* by José Saramago, Chapis looked for the scholar and compañero to tell him not only that she did not like his book but also that she was going to write her own version of the issue. Does it matter if she ended up finding Saramago, if she told him this, if she wrote her version? Or is her decision to do it what matters?

And with Tata Don Juan, does he matter only because of his last names "Chávez Alonso," his Purépecha blood, the hat that covered him and showed him more, as if he wore a balaclava? Or does he also matter because of the paths honored by his native step on different continents?

The children murdered in the ABC Daycare in Hermosillo, Sonora, Mexico, who barely garnered a few letters of biography, do they matter because of the lines and minutes that they managed to get in the media? Or do they matter because of the blood that blood and life gave them, and now insists on a dignified stubbornness that seeks justice? Because those boys and girls also matter now, although they are absent, because of the fathers and mothers that they gave birth to with their death.

Because justice, friends and enemies, also is preventing injustice from repeating itself or changing its name, face, flag, or ideological, political, racial, or gender pretext.

I mean that we (and others like us, many, all) fight to be better, and we accept when reality tells us that we have not achieved it, but we do not stop fighting because of this.

Because it's not as though we do not honor our dead here. We do. But we do it by fighting. Every day, all the time. And we do this until we're looking at the ground, first at ground level, then from underneath, covering ourselves with the compañero step.

Anyway, the pages get longer and with them grows the certainty that nobody cares about all this, that it is not important, that it is not what the-nation-the-historical-moment-the-situation demands, that it is better to tell a story . . . or make a biography . . . or build a monument.

And of these three things, I am fully convinced that the first is the only one that's worth it.

So I will tell you, just as Durito narrated it to me, the story of the cat-dog (note: now read "Rewind 3").

All right. Cheers and, with the dead, looketh above all at the path that their step walked, since it still needs steps to walk it.

Marcos adjusting his balaclava with macabre flirtation.

P.S. WHICH TAKES SIDES IN A TRULY CURRENT DEBATE. "Video games are the continuation of war by other means," Durito proclaims. And he adds: "In the age-old struggle between PlayStation and Xbox fanatics, there can only be one loser: the player." I did not dare to ask him what he was getting at, but I suppose that more than one person will understand.

P.P.S. TOO LONG TO FIT IN A TWEET (it must be because of how bulky the bill is). The self-proclaimed "governor" of Chiapas, Mexico, has solemnly declared that his administration "has tightened its belt" with an austerity program. To demonstrate its decision, more than ten million dollars have been spent on a national publicity campaign whose enormity and costliness do not make it less ridiculous . . . and illegal.[2] But since some media outlets get their cut, the "callow," "inexperienced," and "immature" employee of a business that is not a party, nor green, nor environmentalist, nor Mexican (well, he is not even governor, so why get hung up on details) is now—in the pages and segments of the same press that attacked him for being a "brat"—a "statesman" who does not spend money on his own personal advancement, but "on drawing tourism to Chiapas." Yes, my dear, now travel agencies launch the tourism package "Meet Güero Velasco,"

---

2   In the midst of budget cuts, the Chiapas government had been spending millions of dollars on a national publicity campaign to draw tourists to the state.

part of the "all included" plan that comes with a set of blinders to not see the groups of paramilitaries or the misery and crime that abound in Chiapas's main cities (Tuxtla Gutiérrez, San Cristóbal de las Casas, Comitán, Tapachula, Palenque), in a state where the indigenous are supposed to be the poor ones, not the mestizos. If the great thief, Juan Sabines Guerrero, paid tons of money to the media to simulate government where there was only dispossession, the current "rich kid" of local politics pays more because he has learned from the current federal executive (I think his name is Enrique Manlio Emilio . . . right? Now do you see why it's bad not to have a Twitter account?) that it is possible to go from a judicial ingrate to a list of 2018 presidential candidates with only a few tens of millions of dollars, some good Photoshopping, and a soap opera.

P.P.P.S. ON REITERATED CIRCUMSTANCE. Allow me, ma'am, sir, miss, young man, other.[3] Allow me to, impertinent at last, not let you close the door and be left alone, brooding over your frustration and looking for those responsible, which is like the fury of those who have a fixed altar and a changing idol. And if I don't use my foot to stop you from closing the door and staying safe in your castle of dogmas, and instead stick my nose where it doesn't belong, then blame my nose, in itself already impertinent in size and shape. Go on, allow me to interrupt your muffled, dry, sterile, useless hatred.[4]

Come, quiet down, take a seat, breathe deeply. Be strong and act with reasoned sensibility, like those couples that break up "like mature adults" even though they are dying to break the aforementioned's skull.

So when you get something, it's from your efforts alone? Ah, but when you reap loss, then responsibility is democratized . . . and you exclude yourselves. "Forums are a farce," you proclaimed. "No masked people allowed," you ordained (and don't even think about filing a complaint with CONAPRED[5] for discrimination based on dress). "Only we alone shall triumph and the nation will be eternally grateful to us; our names will be in textbooks, congresses, statues, museums," you rejoice in advance.

Then what happened happened, and like before, now you turn to see who to blame for the failure of that fight above. "There was not enough

---

3   *Otroa*: someone who is neither male nor female.
4   Shortly before this communique was released, the Mexican Congress passed an energy reform bill allowing privatization of the oil industry, which had previously been unconstitutional. In this paragraph and those that follow, Marcos mocks the López Obrador movement's attempts to fight this bill's passage.
5   National Council to Prevent Discrimination (Consejo Nacional para Prevenir la Discriminación).

unity," you say, but you think, "there was not enough subordination to our leadership."

Dispossession disguised as constitutional reform did not begin in this administration. Its formalization began with Carlos Salinas de Gortari and his reform to Article 27. Agrarian dispossession was then "covered" by the same lies that now surround the misnamed reforms: now the Mexican countryside is completely destroyed, as if a bundle of atomic bombs had leveled it. And it is happening now with all reforms. Gas, electricity, education, justice—everything will be more expensive, lower quality, scarcer.

Before that and even before the current reforms, native peoples were and are dispossessed of their territories, which also belong to the nation. Modern liquid gold—water, not oil—has been stolen without this drawing attention in the mass media. The theft of subsoil, so clearly denounced in the Tata Juan Chávez Alonso seminar by the Indigenous National Congress, got a mere few reluctant lines in the paid press that today laments the fact that THE PEOPLE—that pipe dream so characteristic in politics and the media—are not doing anything to stop the legal and illegitimate theft that is called "energy reform." Dispossession is every day and everywhere. But not until now have people said that the homeland was betrayed.

And now you, deaf before, are outraged because people are not listening to or following you.

And you say that nothing gets done because nothing gets seen. You say and say to yourself: "There is value in what *I* do or what is done under my tutelage, in my calendar, and in my geography. The rest does not exist because I do not see it."

And how could you see something if you use the blinders that Power gives you?

Now you discover that the state not only refuses to be a shock absorber in the windstorm of dispossession that is neoliberalism, but also hurries off to vie for the crumbs that true Power casts its way?

Look, the thing is that the world is round; it spins; it changes. And there is little or no use for that catalog of dual indications: left and right, reactionary and progressive, old and modern, and synonyms and antonyms so stylish in the politics of above.

Look, what's happening, plain and simple, is that your thought is decrepit.

And its defeat began at the same time that you decided to embrace those above (using the old trick—turned against you now—of right-left-progressive-reactionary, inventing pretexts and dressing them up in the same words that trap you today), forgetting that those above do not accept embraces, only kneeling.

No, it's not that you don't have ideas and flags. It's just that they are rickety. It does not matter how much you dress them in modernity, nor how many high-sounding words are said about them, nor how many tweets repeat them, nor how many likes and comments they accumulate.

You, who were waiting for a proclamation, anonymous blood spilt, the bugle with its warlike tone, the eight columns, the images with blood offered on the altar of the homeland that—missing more—you and only you are to redeem.

/ *No my dear, if I tell you that Zapatismo is no longer what it was before, do you remember how almost twenty years ago we were excited by the images of deaths so anonymous that they were not given faces or names, so far away, so indigenous, so Chiapanecan? / By the way, is Ocosingo in the Middle East? / Ah, and your initiatives, so brilliant when there was a stage for us. / On the other hand, who can take someone seriously when they refuse to enlist in the fashionable march or movement* (note: they're not the same thing, learn to tell the difference)? *Or refuse to analyze it, classify it, judge it, archive it? / That said, they are finished, now they don't even invite the press to their celebrations, what can they celebrate if it's not our acquittal or conviction? / Ah, but what we will never forgive those Zapatones for, aside from the fact that they're not all dead—and thus have denied us the right to manage their dead in the long labyrinth of mausoleums, ballads, "you have not died, comrade, your death shall be administered"—is that they have also made their dead so . . . so . . . so rebellious. /*

And nothing, since instead of that . . . postscripts!

I already know that you don't care, but for the masked people over here, the fight that matters is not the one that has been won or lost. It is the one ahead, and calendars and geographies are being prepared for it.

There are no definitive battles, neither for winners nor for losers. The fight will continue, and those who now bask in triumph will see their world collapse.

As for the rest, don't worry. You have not lost anything because you have not really fought for anything. The only thing you have done is delegate to someone else the task of attaining a monopoly on a victory that will never come.

Those above will fall, undoubtedly. But their collapse will not be the product of a monopolized and exclusionary fight that is a fanatic of itself.

If you like, keep pulling from above; you will celebrate each small movement of the monolith, but the cord will break again and again.

Statues and authoritarianisms are knocked down from below, so that there is no foundation left for a new bust to substitute the previous one.

Meanwhile, in my humble opinion, the only thing worth doing up above is what birds do: shitting.

All right walnut ice cream, whilst it may be cold out.

Marcos getting ready for . . .

Rewind 1:
When the Dead Are Silent Out Loud

(Which reflects on the absent, on biographies, describes Durito's first encounter with the cat-dog, and talks about other issues that are beside the point, as the impertinent postscript will tell)

November–December 2013.

> Methinks we have hugely mistaken this matter of Life and Death. Methinks that what they call my shadow here on earth is my true substance. Methinks that in looking at things spiritual, we are too much like oysters observing the sun through the water, and thinking that thick water the thinnest of air. Methinks my body is but the lees of my better being. In fact take my body who will, take it I say, it is not me.
> —Herman Melville, *Moby Dick*

For a long time I have argued that the majority of biographies are nothing more than a documented lie, and sometimes, but not always, a well-written one. The average biographer has a preexisting belief, and their margin for tolerance is very limited, if not nonexistent. With this belief, they begin to rummage through the puzzle of a life that is foreign to them (thus their interest in writing the biography) and collect the false pieces that allow them to document their own belief, not the life in summary.

The truth is that we could perhaps know with certainty the person's date and place of birth, and in some cases, date and place of death. Aside from that, the majority of biographies ought to be categorized as "historical fiction" or "science fiction."

What is it then that remains of a life? A little or a lot, we say.

A little or a lot, depending on memory.

Or, rather, on the fragments that that life imprinted on collective memory.

If this is not worthy for biographers and editors, it matters little for common people. It tends to be that what really matters does not show up in the media and cannot be measured with surveys.

Ergo, for an absent person we only have arbitrary pieces of the complex puzzle made of shreds, frays, and trends that are known as "life."

So, with this confusing beginning, allow me to hold up a few of those fragmented pieces to embrace and embrace ourselves for the step that today we are missing and need . . .

⁓

A concert in the Mexican silence. Don Juan Chávez Alonso, Purépecha, Zapatista, and Mexican, makes a gesture as if ridding himself of an annoying insect. It is his response to the apology I make for one of my clumsy outbursts. We are in Cucapá territory, in the middle of a sandy lot. In those geographic coordinates and when the calendar indicates the Sixth Declaration 2006 in the northwest of Mexico, in the large tent that serves as his lodging, Don Juan grabs a guitar and asks if we want to listen to something that he composed. He barely tunes it and begins a concert that, without any lyrics, describes the Zapatista uprising from January 1, 1994, to Commander Ramona's presence in the formation of the Indigenous National Congress.

A silence then, as if it were another note.

A silence in which our dead were silent out loud.

⁓

Also in the Mexican Northwest, Power's bloody madness paints the calendar of below with still unpunished absurdities. June 5, 2009. Governmental greed and despotism have set fire to a day care. The mortal victims, forty-nine children, are the casualties when compromising archives are destroyed. The absurdity of parents burying their children is followed by a weak and corrupt justice: those responsible do not receive an arrest warrant, but appointments in the cabinet of the criminal who—under National Action's blue—will try to hide the bloodbath that he plunged the entire country into.

Where biographers close their notes "because a few years of life are not profitable," the history of below opens its notebook of other absurdities: with their unjust absence, these infants and toddlers have given birth to other men and women. Their fathers and mothers have since then demanded the greatest justice: injustice not repeating itself.

❧

"The problem with life is that, in the end, it kills you," said Durito, whose whimsical stories of knights entertained Chapis so much. Although she would have asked, with that impertinent mixture of naivety and sincerity that bewildered those who did not know her, "and why a problem?" Don Durito of the Lacandon Jungle, beetle by birth and knight errant by trade, would have avoided quarreling with her, given that according to a so-called rule of knighthood, a lady must not be contradicted (above all if the lady in question has a good deal of influence "in high places," added Durito, who knew that Chapis was religious, a nun, a sister, or whatever you want to call women who make a life and profession of faith).

Chapis did not know us. I mean, not like those who look at us from outside and write, speak . . . or misspeak about us (you've already seen how fashions are fleeting). Chapis was with us. And she was for some time before an impertinent beetle showed up in the mountains of the Mexican Southeast to declare himself a knight errant.

And maybe being in us was why Chapis did not seem so troubled by life and death. Like that attitude that is so much ours, the Neozapatistas', in which everything is inverted and death is not what worries us and keeps us busy, but life.

But Chapis was not only in us. It is clear that we were only one part of her walk. And if I'm now telling you something about her, it is not to provide notes for her biography, but to tell you what we feel here. Because this believer's story, her story with us, is one of those that makes fanatical atheists doubt themselves.

"Is religion the opium of the people?" I don't know. What I do know is that the most brilliant explanation I have heard on the destruction and depopulation that neoliberal globalization carries out in a given territory did not come from a Marxist-Leninist-atheist-and-some-more-*ists* theoretician, but . . . from a Christian, apostolic, and Roman Catholic priest, signatory to the Sixth Declaration, banished by the high clergy ("for thinking too much," he told me as if apologizing) to one of the geographic deserts on the Mexican Plateau.

I think (perhaps I am mistaken, it would not be the first time and certainly will not be the last) that many people, if not everyone, who approached what is known as *Neozapatismo* did so looking for answers to questions asked in each of their personal histories, according to their calendar and geography. And they only took the time necessary to find the answer. When they realized that the answer was the most problematic monosyllable of all time, they turned elsewhere and walked off that way. It does not matter how much they say and tell themselves that they are still here: they left. Some people more quickly than others. And the majority of them do not look at us, or do so with the same distance and intellectual scorn hoisted high on calendars before the sun rose on January 1994.

I think I have said it before, in some other missive, I'm not sure. But anyway, I'll say or repeat here that the dangerous monosyllable is "you." Like that, with lower-case letters, because that response was and is intimate for everyone. And everyone takes it with their respective terror.

Because the fight is collective, but the decision to fight is individual, personal, intimate, as is the decision to continue or give up.

Am I saying that the few people who stayed (and I'm not talking about geography but about the heart) have not found that answer? No. What I am trying to say is that Chapis did not come looking for that answer to her personal question. She already knew the answer and had made that "you" her path and goal: her being a believer and being consistent.

Many others like her, but different, had already responded in other calendars and geographies. Atheists and believers. Men, women, and *others*[1] from all calendars. They are the ones who always, dead or alive, put themselves in front of Power, not as victims, but to challenge it with the manifold flag of the Left from below. They are our compañeras, compañeros, and compañeroas . . . although in the majority of cases neither they nor we know it . . . yet.

Because rebellion, friends and enemies, is not the exclusive domain of the Neozapatistas. It is humanity's. And that is something that must be celebrated. Everywhere, every day, all the time. Because rebellion is also a celebration.

---

1   *Otroa*: someone who is neither male nor female.

The bridges that, from all corners of planet earth, have extended to these lands and skies are neither few nor weak. Sometimes with looks, sometimes with words, always with our struggle, we have crossed them to embrace that other who resists and struggles.

Maybe "being compañeros" is about that—about crossing bridges—and not about something else.

Like in that embrace made letters for Chapis's sisters who, like us, miss her and, like us, need her.

༄

Impunity, my dear Matías, is something that only justice can grant; it is Justice exercising injustice.
—Tomás Segovia, in *Cartas Cabales*

I have said before that, in my humble opinion, everyone is the hero of their own individual story. And that in the sedating complacency of telling "this is my personal story," events and nonevents are edited out, the most incredible fantasies are invented, and telling anecdotes looks too much like the accounting of the scrooge who steals what isn't theirs.

The ancestral zeal for transcending one's own death finds that biographies are the substitute for the elixir of eternal youth. Of course, offspring as well. But the biography is, to put it one way, "more perfect." It is not someone who resembles you, it is the "me" extended in time thanks to the "magic" of the biography.

The biographer from above goes to documents of the period, perhaps to testimonies by family members, friends, or compañer@s of the life whose death is appropriated. The "documents" have the same accuracy as weather forecasts, and the testimonies obviate the fine line between "I think that . . ." and "I know that . . ." And so the biography's "truthfulness" is measured by the number of footnotes. The same holds for biographies as for governmental "image-management" expense invoices: the bulkier they are, the more accurate they are.

With the Internet, Twitter, Facebook, and the like, today biographical myths round out their fallacies and voilà, a story is rebuilt for a life, or fragments of it, that has little or nothing to do with the real story. But it does not matter, because the biography is published, printed, circulated; it is read, cited, recited . . . just like lies.

Check in the modern documentary sources for future biographies: Wikipedia and blogs, Facebook and the respective "profiles." Now compare this with reality:

Does it not give you shivers to realize that perhaps, in the future . . .

Carlos Salinas de Gortari will be "the visionary who understood that selling a Nation was, in addition to being a family business (of course, understanding family to mean both blood and political family), an act of modern patriotism," and not the leader of a band of traitors (don't play stupid, several of those who supported the reform to constitutional Article 27—the watershed moment for the nation-state's capitulation in Mexico—are there in the "mature and responsible" opposition).

Ernesto Zedillo Ponce de León will not be the "statesman" who brought an entire nation from one crisis to a worse one (in addition to being one of the intellectual authors of the Acteal massacre, along with Emilio Chuayffet and Mario Renán Castillo), but instead one who took "the country's reins" with a singular sense of humor . . . to end up being what he always was: a second-class employee of a multinational corporation.

Vicente Fox will be proof that the positions of president of a republic and of a soft-drink subsidiary are interchangeable . . . and that both positions can be held by useless people.

Felipe Calderón Hinojosa will be a "brave president" (for others to die) and not a psychopath who stole the weapon (the presidency) for his war games . . . and who ended up being what he always was: a second-class employee of a multinational corporation.

Enrique Peña Nieto will be an educated and intelligent president ("well, he's ignorant and stupid but able," is the new profile being built for him in circles of political analysts), and not a functional illiterate (oh well, as the popular proverb goes: "what nature does not provide, Monex does not buy").[2]

Ah, biographies. Often they are autobiographies, even if their descendants (or cronies) are those who promote them and adorn their family tree.

The criminals of the Mexican political class who have misgoverned these lands shall continue to be unpunished criminals for those who have suffered from their disgraces. It does not matter how many lines are paid for in the paid media, nor how much is spent on spectacles in the streets, on written press, on the radio and television. From Díaz (Porfirio and Gustavo) to Calderón and Peña, from Castellanos and Sabines to Albores

---

2   In the aftermath of the 2012 general election, López Obrador accused the PRI presidential candidate Peña Nieto of having funded his campaign through illicit funds channeled through the Monex financial institution and of having distributed prepaid electronic gift cards issued by Monex to bribe prospective voters.

and Velasco, the only mediator is oversight (via social networks, because in the paid media they are still "responsible and mature people") from the rich kids' ridiculous frivolity.

But the world is round, and in the politics of above's continuous rise and fall, in a short time one can go from the cover of *Hola* to "WANTED: DANGEROUS CRIMINAL,"[3] from the NAFTA December jamboree to the hangover of the Zapatista uprising, from "man of the year" to the "hunger strike" with chic brand-name bottled water (oh well, my dear, even for protests there are social classes), from the applause for bad jokes to the putative filicide in the making, from nepotism and corruption garnished with witty ideas to investigation for links to drug trafficking, from extra-large military uniforms to blood-stained fearful exile, from the traitorous December jubilee to . . .

❧

With all this and what's to come, am I saying that there is no need to write/read biographies? No, but what makes history's old wheel go round are collectives, not individuals. Historiography is nurtured by individualities; history learns from peoples.

Am I saying that there is no need to write/study history? No, but what I am saying is that it is better to make it the only way it is done: with others and organized.

Because, friends and enemies, when individual, rebellion is beautiful. But when collective and organized, it is terrifying and wonderful. The first is material for biographies; the second is what makes history.

❧

And not with words, we embrace our Zapatista compañeros and compañeras, atheists and believers,
  those who at night carried a backpack and history on their shoulders,
   those who took lightning and thunder with their hands,
    those who put on their boots without a future,
     those who covered their face and name,
      those who, expecting nothing in exchange, died in the long night
       so that others, everyone, one morning yet to come,
        may see the day as it must be seen:
         head-on, standing up, and with a bright gaze and heart.

---

3   Here and below, Marcos is making allusions to contemporary Mexican political figures.

For them neither biographies nor museums.
For them our memory and rebellion.
For them our cry:
freedom! Freedom! FREEDOM!
Alright. Cheers and may our steps be as great as our dead.

Marcos.

P.S. ON OBVIOUS INSTRUCTIONS. Now do be so kind as to read, in reverse-date order, "Rewind 1" through "Rewind 3," and maybe you'll find the cat-dog and some uncertainties will be cleared up. And yes, you can be sure that more questions will come up.

P.P.S. WHICH RESPONDS TO, REQUESTS FROM, THE PAID ME-DIA. Ah! A moving effort by the contras[4] in the paid media to try to provide arguments to the few contra readers/listeners/viewers who remain. But, feeling generous for the Christmas season, I'll send you a few tips here for you to use as journalistic material:
– If the Zapatista indigenous communities' conditions are the same as twenty years ago and the quality of life has not advanced at all, why does the EZLN—as it did in 1994 with the paid press—"open" its doors with the Escuelita for people from below to directly see and understand what there is here WITHOUT INTERMEDIARIES?
And now that I'm in "interrogation mode," why, in the same period, did the paid media's number of readers/listeners/viewers also drop exponentially? *Psst, psst, you can respond that you do not have fewer readers/ listeners/viewers—that would reduce advertising and hush money—what's happening is that now they are more "selective."*
– You ask, "What has the EZLN done for indigenous communities?" And we are responding with direct testimony from tens of thousands of our compañeros and compañeras.
Now owners and shareholders, executives and bosses, answer this:
What have you done, in these twenty years, for media workers, one of the sectors hit hardest by the crime adopted and fueled by the regime that you so adore? What have you done for the journalists, the threatened, kidnapped, and murdered journalists? And for their family members? What have you done to improve your workers' living conditions? Have you increased their salary so that they have a dignified life and do

---

4   A metaphorical reference to the right-wing, reactionary "Contras" that operated in Nicaragua in the 1980s.

not have to sell their word or their silence in the face of reality? Have you created conditions so they can have a respectable retirement after years of working for you? Have you given them job security? I mean, does a reporter's job no longer depend on the mood of the editor in chief or on sexual "favors" or favors of any another nature, demanded of all genders?

What have you done so that being a media worker is an honor that does not come at the price of losing one's freedom or life for being honest?

Can you say that your work is more respected by rulers and the governed than twenty years ago?

What have you done to counter imposed or tolerated censorship? Can you say that your readers/listeners/viewers are better informed than twenty years ago? Can you say that you have more credibility than twenty years ago? Can you say that you survive thanks to your readers/listeners/viewers and not because of advertising, largely by the government?

Answer that for your workers and readers/listeners/viewers, just as we answer our compañeros and compañeras.

Oh, come on, don't be sad. We are not the only ones who have escaped your role as judge, jury, and executioner, begging for your mercy and always receiving your condemnation. There is also, for example, reality.

All right nine or, better yet, sixty-nine.

Marcos telling himself that a thumbs-down is better than a thumb-sideways.

It is Zapatista territory, it is Chiapas, it is Mexico, it is Latin America, it is Earth. And it is December 2013, it is cold like twenty years ago, and, like then, today a flag keeps us warm: the flag of rebellion.

Pain and Rage

Zapatista Army of National Liberation. Mexico.

May 8, 2014.

To the compañeras and compañeros of the Sixth Declaration:

Compas:

As a matter of fact, the communique was already ready. Succinct, precise, clear, as communiques should be. But . . . hmm . . . maybe later.

Because now the meeting with the support base compañeras and compañeros from La Realidad is beginning.

We are listening to them.

The tone and emotions of their voice has been known for some time: pain and rage.

So it occurs to me that a communique is not going to reflect that.

Well, not entirely.

True, maybe a letter wouldn't either, but at least with these words I can try, even if it is a pallid reflection.

Because . . .

Pain and rage were what made us challenge everything and everyone twenty years ago.

And pain and rage are what now make us lace up our boots again, put on our uniforms, holster up our pistols, and cover our faces.

And now put on my old and tattered hat with three red five-pointed stars.

Pain and rage are what have brought our steps to La Realidad.

Moments ago—after we explained that we had come in response to the petition by support bases from the Good Government Committee—a support-base compañero, a teacher for the course "Freedom according to the Zapatistas," told us in more or less these words:

"Of course we are telling you compañero subcommander, were it that we are not Zapatistas, a while ago we would have taken revenge and there would have been a massacre. Because we are very angry about what they did to compañero Galeano. But, well, we are Zapatistas and it is not about revenge but about justice. So we are waiting for what you are going to tell us and we are going to do that."

When I heard this, I felt envy and sorrow.

Envy for those who had the privilege of having as teachers men and women like Galeano and like the man talking now. Thousands of men and women from across the world have had that fortune.[1]

And sorrow for those who will no longer have Galeano as a teacher.

Compañero Subcommander Moisés has had to make a difficult decision. His decision is final and, if you ask for my opinion (which nobody has), unquestionable. He has decided to indefinitely suspend the meeting and exchange with native peoples and their organizations in the Indigenous National Congress. And he has also decided to suspend the ceremony that we prepared for our absent compañero Don Luis Villoro Toranzo, and to suspend our contribution to the "Ethics in the face of Dispossession" seminar organized by artist and intellectual compas from Mexico and the world.

What brought him to that decision? Well, the initial results of the investigation, as well as information that we received, leave no doubt that

1. It was a preplanned attack, organized militarily and carried out with malice, premeditation, and an advantageous position. And it is an attack occurring in a climate created and fueled from above.

2. There is involvement from the leadership of the CIOAC-H,[2] the Green Party[3] (the name with which the PRI governs in Chiapas), the National Action Party, and the Institutional Revolutionary Party.

3. At the very least, the Chiapas state government is implicated. The federal government's level of involvement has yet to be determined.

A woman from the contras has come to tell us that it was in fact planned and that it was in fact the plan to "screw over" Galeano.

---

1   Galeano was one of the teachers for the "Escuelita on Freedom according to the Zapatistas." See above, p. 217, n. 9.

2   Independent Center of Agricultural Workers and Peasants–Historic (Central Independiente de Obreros Agrícolas y Campesinos–Histórica).

3   Environmentalist Green Party of Mexico (Partido Verde Ecologista de México), affiliated with the PRI and part of the Global Greens.

In sum: it was not a community problem, where two sides face off in the heat of the moment. It was something planned: first the provocation by destroying the school and clinic, knowing that our compañeros did not have firearms and that they would go to defend what they had humbly built with their efforts; then the positions that the aggressors took, predicting the path that they would follow from the caracol to the school; and finally the crossfire on our compañeros.

In that ambush, our compañeros were wounded with firearms.

What happened with compañero Galeano is chilling: he did not fall in the ambush, he was surrounded by fifteen or twenty paramilitaries (that is indeed what they are, their tactics are those of paramilitaries[4]); compañero Galeano challenged them in hand-to-hand combat, without firearms; they swung their sticks at him and he jumped from side to side, dodging the blows and disarming his opponents.

After seeing that they couldn't fight him, they shot at him, and a bullet to his leg knocked him down. After that came the barbarity: they went over him, beat him and struck him with machetes. Another bullet to his chest mortally wounded him. They kept beating him. And after seeing that he was still breathing, a coward shot him in the head.

He was shot three times in cold blood. And those three shots when he was surrounded, unarmed, and without surrender. His body was dragged by his murderers about eighty yards and they tossed it aside.

Compañero Galeano was alone. His body lying in the middle of what once was encampment territory, for men and women from across the world who came to the "peace encampment" in La Realidad. And the compañeras, the Zapatista women from La Realidad, were the ones who defied fear and went to retrieve his body.

Yes, there is a photo of compañero Galeano. The image shows all the wounds and fuels the pain and the rage, although listening to the accounts needs no reinforcement. Of course, I understand that photo could offend the sensibilities of the Spanish-nationalist royalty, and so it is better to put up a photo of a brazenly fabricated crime scene, with a few injuries, and for reporters—mobilized by the Chiapas government—to begin to sell the lie of a confrontation.[5] "He who pays, commands." Because there are classes, my dear. The Spanish monarchy is one thing, and another the "damn" rebel Indians that send you to AMLO's ranch just because there, a few steps away, they are watching over compañero Galeano's still-bloody body.

---

4   Here "paramilitaries" means military groups armed, funded, and trained by the government.

5   Many media outlets falsely reported that this attack was part of an "intracommunal conflict" or that there were hostilities on both sides.

CIOAC-Historic, its rival CIOAC-Independent, and other "peasant" organizations like ORCAO, ORUGA, URPA, and the rest live by causing confrontations. They know that causing problems in communities where we have a presence is pleasing to governments. And that they tend to be rewarded for their wrongs against us with projects and with wads of cash for their leaders.[6]

In the words of an official from Manuel Velasco's government: "It is better for us when the Zapatistas are busy with artificially created problems, instead of doing activities where 'güeros'[7] come from all over the place." That's what he said: "güeros." Yeah, it is comical that the servant of a "güero" expresses himself that way.

Each time the leaders of these "peasant" organizations see their budget dwindle from the jamborees they throw for themselves, they organize a problem and go to the Chiapas government so that it will pay them to "calm down."

This "modus vivendi" of leaders that do not even know the difference between "sand" and "gravel" began with the PRI's ill-remembered "Kibbles" Albores, was taken up again with the López Obrador supporter Juan Sabines, and is maintained with the self-styled environmentalist Manuel "el güero" Velasco.

Wait a minute . . .

Now a compañero is talking. Crying, yes. But we all know that they are tears of rage. With halting words he says what everyone feels, what we all feel: we do not want revenge, we want justice.

Another interrupts: "Compañero subcommander, don't misunderstand our tears, they are not tears of sadness, they are tears of rebellion."

Now a report comes in from a meeting of the CIOAC-H's leaders. The leaders say, textually: "It is not possible to negotiate with the EZLN with money. But once everyone in the newspaper is arrested, locked up for four or five years, and after the problem subsides, it will be possible to negotiate with the government for their freedom." Another adds: "Or we can say that one of ours died and it will be a tie, one death on each side, and the Zapatistas will calm down. We'll invent a death or kill someone ourselves and the problem will be solved."

In sum, the letter goes on and I don't know if you are able to feel what we feel. Anyway, Subcommander Moisés has given me the task of

---

6   Paramilitary groups receive both cash and aid from government "humanitarian" efforts.

7   In Mexico, *güero* is a term used to refer to people with white skin, regardless of their race or nationality. Because of his pale complexion, Manuel Velasco, who has been governor of Chiapas since 2012, adopted the nickname "el *Güero,*" which he has used throughout his political career.

notifying you that . . .

Hold on . . .

Now they are talking in the Zapatista assembly in La Realidad.

We have gone out so that they can agree among themselves about a question that they were asked: "The governments go after the EZLN command, you know this well because you were there during the 1995 betrayal. So, do you want us here to see about this problem and see that justice is served, or do you want us to go somewhere else? Because all of you may now suffer the direct persecution of governments and their police and soldiers."

Now I listen to a young man. Fifteen years old. I am told that he is Galeano's son. I look out and it's true: although he's real young, he is a Galeano in training. He tells us to stay, that they trust us for justice and to find those who murdered his dad. And that they are willing to do whatever it takes. The voices in favor of this multiply. The compañeros talk. The compañeras talk, and even the children stop crying: the women were the ones who reconnected the water system, in spite of the fact that the paramilitaries threatened them. "They are brave," says a man, a war veteran.

We stay; that is the agreement.

Subcommander Moisés gives some monetary support to the widow.

The assembly disperses. Although it is possible to see that everyone's step is firm again and that there is another light in their gaze.

What was I talking about? Ah, yes. Subcommander Moisés has given me the task of notifying you that May and June's public activities have been suspended indefinitely, as have the courses on "Freedom according to the Zapatistas." So there you see the cancellations and the rest.

Wait . . .

Now we are being told that the so-called Acteal Model is starting to be fueled above: "It was an intra-communal conflict over a sand bank." Hmm . . . and so continues the militarization, the domesticated press's hysterical clamor, the shams, the lies, the persecution. It is no coincidence that old Chuayffet[8] is still there, now with studious disciples in the Chiapas government and "peasant" organizations.

We already know what's next.

But what I want to do is take advantage of these lines to ask you:

Pain and rage are what have brought us here. If you are able to feel this too, where does it take you?

---

8   Emilio Chuayffet is a PRI politician who President Zedillo appointed as secretary of the interior in 1995. He resigned from his post in 1998 following accusations that the federal government was responsible for the Acteal massacre, in which forty-five people were killed while attending church. At the time Marcos was writing this communique, Chuayffet was secretary of education (2012–2015).

Because we are here, in reality. Where we always have been.

And you?

All right. Cheers and outrage.

From the mountains of the Mexican Southeast.

Insurgent Subcommander Marcos.

Mexico, May 2014. In the twentieth year since the beginning of the war against oblivion.

P.S. The investigations are being led by Subcommander Moisés. He will be informing you of the results, or he through myself.

Another P.S. If you ask me to summarize our laborious advance in a few words, they would be: our efforts are for peace, their efforts are for war.

Further Reading

The literature on the Zapatistas is now vast. The following are good starting points that introduce the movement: Gloria Muñoz Ramírez's *The Fire and the Word* (San Francisco: City Lights Books, 2008), which outlines the Zapatistas' history, much of it in their own words; John Ross's highly readable trilogy mentioned in the introduction (p. 10); John Holloway and Eloína Peláez's *Zapatista! Reinventing Revolution in Mexico* (London: Pluto, 1998); and Alex Khasnabish's *Zapatistas: Rebellion from the Grassroots to the Global* (London: Zed Books, 2010). Also recommended are Mihalis Mentinis's *Zapatistas: The Chiapas Revolt and What It Means for Radical Politics* (London: Pluto, 2006); and Jeff Conant's *A Poetics of Resistance: The Revolutionary Public Relations of the Zapatista Insurgency* (Oakland, CA: AK Press, 2010). Finally, there is Tom Hayden's *The Zapatista Reader* (New York: Thunder's Mouth, 2002), a highly valuable collection of pieces, many translated for the first time into English, penned by a host of contributors, including some very eminent authors. Works in English either by Subcommander Marcos himself or written specifically about him are listed below.

Important documentary films in English include Cristián Calónico's *Marcos: Word and History* (Producciones Marca Diablo, 1995); Nettie Wild's *A Place Called Chiapas* (New Yorker Video, 1998); Big Noise Films' *Zapatista* (1998) and *Storm from the Mountain* (2001); and Francesca Nava's *The Other Mexico* (2008).

There are also numerous other texts, like those in this book, that outline the Zapatistas' political theory and practice. The Sixth Declaration of the Lacandon Jungle (sixthdeclaration.blogspot.com) is the central exposition of the Zapatistas' political platform, while the Escuelita Textbooks (escuelitabooks.blogspot.com) provide detailed accounts of daily life and political struggle in Zapatista communities.

All of the Zapatistas' communiqués are published in Spanish on Enlace Zapatista (enlacezapatista.ezln.org.mx), the Zapatistas' official website, and the site also has English translations of all CCRI communiqués from the past several years.

Other websites with useful information on the Zapatistas and English translations of Zapatista communiqués, denunciations, and other important documents include the Irish Mexico Group (http://www.struggle.ws/mexico/ezlnco.html); Europa Zapatista (www.europazapatista.org/?tags=pl-en); and Ours Reemerging Translations (galestranslations.blogspot.com).

Subcommander Marcos's Words

Writings

Autonomedia. *¡Zapatistas! Documents of the New Mexican Revolution.* New York: Autonomedia, 1994.

_____. *Conversations with Durito: Stories of the Zapatistas and Neoliberalism.* New York: Autonomedia, 2005.

Clarke, Ben, and Clifton Ross. *Voices of Fire: Communiqués and Interviews from the Zapatista Army of National Liberation.* Revised ed. San Francisco: Freedom Voices, 2000.

Ross, John, and Frank Bardacke, eds. *Shadows of a Tender Fury: The Communiqués of Subcomandante Marcos and the EZLN.* New York: Monthly Review Press, 1995.

Ruggiero, Greg, and Stewart Shahulka, eds. *Zapatista Encuentro: Documents from the 1996 Encounter for Humanity and Against Neoliberalism.* New York: Seven Stories, 1998.

Subcomandante Marcos. "Marcos on Independent Media," January 31 and February 1, 1997. http://struggle.ws/mexico/ezln/1997/marcos_inter_media_feb.html.

_____. *The Story of Colors / La Historia de los Colores.* El Paso: Cinco Puntos, 1999.

_____. *Our Word Is Our Weapon.* Edited by Juana Ponce de León. New York: Seven Stories, 2001.

_____. *Questions and Swords.* El Paso: Cinco Puntos, 2001.

_____. *Zapatista Stories.* Translated by Dinah Livingstone. London:

Katabasis, 2001.

———. "The World: Seven Thoughts in May of 2003." *Rebeldía*, no. 7 (2003). English translation at http://www.cuestiones.ws/revista/n15/ago03-mex-eng-marcos.htm.

———. *Chiapas: Resistance and Rebellion.* Coimbatore, India: Vitiyal Pathippagam, 2005.

———. *The Other Campaign.* San Francisco: City Lights, 2006.

———. *The Speed of Dreams.* San Francisco: City Lights, 2007.

———. "Third Letter to Don Luis Villoro in the Interchange on Ethics and Politics," July–August 2011. El Kilombo, http://www.elkilombo. org/third-letter-to-don-luis-villoro-in-the-interchange-on-ethics-and-politics/.

———. "We Don't Know You Yet?" December 29, 2012. Enlace Zapatista, http://enlacezapatista.ezln.org.mx/2013/01/07/we-don%C2%B4t-know-you-yet/.

———. "The Method, the Bibliography, and a Drone Deep in the Mountains of the Mexican Southeast," May 4, 2015. Enlace Zapatista, http://enlacezapatista.ezln.org.mx/2015/06/19/the-method-the-bib-liography-and-a-drone-deep-in-the-mountains-of-the-mexican-southeast/.

———. *Critical Thought in the Face of the Capitalist Hydra.* Durham, NC: PaperBoat, 2016.

Vodovnik, Žiga, ed. *Ya Basta! Ten Years of the Zapatista Uprising.* Oakland, CA: AK Press, 2004.

Interviews

Benjamin, Medea. "Interview: Subcomandante Marcos." In *First World, Ha Ha Ha!*, edited by Elaine Katzenberger, 57–70. San Francisco: City Lights, 1995.

Blixen, Samuel, and Carlos Fazio. "Interview with Marcos about Neoliberalism, the National State and Democracy." *Brecha* (Uruguay), Autumn 1995. English version available at http://struggle.ws/mexico/ezln/inter_marcos_aut95.html.

de Huerta, Marta Duran, and Nicholas Higgins. "An Interview with Subcomandante Insurgente Marcos, Spokesperson and Military Commander of the Zapatista National Liberation Army (EZLN)." *International Affairs* 75, no. 2 (April 1999): 269–79.

El Kilombo. *Beyond Resistance: Everything: An Interview with*

Subcomandante Insurgente Marcos. Durham, NC: PaperBoat, 2007.

García Márquez, Gabriel, and Roberto Pombo. "The Punch Card and the Hour Glass: Interview with Subcomandante Marcos." *New Left Review* 9 (May–June 2001): 69–79. Available at http://struggle.ws/mexico/ezln/2001/marcos/gg_interview.html.

Landau, Saul. "In the Jungle with Marcos." *Progressive*, March 1, 1996, 25–30. Available at https://www.thefreelibrary.com/In+the+jungle+with+Marcos.-a018049702.

McCaughan, Michael. 1995. "An Interview with Subcomandante Marcos." *NACLA Report on the Americas* 28, no. 1 (July–August 1995): 35–37.

Monsiváis, Carlos, and Hermann Bellinghausen. Marcos Interview," January 8, 2001. Originally published in *La Jornada*. Available at http://www.struggle.ws/mexico/ezln/2001/marcos_interview_jan.html.

Rodríguez Lascano, Sergio. "The Extra Element: Organization. An Exclusive Interview with Zapatista Subcomandante Marcos: Part I." *Rebeldía*, May 30, 2006. Available at http://www.narconews.com/Issue41/article1856.html.

———. "A Message for the Intellectuals and their 'Magnificent Alibi to Avoid Struggle and Confrontation.' An Exclusive Interview with Zapatista Subcomandante Marcos: Part II." *Rebeldía*, May 31, 2006. Available at http://www.narconews.com/Issue41/article1857.html.

———. "A Different Path for Latin America Rides through Mexico. An Exclusive Interview with Zapatista Subcomandante Marcos: Part III." *Rebeldía*, May 31, 2006. Available at http://www.narconews.com/Issue41/article1861.html.

———. "If You Listen, Mexico 2006 Seems a lot Like Chiapas in 1992. An Exclusive Interview with Zapatista Subcomandante Marcos: Part IV." *Rebeldía*, June 1, 2006. Available at http://www.narconews.com/Issue41/article1865.html.

Simon, Joel. "The Marcos Mystery: A Chat with the Subcommander of Spin." *Columbia Journalism Review*, no. 33 (September–October 1994): 9–11. Reprinted in *The Zapatista Reader*, edited by Tom Hayden, 45–47 (New York: Thunder's Mouth, 2002).

Subcomandante Marcos. "First Interviews with Marcos," January 1, 1994. Originally published in *La Jornada*. Available at http://www.struggle.ws/mexico/ezln/marcos_interview_jan94.html.

———. "Interview with Subcomandante Marcos," May 11, 1994. From Infoshop Berkeley. Available at http://www.struggle.ws/mexico/ezln/anmarin.html.

————. "December 1994 Interview with Marcos," December 9, 1994. Interview by Epigmenio Ibarra, originally published in *La Jornada*. Available at http://www.struggle.ws/mexico/ezln/inter_marcos_dec94.html.

————. "Interview with Marcos," August 25, 1995. Originally published in *La Jornada*. Available at http://www.struggle.ws/mexico/ezln/inter_marcos_consult_aug95.html.

————. "Never Again a Mexico without Us," November 25, 1997. Article by Beto Del Sereno, published in *In Motion*. Available at http://www.inmotionmagazine.com/chiapas2.html.

————. "15 Years since the formation of the EZLN," November 16, 1998. Originally published in *La Jornada*. Available at http://www.struggle.ws/mexico/ezln/1998/inter_marcos_nov98.html.

————. "Bellinghausen Interviews Marcos about Consulta," March 10 and 11, 1999. Originally published in *La Jornada*. Available at http://struggle.ws/mexico/ezln/1999/inter_marcos_consul_mar.html.

————. "Marcos on Peace, 3 Conditions and Globalisation," January 28, 2001. Originally published in *La Jornada*. Available at http://www.struggle.ws/mexico/ezln/2001/marcos_inter_jan28.html.

Works on Subcommander Marcos

Substantial Studies

Di Piramo, Daniela. *Political Leadership in Zapatista Mexico: Marcos, Celebrity, and Charismatic Authority*. Boulder, CO: FirstForumPress, 2010.

————. "Beyond Modernity: Irony, Fantasy, and the Challenge to Grand Narratives in Subcomandante Marcos's Tales." *Mexican Studies / Estudios Mexicanos* 27, no. 1 (Winter 2011): 177–205.

Guillermoprieto, Alma. "Zapata's Heirs," 185–206, and "The Unmasking," 207–23. In *Looking for History: Dispatches from Latin America*, by Alma Guillermoprieto. New York: Vintage Books, 2002.

Henck, Nick. *Subcommander Marcos: The Man and the Mask*. Durham, NC: Duke University Press, 2007.

————. "Laying a Ghost to Rest: Subcommander Marcos' Playing of the Indigenous Card." *Estudios Mexicanos / Mexican Studies* 25, no. 1 (Winter 2009): 155–70.

————. "Subcommander Marcos and Mexico's Public Intellectuals: Octavio Rodríguez Araujo, Carlos Monsiváis, Elena Poniatowska and Pablo González Casanova." *A Contracorriente* 9, no. 1 (Fall 2011): 287–335.

————. "Subcommander Marcos' Discourse on Mexico's Intellectual Class." *Asian Journal of Latin American Studies* 25, no. 1 (2012): 35–73.

————. "The Subcommander and the Sardinian: Marcos and Gramsci." *Estudios Mexicanos / Mexican Studies* 29, no. 2 (Summer 2013): 428–58.

————. "Subcomandante Marcos: The Latest Reader." *The Latin Americanist* 58, no. 2 (June 2014): 49–73.

————. "Adiós Marcos: A Fond Farewell to the Subcommander Who Simply Ceased to Exist." *A Contracorriente* 12, no. 2 (Winter 2015): 401–21.

————. *Insurgent Marcos: The Political-Philosophical Formation of the Zapatista Subcommander*. Raleigh, NC: Editorial Contracorriente, 2016.

Herlinghaus, Hermann. "Subcomandante Marcos: Narrative Policy and Epistemological Project." *Journal of Latin American Cultural Studies* 14, no. 1 (March 2005): 53–74.

Higgins, Nicholas P. "Visible Indians: Subcomandante Marcos and the 'Indianization' of the Zapatista Army of National Liberation." In *Understanding the Chiapas Rebellion: Modernist Visions and the Invisible Indian*, by Nicholas P. Higgins, 153–71. Austin: University of Texas Press, 2004.

Jörgensen, Beth. "Making History: Subcomandante Marcos in the Mexican Chronicle." In *Documents in Crisis: Nonfiction Literatures in Twentieth-Century Mexico*, by Beth Jörgensen, 161–90. New York: State University of New York Press, 2011.

Krauze, Enrique. "Subcomandante Marcos: The Rise and Fall of a Guerrillero." In *Redeemers: Ideas and Power in Latin America*, by Enrique Krauze, 433–48. New York: HarperCollins, 2011.

Martín, Desirée A. "Todos Somos Santos: Subcomandante Marcos and the EZLN." In *Borderlands Saints: Secular Sanctity in Chicano/a and Mexican Culture*, by Desirée A. Martín, 142–81. New Brunswick, NJ: Rutgers University Press, 2014.

Mato, Shigeko. "Subcomandante Marcos' Performance: Intellectual Consciousness and Appropriation." In *Co-optation, Complicity, and Representation: Desire and Limits for Intellectuals in Twentieth-Century Mexican Fiction*, by Shigeko Mato, 99–130. New York: Peter Lang, 2010.

Oppenheimer, Andrés. "Marcos," 61–82, and "Unmasking Marcos," 235–62. In *Bordering on Chaos*, by Andrés Oppenheimer. Boston: Little, Brown and Company, 1998.

Weinberg, Bill. "Behind the Lines with Marcos." In *Homage to Chiapas*, by Bill Weinberg, 118–32. London: Verso, 2000.

Shorter Studies

Bob, Clifford. "The Making of an Anti-Globalization Icon: Mexico's Zapatista Uprising." In *The Marketing of Rebellion: Insurgents, Media, and International Activism*, by Clifford Bob, 117–77, esp. 161–64. New York: Cambridge University Press, 2005.

Gogol, Eugene. "Mexico's Revolutionary Forms of Organization: The Zapatistas and the Indigenous Autonomous Communities in Resistance," 119–51, and "The Zapatistas and the Dialectic," 402–13. In *Utopia and the Dialectic in Latin American Liberation*, by Eugene Gogol. Brill: Leiden, 2016.

Graebner, Cornelia. "Subcomandante Insurgente Marcos." In *The Literary Encyclopedia* (online), 2011. http://www.litencyc.com/.

Henck, Nick. "Subcomandante Marcos." In *Iconic Mexico: An Encyclopedia from Acapulco to Zócalo*, edited by Eric Zolov, 556–62. Santa Barbara, CA: ABC-CLIO, 2015.

Klein, Naomi. "The Unknown Icon." In *The Zapatista Reader*, edited by Tom Hayden, 114–23. New York: Thunder's Mouth, 2002.

Monsiváis, Carlos. "From the Subsoil to the Mask that Reveals." In *The Zapatista Reader*, edited by Tom Hayden, 123–32. New York: Thunder's Mouth, 2002.

Montalbán, Manuel Vázquez. "Marcos: Mestizo Culture on the Move." In *The Zapatista Reader*, edited by Tom Hayden, 472–83. New York: Thunder's Mouth, 2002.

Poniatowska, Elena. "Voices from the Jungle: Subcommander Marcos and Culture." In *The Zapatista Reader*, edited by Tom Hayden, 73–81. New York: Thunder's Mouth, 2002.

Stavans, Ilan. "Unmasking Marcos." In *The Zapatista Reader*, edited by Tom Hayden, 386–95. New York: Thunder's Mouth, 2002.

Steele, Cynthia. "The Rainforest Chronicle of Subcomandante Marcos." In *The Contemporary Mexican Chronicle*, edited by Ignacio Corona and Beth E. Jörgensen, 245–55. New York: State University of New York Press, 2002.

Tormey, Simon. "*Ya Basta!*: A Brief Excursus on Marcos and 'Zapatismo.'" In *Anti-Capitalism: A Beginner's Guide*, by Simon Tormey, 129–36. Oxford: Oneworld, 2004.

Vanden Berghe, Kristine, and Bart Maddens. "Ethnocentrism, Nationalism and Post-nationalism in the Tales of Subcomandante Marcos." *Mexican Studies / Estudios Mexicanos* 20, no. 1 (2004): 123–44.

AK Press is small, in terms of staff and resources, but we also manage to be one of the world's most productive anarchist publishing houses. We publish close to twenty books every year, and distribute thousands of other titles published by like-minded independent presses and projects from around the globe. We're entirely worker-run and democratically managed. We operate without a corporate structure—no boss, no managers, no bullshit.

The Friends of AK program is a way you can directly contribute to the continued existence of AK Press, and ensure that we're able to keep publishing books like this one! Friends pay $25 a month directly into our publishing account ($30 for Canada, $35 for international), and receive a copy of every book AK Press publishes for the duration of their membership! Friends also receive a discount on anything they order from our website or buy at a table: 50% on AK titles, and 20% on everything else. We have a Friends of AK ebook program as well: $15 a month gets you an electronic copy of every book we publish for the duration of your membership. You can even sponsor a very discounted membership for someone in prison.

Email friendsofak@akpress.org for more info, or visit the Friends of AK Press website: https://www.akpress.org/friends.html

There are always great book projects in the works—so sign up now to become a Friend of AK Press, and let the presses roll!